YESTERDAY'S WINGS

YESTERDAY'S WINGS

TEXT BY JOSEPH E. BROWN

PHOTOGRAPHS BY DAN GURAVICH

DOUBLEDAY & COMPANY, INC.
GARDEN CITY, NEW YORK
1982

Library of Congress Cataloging in Publication Data

Brown, Joseph E., 1929–
    Yesterday's wings.

    Includes index.
    1. Airplanes, Military.   2. Confederate Air Force—
History.   I. Guravich, Dan.   II. Title.
UG1240.B76   358.4′183′09044
AACR2
ISBN: 0-385-12053-2
Library of Congress Catalog Card Number 77–82930

Photograph Credits
Color Photographs by Dan Guravich

Black and White Photographs
By Dan Guravich: page 2 (bottom), 6, 8, 10, 11, 20, 24, 30, 33, 40, 51 (top), 53, 56, 71, 83
(bottom), 94, 96, 99, 102, 103, 104, 108, 111, 113, 131, 134, 135 (bottom), 138, 139, 142,
143, 144, 145, 152, 153, 158, 159, 163, 166, 168 (bottom), 171 (bottom), 184, 186, 188, 189
(right), 191, 193, 194, 195, 196

Lockheed Aircraft Corporation: page 55

Fairchild Republic Company: page 73

All others courtesy Confederate Air Force

Designed by Virginia M. Soulé

CONTENTS

SAVED
FROM EXTINCTION

1

Just outside the city limits of Aberdeen, Maryland, a chill spring wind rustles the grass that wanders across a meadow and then disappears over a low-lying knoll. The wind is the only sound the visitor hears, for the eight huge four-engined B-29 Superfortress bombers are cold and silent now, helpless, forlorn skeletons of fabric and aluminum that have been left in this meadow to rust away their final years. The sign outside the gate reads "Aberdeen Proving Ground" but in reality the sprawling acreage is a graveyard . . . and a sad reminder of the way that man forgets and discards the machines that have served him well, when their usefulness to him ends. More than three decades earlier, B-29s rumbled aloft in an endless stream from tiny dots of Pacific coral and volcanic lava to pummel targets in Japan. One predawn August morning in 1945, one of them dropped a special, top-secret, hush-hush bomb on a city named Hiroshima and World War II ended shortly thereafter with a tremendous savings in American lives. That, however, was years ago. Now the great planes that brought the most tumultuous war in history to an early close sprawl helplessly across a Maryland meadow, forgotten by all but a few who come here to riddle their already-tattered skeletons with Space Age projectiles. The years of neglect are apparent. The control fabric of the B-29s rotted away long ago. Their tires no longer hold air. The electrical wiring that made them go snakes out of their sides and across the meadow like so much tired spaghetti. Parts that had any value at all were long ago ripped away and sold as surplus.

Change location now to Phoenix, Arizona. A few miles outside the southwest city, at Litchfield Park Naval Air Station, are kept hundreds of other World War II era fighters and bombers. Row upon row they sit, wing tip to wing tip, their once-howling engines now silent or even missing, their once-bright war paint faded under the desert sun. To save room, their keepers have ignominiously stacked some of the planes side to side and nose down into the earth, so that even in the winter of their years they no longer point toward the blue yonder they knew so well.

There are other Litchfield Parks and Aberdeens scattered around the United

Mute ghosts of history's greatest war, B-29 Superfortress heavy bombers squat forlornly in the California desert. Although the dry environment was deliberately chosen for its absence of corrosion-causing humidity, these planes and thousands of others nevertheless were scheduled for scrapping. Only intervention by a group of concerned former military fliers prevented total destruction.

Their engines quiet now, hundreds of World War II fighters, bombers, and auxiliary airplanes await the smelter at a surplus disposal field near Tucson, Arizona.

States, boneyards of aviation all. In total, an estimated 300,000 combat aircraft were rushed off American production lines between the time of the attack on Pearl Harbor on December 7, 1941, and the end of World War II three and a half years later. Some were sent to other nations as the nucleus of postwar air forces. A small number were sold as surplus to private individuals. Thousands perished in battle. But the lion's share wound up in open-air storage areas, later to be scrapped.

They were the last of a breed, these feisty, individualistic, sometimes cantankerous but always valuable fighters and bombers. They represent the last of the era of propeller-driven combat airplanes and as such they were the best and most efficient ever built. They were the classic B-17 Flying Fortresses, the twin-tailed P-38 Lightnings, the uniquely rear-engined P-39 Airacobras, the carrier-borne F6F Hellcats, Corsairs, and Avengers. But at places like Aberdeen and Litchfield Park after the war, when they were no longer needed, and when they were made obsolete overnight by an emerging generation of whisper-smooth jets, they became just so much smelter fodder.

Almost all of them, anyway . . .

High above the lush, moist Lower Rio Grande Valley of Texas, a tiny dot

The restoration of any airplane abandoned for years is an enormous challenge. How much time, ingenuity, and patience would be needed, for instance, to make this World War II era engine roar to life again?

streaks above the fields of cotton and citrus, then points its nose toward the billowing white cumulus clouds above. Nothing unusual about that in this valley, where the crop duster is aviation's king, and where the moan of his engine is heard daily. But now there is another plane, flying lower, and its engine suddenly rips open the silence. Approaching at high speed, it is easily seen now in detail, a brown-painted single-engined plane with huge shark's teeth painted on its engine cowling. No doubt about it, it is a P-40 Warhawk, the same plane flown by a handful of legendary volunteers out of China in the harrowing months before Pearl Harbor brought the United States into the global conflict. Not far behind the Warhawk comes another plane of the World War II era. To a youngster, it is but a photograph in a history book, but to anyone over forty-five, it conjures memories as vivid as yesterday. It is a P-38, winging in at almost treetop level. Soon, the Texas sky is filled with other airplanes that cleared the air in the 1940s, when the world was both younger and threatened with annihilation, and when these planes were at home in places like Sicily, Guam, Britain, North Africa and New Guinea.

Survivors of the war in which combat aviation came into its own, they are the aircraft of the Ghost Squadron of the Confederate Air Force. Like the few sister planes that somehow evaded the smelter and scrap heap after V-J Day, they are museum pieces but with a difference: all are *flying* today.

The men who fly these planes, and who have saved them from oblivion with pride, hard-earned cash, and more than a smattering of tender loving care, are honorary "colonels" in the CAF, perhaps the most unusual historical aviation organization in the world today. A few of the planes they have saved are one-of-a-kind survivors of the war period; all are considered extremely rare, a cross section of a period when American technology and industrial capacity overcame a ten-year deficit yielded to its enemies and provided the means for their defeat.

The inspiration for the Confederate Air Force was pure happenstance. One blistering midsummer day in 1951, a Texas crop duster named Lloyd Nolen bought a Curtiss P-40 from a private owner in Phoenix, who had obtained it earlier in a military surplus sale in Canada. A World War II flight instructor, Nolen had never lost the itch to keep on flying when war clouds parted in 1945, and the P-40 seemed a sure-fire way of scratching it.

Though Nolen recalls that flying the old warplane "never ceased being fun," he was soon fidgeting to own something faster and sleeker. Flying a World War II vintage fighter proved the inspiration for what later was to become the Confederate Air Force, but Nolen yearned for a later-model plane.

The Korean War had begun in June 1950. Although jets were now on the military scene, American pilots were still flying a few planes of the World War II period when the Korean action began. Among them was the North American P-51 Mustang, one of the hottest World War II fighters, which Nolen had had his eye on for some time.

In 1952, hoping to scrape up enough cash to buy a surplus P-51, Nolen sold his P-40 and began negotiating for the purchase of a Mustang. Almost as the deal was being closed, the Pentagon issued an order recalling *all* P-51s for duty in Korea. It was a major disappointment for Nolen. Five more years were to pass until, the Korean War over, he would get to fly a P-51.

The purchase that eventually got a P-51, in 1957, involved Nolen and a group of crop duster friends. They pooled their resources and bought the World War II fighter from a private owner in El Paso. Little restoration was required, and they soon were taking turns putting the craft through its paces.

Typical of the kind of up-by-the-bootstraps restoration project faced by the Confederate Air Force.

One more example of a military aircraft, once scheduled for scrapping, awaiting the patient touch of the CAF.

One Sunday in the fall of 1957, as Nolen remembers it, the group discovered that some wag had painted the words "Confederate Air Force" on the Mustang's fuselage. "We never found out who that gagster was," Nolen remembers, "but the words seemed to fit. My buddies and I stared at the words, began to laugh out loud, then gave each other a playful salute. That was the day we count as the unofficial beginning of the Confederate Air Force, even though at the time we had one plane."

Two years later, in 1959, Nolen heard that another World War II classic, a Grumman F8F Bearcat, was for sale at Litchfield Park, Arizona. Completed too late for actual wartime service, the Bearcat nonetheless was considered of World War II vintage, an advanced later relative of two other Grumman "cat" fighters turned out for Navy duty: the F4F Wildcat and F6F Hellcat.

"We actually bought two Bearcats at Litchfield," Nolen recalls, "but what I saw around me that day in Arizona nearly made me cry. Dozens of other World War II planes—fighters, bombers, patrol planes, trainers—were being stripped of their instruments and other worthwhile parts, chopped up by bulldozers, and then heaved into a huge smelter to be destroyed forever."

Angrily, Nolen termed what he saw "a disgrace, a waste, and an affront to history." Returning home to Mercedes, Texas, he made a series of telephone calls around the country only to hear the same story repeated: no substantial effort had been made anywhere to save, for historical purposes, examples of the more than 300,000 fighting aircraft turned out by American factories from 1939 to 1945 to engage in combat in the skies over Europe and the Pacific. To be sure, there were a few in museums, but even fewer in *flying* condition.

The Navy later, in 1964, set aside some of its World War II planes as museum displays at Pensacola, Florida. The Smithsonian Institution had added

The man whose anger started it all: "Colonel" Lloyd Nolen, founder of the Confederate Air Force.

World War II types to its well-established aviation museum in Washington, D.C. A few, bought as surplus by private owners, were scattered at small airfields around the country. Another handful were preserved as memorials to flying heroes. In Valparaiso, Florida, for example, a B-25 Mitchell bomber is displayed as a tribute to Lieutenant General James Doolittle, who, as a lieutenant colonel, led a flight of its sisters on a daring daylight raid over Tokyo in early 1942. A P-38 Lightning is similarly preserved at Poplar, Wisconsin, hometown of the late Richard Bong, whose skill and courage at the controls of Lightnings in the South Pacific ranked him as America's "ace of aces" during that conflict. And in Memphis, historically minded citizens put together the means to permanently exhibit a venerable B-17 Flying Fortress bearing the city's name, the *Memphis Belle,* which was the first B-17 to fly twenty-five missions over Europe.

Perhaps the best static collection of World War II combat aircraft is that maintained by the U. S. Air Force at Wright-Patterson Air Force Base at Dayton, Ohio. Its origin dating back to 1923, the nonprofit Air Force Museum, Inc., was chartered in 1960 and today boasts of more than eighty historic military airplanes in its main building alone, with another twenty attracting more than 1 million visitors each year on runways and aprons outside. Altogether, the Air Force Museum covers four hundred acres and is financed entirely by memberships and donations. Included in the World War II part of the collection are a P-38, P-39, P-47, and P-51 fighters, a British Spitfire, a B-25 Mitchell, a B-17 Flying Fortress and a B-29 Superfortress bomber, and several transport and support aircraft. (There's also a Russian MIG exhibited; the Air Force paid a North Korean defector $100,000 for it during the Korean War.)

His own flying career having been nurtured during the war years, Lloyd Nolen sympathized with the various efforts to retain a sense of the historical aviation perspective of the period. But aside from static collections in museums, and a handful of personally owned surplus planes that former military pilots like himself had purchased, most World War II planes by the early fifties were facing extinction as certain as that of the dodo and the passenger pigeon.

The end result of Nolen's anger, the restored and flying planes of the CAF, today sprawls across a sweeping asphalt runway in Harlingen, Texas. There, fully restored, wearing combat paint and ready to fly, are lined up no less than 100 aircraft of World War II. On that apron are flyable examples of most of the major planes that saw combat between 1939 and 1945, including selected examples of British and German planes.

The underlying motives of the CAF are far more serious than the magnolia and mint julep name would imply. "We called ourselves 'rebels' in the beginning because we were doing just that—rebelling against the wanton destruction of airplanes that should have been preserved for historical purposes," Nolen explains. "We started the CAF tongue-in-cheek, a sort of hobby, never dreaming it would eventually grow into a group with more than 6,500 members, a budget of more than $5 million a year, an investment of more than $7 million in airplanes and facilities, and support coming from every corner of the country.

"We wear Texas-style wide-brimmed Stetson hats and gray uniforms with shoulder patches displaying the American flag, and we decided that all our members would hold the rank of 'colonel.' But it wasn't long after we launched the CAF that we discovered that our hobby was to become a significant, serious, patriotic endeavor."

To a generation yet unborn on V-J Day, the dewy-eyed nostalgic tug evoked by the World War II airplane may be understandably difficult to accept. Compared to today's generation of swift, sleek, highly efficient jets, the 1939–45 war

Saved from extinction! Three World War II fighters—top to bottom, a P-40 Warhawk, a P-47 Thunderbolt, and a P-51 Mustang—roar over the Texas Lower Rio Grande Valley in tight formation. The three were among the first planes restored by the CAF.

birds were, admittedly, among the noisiest, most temperamental, never-fraying machines ever to roll off an assembly line. Even when idling, for instance, the backfiring snort of the B-25's twin 1,700-horsepower engines suggests imminent Armageddon, and the flaming belch from its exhaust manifolds seems calculated to singe the fur of a jack rabbit fifty yards away, or, failing that, to overcome the poor animal by smoke inhalation. Frank Tallman, the late movie stunt flier who assembled an entire squadron of B-25s for the movie *Catch-22,* once noted wryly that the aircraft's design "is more in keeping with Zasu Pitts than Rita Hayworth, and the 'greenhouse' in the nose may well have been designed by the same man who laid out the aviary at the Brooklyn Zoo."

The B-25's close cousin, the Martin B-26 Marauder, was universally nicknamed "The Widowmaker," a backhanded tribute to its temperamental handling characteristics, particularly its death-defying high landing speed. The B-17, despite its glowing press clippings, "was a sitting duck for frontal attacks, burned easily, and had enough systems troubles to give the plumber's guild a nightmare," Frank Tallman also observed. And as unsettling to the pilots who flew it was the highly vaunted P-39 Airacobra; more irritating than the constant vibration of the drive shaft leading between the pilot's legs to the rear-mounted engine was the constant specter of being crushed to death should a belly landing occur.

Despite their cantankerous and sometimes frightening nature, however, World War II aircraft—particularly the fighters developed toward the end of the war—continue to fascinate flier and nonflier alike. No pilot can help but be excited by the performance characteristics of World War II airplanes. Their rate of climb, their ability to do aerobatics in tight situations, their response—it's a vastly different world from that of either the slower, bamboo-and-bailing-wire airplanes of World War I or the high-performance jets of today. They didn't have the glamour of World War I planes, but neither were they the coldly impersonal machines of the Jet Age. They were just a damned exciting generation of aircraft.

The CAF's flying colonels confess various motives for gathering once a year to fly these old planes in mock combat. C. A. Skiles, a graying senior airline captain with Pan American, launched his aviation career piloting flying boats across the Atlantic. Until his death in a tragic air crash in 1975, he sat at the controls of a venerable PBY Catalina amphibian, one of the few left in circulation in the world. For a living, Skiles until his death flew 707 jetliners between the East Coast and Latin America. By comparison, switching to the 160-mile-an-hour Catalina was an exaggerated comedown from the proverbial tortoise to the hare, but Skiles liked to remark that for pure joy of flight, he'd take the PBY any day. "Today's airplanes are considerably faster and probably safer than the planes of yesterday," he once put it, "but they're also a lot less *fun.*"

For Dr. Hal Fenner, an orthopedist from Hobbs, New Mexico, piloting a B-25 Mitchell bomber is the culmination of many months of restoration work. "I'd wanted to fly the B-25," he says, "ever since the Air Force, when I was in flight school, discovered I was totally color blind and washed me out. Denied the opportunity then, I had to wait twenty more years until I found my own airplane, a has-been buried up to its axles in mud at a small California airfield."

And for others, the CAF is a means of finally breathing life into boyhood dreams. "I was a youngster during World War II," says astronaut Joe Engle, who piloted the X-15 rocketship that preceded manned space flight, "and it wasn't until the jets came in that I sat in a cockpit for real. During the war, I was a member of the Junior Flying Tigers; now, thanks to the CAF, I fly a P-40 and finally do what I hungered to do as a kid."

In a world where the antihero is welcomed and accorded respect, aviation continues to attract men and women who are the ultimate individualists. And, in turn, these individualists—the test pilots, airline captains, and crop dusters—are held in awe by most little boys . . . and many adults. This may help explain why the CAF has mushroomed so since its origin, but the success still astonishes Lloyd Nolen.

"When we launched the Ghost Squadron (that's a name which seems very appropriate) none of us dreamed we'd wind up with an air force larger than those of many small nations." In an average year, more than 3,000,000 Americans attend CAF air shows around the country; an estimated 105,000 showed up in Harlingen alone for one recent annual four-day homecoming show. From its original membership of less than a dozen, the Ghost Squadron has expanded its roster to more than 6,500, including two United States senators, four astronauts, assorted business executives, and as might be expected, a wide variety of pilots.

After Nolen acquired his P-40 in 1951, and watched as the Litchfield Park smelters consumed their prey, the underlying motif for the CAF suddenly hit him: if possible, why not acquire as many different types of World War II fighters and interceptors as funds would permit, restore them to flying condition, and put them all under one roof somewhere in Texas?

"Like many pilots, fighters appealed most to me," he explains. "And the fighters of World War II were classics in every way. That's all we had in mind in the beginning—fighters of every description."

Nolen and his partners now had two different types of fighters and, like the first-time boat owner stung with the urge to buy something longer, faster, and more expensive, they immediately began to dream of owning a third: a

Astronaut Joe Engle trained for a mission in outer space, but as a member of the CAF he flies much closer to earth. His favorite plane: the Curtiss P-40 Warhawk, famed member of China's Flying Tigers.

Army Air Corps World War II fighters were the first planes restored and flown by the Confederate Air Force. Generating considerable enthusiasm for its mission, however, the Texas "flying museum" soon began adding other types, such as these Navy craft lined up at Harlingen.

Lockheed P-38 Lightning, easily one of the fastest and most maneuverable of the World War II fighters.

"But as we checked around the country, we discovered that out of the more than nine thousand P-38s built, less than a dozen survived. It was then we decided that if the CAF was to perform a very significant historical service, we had to move fast."

Nolen and M. L. "Lefty" Gardner, another of the CAF's earliest members, finally found a restorable P-38 and next added an F4U Corsair, the single-engined Navy fighter that first saw service with the Marines on Guadalcanal in 1943 and was still active in Korea ten years later . . . the longest life of any American fighter. "The Corsair was typical of the aircraft the CAF was acquiring, in terms of both its unique history and the way in which we acquired it. During the Korean War, a Corsair—that's a propeller-driven airplane, remember—was credited with shooting down a MIG-15 jet; during World War II, a Navy pilot named Klingman, discovering that his guns were jammed, destroyed a Japanese photo plane by moving in close and sawing off its rudder and elevators with his own prop! Like most of the other planes, though, the Corsair had become an endangered species by the mid-fifties, and we had to search long and hard before finding a suitable one, deserted on a small airstrip in Arizona."

Even scarcer was the P-47 Thunderbolt, at 13,000 pounds the heaviest single-engined fighter ever built in the United States. During World War II, more than 15,000 Thunderbolts came off the production line, flew more than one-half-million combat sorties, dropped 132,000 tons of bombs. The P-47 also added considerably to aviation technology; in 1943, Colonel Cass Hough reached Mach 1—the speed of sound at sea level—in a dive over Bovington, England. But by the late 1950s, not a single "Jug," as it was nicknamed, could be located in the United States.

A puzzled Nolen was soon to learn the reason: all P-47s that had survived the scrap pile had been sold to Nicaragua. "Dick Disney, Lefty, and I flew down there," Nolen remembers. "I guess they thought we were crazy, asking to buy back a bunch of planes that by the book were years obsolete. But we were convincing arm-twisters; we came back from Latin America with our 'Jug.' We later acquired six more from Peru."

By 1966, the CAF had grown into a respectable aerial armada. Still housed at a small private airfield in Mercedes, Texas, its operators began worrying about a new problem: elbow room. That concern vanished when city fathers of the agricultural community of Harlingen, ten miles away, saw in the fledgling CAF the germ of a plan to encourage tourists to visit a corner of the country which otherwise was too far off the beaten path to attract much attention.

Harlingen had a fine airstrip, a leftover from World War II when the community's Rebel Field had been an Army Air Corps gunnery training facility, and several unused hangars. By 1968, the CAF had 170 officer-members and an investment of $306,000 in airplanes; spurred by the enthusiasm that was now spreading even beyond the borders of Texas, the CAF moved to Harlingen in that year to become what doubtless is the most unusual tourist attraction of the Lower Rio Grande Valley.

One day a stranger approached Nolen at CAF headquarters. "Remember," Nolen recalls the incident now with a wide grin, "up to then we were strictly fighter pilots; we hadn't even thought of any other kind of airplane. Some guy offered to sell us a B-25 for $4,000 and we found ourselves collecting bombers."

The first bomber—a twin-engined B-25 Mitchell—became the nucleus of

Locating a restorable P-47 Thunderbolt was one of the CAF's toughest missions; not a single one could be found in the United States. The solution? Look elsewhere. The CAF did; this "Jug" was one of seven acquired in Nicaragua and Peru.

A restored Thunderbolt on public display at CAF headquarters.

Rebuilt and ready to fly, the CAF's first seven fighter planes stand wing tip to wing tip in Harlingen in 1962.

The first two restorations in the CAF's Bomber Wing: an A-26 Invader, left, and a B-25 Mitchell. The Mitchell was the Ghost Squadron's first bomber purchase. This photograph was taken in Harlingen in 1966.

what today is an entire wing of the CAF. It includes two B-17 Flying Fortresses, a B-24 Liberator, three B-25s, a B-26 Marauder, an A-20 Havoc, an A-26 Invader, and the largest, longest-range propeller-driven bomber ever built, the B-29 Superfortress.

Even later, the CAF decided to add foreign combat aircraft, as well as flying examples of American and foreign patrol planes, transports, and trainers. The CAF's Foreign Wing today includes two British Spitfires, a German Heinkel bomber, and four German Me-109 fighters. The Transport Wing flies venerable World War II types: the C-45, C-47, C-54, and C-46 and the German Junkers Ju-52. There's a Liaison Squadron, too, equipped with a Piper L-4 and a Stinson L-5; recently, a rare German Fieseler Storch and Messerschmitt Me-108 joined the unit. Last but not least is the CAF's Sikorsky R-4B helicopter, the first helicopter to enter military service, plus a string of venerable training aircraft, and an extremely rare CG-4A combat glider.

As the CAF's aircraft collection continued to grow through the sixties, so did its related facilities . . . and problems. One of the biggest annual headaches faced by the flying colonels is money. In many aviation organizations, costs are kept at a minimum because the aircraft involved are privately owned and privately maintained. In the case of the CAF, however, most are owned by the organization.

Since its inception, the CAF's unique method of aircraft sponsorship has proven successful. The CAF sponsor can enjoy the same thrills, excitement, and satisfaction of owning his own classic World War II combat aircraft at only a fraction of the cost. He also has the privilege of participating in a worthwhile patriotic and educational endeavor.

For an out-of-pocket cost ranging from a few dollars to several thousand, aviation-minded citizens may participate in the Ghost Squadron's history-preserving effort by underwriting needed restoration and maintenance costs, and because the CAF now has been blessed by the Internal Revenue Service as a nonprofit organization, the money spent is tax deductible. Member colonels pay dues of $125 each per year. The CAF covers the rest of its expenses from voluntary donations and sponsorships. Its highly popular Harlingen air show and its small but historically accurate flight museum at Rebel Field have begun to put a small amount of money in the maintenance fund. They attract a deluge of visitors each year, which generates additional revenue.

By 1971, the original objectives of the CAF were reached—the collection of major types of American World War II combat aircraft in flying condition, with trainers, foreign planes, and auxiliaries added for good measure had been completed. The total is flexible; as new plane types are added duplicate types may be sold. In addition, more than forty other combat planes are owned privately by members. But over all, the collection—as a *flying* museum—is the only one of its kind in the world, and sometimes when the fighters or bombers group up in formation, what the visitor to Harlingen sees is a sight that has not been repeated since World War II. During the 1975 air show, for instance, the CAF flew in formation its entire bomber wing, consisting of six planes wing to wing. It was the first time the planes had flown together, anywhere in the world, in more than thirty years. On September 6, 1961, four years after its informal organization, the CAF was legally chartered as a nonprofit Texas corporation.

Locating restorable aircraft continues year by year, and as time passes, the finding becomes increasingly difficult. But by now, the word of what the CAF is

An A-26 Invader, painted in the colors of the 386th Bomb Group of the Ninth Air Force, flies in formation with a Republic P-47D Thunderbolt, bearing the insignia of the Fifth Air Force.

trying to accomplish has permeated aviation circles the world over, and occasionally help comes in from unexpected sources.

For several years, as an example, the CAF headquarters had been looking into the possibility of acquiring a PBY Catalina patrol plane, but because of its rarity, the prices asked were beyond the Texans' reach. Nolen's colleagues then learned that an abandoned, derelict PBY was gathering dust at a small airfield near Fort Worth. The owner, a commercial firm located in Oklahoma City, agreed to donate the old ship to the CAF, but when the estimate came in on what it would cost to restore it—$40,000—the groans could be heard from the Gulf of Mexico to the Texas Panhandle. Fortunately, a second PBY was located. Once flown by the Danish Navy under the Lend-Lease program, it had in fact already been unsuccessfully bid on by the CAF when it was released from foreign service and declared surplus. Now it was up for grabs once more. Because of his flying boat experience, C. A. Skiles, the Pan American 707 pilot mentioned earlier, was the logical colonel to do the grabbing, and upon hearing that the PBY was then in California, he was winging westward.

Reaching Monterey, Skiles was surprised to learn that the plane was privately owned by a fellow CAF member, John Church, who was only too happy to drop his asking price by $10,000 when Skiles explained that the ship would become the nucleus of a new CAF Patrol Wing. Skiles dug into his pocket, produced his checkbook, and wrote out a personal check for $5,000 to cover the deposit Church asked. "Nobody told me that the CAF had already formally authorized the purchase of the plane," Skiles remembered later, "so to say that I was a little nervous about that five grand would be the understatement of the year." As it had before, the CAF's membership rallied to the cause; within five weeks, five colonels shelled out $5,000 each as sponsors of the CAF's one-plane Patrol Wing, and with Skiles at the controls the aging PBY finally took off from California on the flight to its new home in the Lower Rio Grande Valley.

Wheels extended, a twin-engined Catalina PBY flying boat prepares for a landing. One of the Navy's most versatile World War II craft, this one once flew with the Danish Navy. Hundreds of others flew patrol missions around the globe and were revered by downed aviators in their role as rescue craft.

The CAF's collection of airplanes is now considered complete. "Technically, we don't have *every* World War II American combat plane," Nolen says, "but we've come as close as humanly possible. We've never been able to find a Navy TBD Devastator torpedo plane, a Brewster Buffalo or a P-61 Black Widow, for instance. Very few Buffalos and Black Widows were built, and the Devastator—it made history in the Battle of Midway—seems absolutely extinct.

"In exchange, though, we've added many foreign combat planes we hadn't planned on in the beginning, and we're mighty proud of what we've achieved."

Thousands of Americans to whom the significant World War II period of aviation would otherwise be limited to lifeless, static aircraft displays in museums or descriptions in books may continue to see them flying once again, recalling the momentous years in which they served not only their nation but the cause of world peace. And in the array of now ancient airplanes that roar over the Lower Rio Grande Valley of Texas each fall, the underlying theory that launched the world's most unusual air force seems well expressed: *Obsolescence is no reason for extinction.*

With the Texas Lower Rio Grande Valley stretched out below as a dramatic backdrop, a lone P-47 Thunderbolt roars through its paces. Obsolete? Not to the CAF's flying colonels.

2

"DAMNED BY WORDS BUT FLOWN TO GLORY"

Few if any World War II fighters were as cursed and condemned yet performed more valiantly for more nations over more of the globe than the sleek, feisty, single-engined Curtiss P-40 Warhawk. Best remembered for its role with Claire Chennault's famed Flying Tigers when its nose was painted with savage shark eyes and teeth, the P-40 technically was obsolete even before the war began. Admittedly, it was overly heavy for its liquid-cooled Allison engine, a drawback that made it a second-rate performer in the three departments where top performance in a fighter is mandatory: speed, rate of climb, and service ceiling. It was also true that despite constant modifications throughout its six years of active service there were basic design characteristics that harried its pilots no end, and which were never fully corrected. Most irritating, perhaps, was the P-40's notorious reputation as a ground looper, an annoyance attributed to its closely spaced landing gear. This was especially nerve-wracking in three-point landings; converting to Warhawks for the North Africa campaign, former Spitfire pilots, trained to land this way, accordioned many a P-40 before they learned to undo the habit and touch down on only the main gear first.

Yet despite its shortcomings, the P-40 saw wider service than any other fighter of World War II. It served on every fighting front in the world from 1939 to 1945 and flew under the colors of twenty-eight Allied nations. The Warhawk was one of only two U. S. Army Air Corps fighters in service during the first month of the war. Only a few got into the air at Pearl Harbor to knock down the first Japanese planes of the Pacific war. Despite the fact that the Japanese destroyed seventy-three Warhawks in the Hawaii attack, most of them on the ground, enough were still available at scattered Pacific outposts to challenge the enemy during the first dark weeks of the war. It was the P-40, along with the Navy's equally outdated F4F Wildcat and Britain's Spitfire, that held off the full fury of the Axis' global attack for many months until late in 1942, while more powerful fighters were being developed. More than any other fighter, perhaps, the heavy but rugged Warhawk truly deserves the adjective *versatile*. Its pilots fought Rommel's Afrika Korps in the burning sands of the Great Western Desert and flew it as well from England, Australia, China, the Philippines. It fought in subzero

The workhorse P-40 Warhawk, which saw service in more military theaters than any other U.S. aircraft. This is the plane that inspired the founding of the Confederate Air Force.

weather, too, in Russia, where P-40s were shipped under the wartime Lend-Lease program; one Red P-40 pilot, discovering his guns frozen solid, started toward acedom in a most unusual way . . . he *rammed* three enemy planes into oblivion. At various times in various theaters, the P-40 was pressed into service as a fighter-bomber, dive-bomber, night fighter, cargo carrier, advanced trainer, rescue aircraft, and escort fighter. "Give me a periscope," Colonel Robert L. Scott, Jr., of the Flying Tigers once quipped, "and I'll turn my P-40 into a submarine!"

Because the P-40 was the earliest land-based fighter to see action in World War II and because its service stretched the length of the war, it was perhaps fitting—though not planned that way—that the gallant little Warhawk was to be the plane that inspired the founding of the Confederate Air Force. There aren't many P-40s around today, despite the fact that Curtiss built 13,783 of them in six years; like most other World War II combat planes, they are as rare as the proverbial hen's teeth, and the total, including even those on static display, probably numbers less than twenty.

The plane that stirred CAF founder Lloyd Nolen's interest in collecting, restoring, and flying World War II combat fighters was itself not an original design but a highly refined successor to the Curtiss P-36 Army pursuit plane. The P-36, which bagged the first "kill" of a German fighter in French Air Force service over France in 1939, evolved in the mid-thirties and was the U. S. Army Air Corps's standard pursuit plane at the time. Powered with a radial engine, it had gained acceptance by many other nations, including England and France, and saw combat action with the RAF in the India-Burma Theater early in the war. The P-40's airframe was adapted basically from the P-36 Hawk, but installation of a liquid-cooled in-line engine permitted Curtiss to streamline its nose and the reduced frontal area helped increase maximum airspeed.

First produced in 1939, the early P-40s immediately impressed pilots with their streamlined fuselages, rugged construction, and the relative ease with which

More than 13,000 P-40s were built in six years, making the Warhawk the "most-produced" of any American World War II type. Here, Astronaut Joe Engle prepares to climb aboard the CAF's Warhawk.

they could be handled in flight. Because of their limited ceiling, P-40s could not accept combat above 15,000 feet, but below that altitude, controlled by skilled pilots, they were holy terrors against the enemy. The most famous P-40 pilot of all, in terms of enemy "kills," was Australian Clive R. Caldwell, commander of the Royal Air Force's 112 Squadron, which won its glory flying against Rommel's Afrika Korps. Caldwell flew 227 operational sorties with the "Desert Air Force," and was credited with twenty and a half enemy planes shot down. His recollection of the P-40 comes from not a single plane, but from twenty-three different ones of the P-40 "Hawk" series:

"My introduction to the Tomahawk P-40-IIB was on being posted to the newly-formed Number 250 Squadron, RAF, the first in the Middle East to be equipped with these aircraft, at the end of April 1941 and with which I remained until posted on December 29, 1941, to command Number 112 Squadron then re-equipping with the Kittyhawk, modified by 112 Squadron in early 1942 to the fighter-bomber role. The first Kittyhawk so converted, tested, and to bomb the enemy was AK 900 on March 10, 1942. Of the two I preferred the Tomahawk as a pilot's aircraft, favouring only the greater lethal density of the Kittyhawk's six .50-caliber guns. Although later on I flew much better-performing fighter aircraft, the Tomahawks were the best the RAF had in the Middle East, and I was glad to be flying them, liked their flush-riveted clean lines and the airplane itself. They were wanting in performance but the Allison engine was honest, hardworking and reliable. The fuel injection which kept it running smoothly in all attitudes was a very good feature. The airplane handled and turned well, gave a fair warning of the approaching stall, recovered from a spin without fuss, and in general had little vice.

"In service they proved strong and rugged and would stand up to a lot of punishment from opposing fire as well as from violent aerobatics. They picked up speed quickly in a dive but at steep angles of dive at high speed considerable strength of arm and leg and/or a lot of activity with the trim gear was needed to keep control. While inferior in performance, particularly at altitude, to the Bf-109 (Me-109) and to the elegant MC202 Folgore, which latter aircraft appeared in the Desert towards the end of 1941, and excited my admiration if not my approval, the Tomahawk seemed to hang on to them well in a steep or vertical dive, operating within its own altitude limitations, performed creditably in a dogfight. The Tomahawk's lack of comparable performance left the initiative mainly with the opposition and it was usual to accept the initial attack in order to engage at our best height. We rarely caught them below us.

"The armament was adequate. The two .50-caliber guns firing through the airscrew were especially useful at close range, the four .30-caliber wing guns were changed over to four 303s to take advantage of the more sophisticated ammunition then available for these guns. The Tomahawk did, however, have one serious fault. The cockpit canopy, when jettisoned from the near-closed or well-forward position, swung inwards through the cockpit, striking the pilot a heavy blow in the face or head. My own experience with this on June 6, 1941, and from which I was very lucky indeed to recover in time, brought this to light with consequent appropriate warning to the pilots. It is greatly to the credit of this aircraft that it stood up to the work so well in the desert and especially of the ground staff for the high degree of serviceability they achieved under the conditions for maintenance, often seemingly impossible, and never less than difficult, in which the Desert Air Force operated."

Another description of how the P-40 handled, especially in aerobatics,

Shark's teeth painted on the cowling of this early CAF acquisition were a trademark of Claire Chennault's famed Flying Tigers. Technically, the "Tigers" were the AVG— the American Volunteer Group.

comes from William H. West, who served as a lieutenant during World War II in the P-40 79th Fighter Group:

"The airplane was a sweet ship to fly but was basically a rudder ship and required strong leg action and a constant readjustment of the rudder trim. Take-off was a condition of full right rudder with an almost gentle but steady application of throttle. The ship started in idle cut-off, prop pitch forward and a couple of belts at the wobble pump by your right knee to make sure that you had hydraulic pressure. Take-off was with mixture control in full rich, somewhere between 56 and 60 inches of mercury and 3,000 rpm. The tail would come up fast and you would break ground at 95–100 mph. If I remember correctly take-off run was between 1,000–1,500 feet depending on gross loaded weight. The rolls on take-off had a unique hum which to this day when I hear the sound on late, late TV movies awakens a strong nostalgic memory. Take-off was accomplished without the use of flaps and with the cowl flaps closed.

"We usually carried a 1,000 pound bomb under the belly or 500 pounders when we couldn't get 1,000 pounders. I don't remember the rate of climb or throttle and rpm setting but as you know the P-40 was never exactly a shooting star when it came to climbing. In the back of my mind it seems that there was not much loss in performance when carrying an external load. Cruise setting was 30 inches of mercury and 2,500 rpm. Indicated airspeed was between 215 and 220 mph. Maximum speed I was ever able to get out of the ship was in a zero lift dive when it hit 425 mph. The ship was a complete rudder airplane and required very heavy and active leg action. Rudder trim was always being adjusted. The ship was not good in large angle deflection shots, but who could hit anything in a large angle deflection shot? In an Allison powered P-40 the ring sight for the guns was almost tangent to the airscoop on top of the nose. The Rolls powered ships had up draft carburetors and a little more clearance over the nose. Incidentally, we only used the P-40F and L. My ship, No. X-55, 'The Empress,' was a P-40L converted back to the F configuration. We added the auxiliary wing tanks and two more .50s to make it a six-gun airplane. This ship had come to the 79th from the 33rd and had been in the L configuration when we received it. Some of our Fs were short-tailed models and would do a left roll in a maximum dive no matter what you might want to do. This was somewhat corrected in the long tailed model but it was still a problem.

"Landing was tricky for new pilots because of the narrow gear. The approach was at 120–130 mph and it quit flying at about 95 mph indicated. Rudder action was very, very frequent and until you became accustomed to the aircraft it would likely as not be bouncing down the runway. Once you knew your aircraft you could goose the engine just at flare out and grease in like a true 'Hot Shot Charlie.' In aerobatics it was big enough to fly through anything you were big enough to try. It had a beautiful slow roll and although placarded against snaps and spins would do them. In a snap it would really snap your head around and in a spin it would wind up very nicely. Spin recovery was very simple—throttle, full left rudder and a very light right stick and turn on a dime and get nine cents in change. You came out facing 180 degrees and just about at stalling speed but you sure could change direction in a hurry. I have used this playing with Mark V Spitfires in North Africa and have turned to meet them head on and surprised the devil out of them in the process. It was a very good dive bomber and strafing airplane with excellent low level reliability. To sum it up— it was a delightful aircraft to fly."

These descriptions mirror opinions of most pilots who flew the P-40, a plane that tended to be temperamental at times, one requiring a lot of muscle to maneuver, below par in performance compared to a few other fighters of the era, but a hard-working, reliable ship nevertheless, which did its job well. In combat, the P-40 had already distinguished itself many months before the Japanese attack on Pearl Harbor. The British and French governments had ordered large numbers of them from Curtiss, although France fell under the German assault before she could fly them in combat; with the war drawing closer to her shores, a desperate Britain lost no time in assuming the French order, and Russia also began receiving P-40s under the Lend-Lease arrangement.

It was in China, however, in the earliest months of its wartime career, that the P-40's reputation as a rough-tough fighter began to skyrocket. This refers, of course, to the 99 Kittyhawks flown by the American Volunteer Group, soon to become the famed Flying Tigers, under the command of Claire Chennault. Although they were in combat less than one year, the Flying Tigers racked up the highest victory ratio of any P-40 group in the war: 286 Japanese aircraft shot down, and as many probables, against a loss of 23 Flying Tigers killed either in aerial combat or in accidents. Some historians place the number of Japanese killed as high as 1,500.

The United States was not at war when the AVG was formed, so the Flying Tigers were civilian volunteers. Yet the combat they saw was as real as any that their uniformed successors would encounter in three and a half years of flying P-40s after Pearl Harbor. The AVG, subject of many books and movies, produced thirty-nine aces by the time the group was disbanded on July 4, 1942; some, including Colonel Robert L. Scott, Jr., who was to bag thirteen Japanese planes as a P-40 aviator, remained in China to form the nucleus of the Army Air Corps's 23rd Fighter Group. Most of the other Flying Tigers remained in combat aviation, some returning to the Air Corps after their separation from the AVG, others to join Navy or Marine Corps units.

A month before the AVG was disbanded, P-40s were an important weapon

Now flying in peace instead of war, a P-40 Warhawk and a P-47 Thunderbolt join up in flying formation for spectators at the annual fall air show.

in the U. S. Navy's defense of the Aleutians against a Japanese naval assault, an attack most naval historians feel was intended as a diversionary maneuver to draw American ships away from their major (and victorious) engagement in the Battle of Midway. Prior to the outbreak of war, P-40s were a mainstay of the Air Corps's continental air defense of the Western Hemisphere. Squadrons were assigned not only to Alaska, but to Pearl Harbor, the Panama Canal, and U.S.-held Pacific outpost islands as well; as a result, periodic pre-Pearl Harbor aviation "war games" gave P-40 pilots at least a smattering of simulated combat experience, which they found to be of considerable value when the real shooting started in December 1941.

In December 1941, with America's entry into the war imminent, twenty-five P-40s and their pilots were ordered to the Aleutians, although only thirteen were in flying condition by the following month and only an even dozen were available when the Japanese fleet occupied the island of Kiska in June, about the time of the Battle of Midway. Japanese intelligence may have underrated the American fighter strength or, worse, overrated its own capacity to overwhelm the American Aleutian defense; in any event, the Imperial Navy was soon to receive an expensive lesson in P-40 combat ferocity, outnumbered or not. First, from occupied Kiska, the Japanese sent observation float planes over the island of

Strictly business, a rebuilt P-40, flown by Colonel Joe Jones, in level flight over Harlingen.

Umnak, where the P-40 fighters were based. The Japanese pilots quickly found that even a dense cloud cover over Umnak was no barrier to determined P-40 defenders; one float plane was shot down immediately and a second scooted home to Kiska heavily damaged. Next, the Japanese carriers *Ryujo* and *Junyo* launched four fighters and four dive-bombers, but eight defending P-40s downed two of each—a total of four—with a loss of only two "Hawks." Until September, when the all-P-40 18th Squadron arrived to bolster the Aleutian defenses, the Japanese, now aware of the P-40's lethal sting in the hands of a determined pilot, played it cozy; only occasionally did they send aircraft within sight of Umnak, and then only for quick look-and-run reconnaissance. The P-40s, meanwhile, had done exactly the job they were intended to do—they kept the enemy off balance until enough American strength was mustered to strike back. That is what happened on September 25, when the Americans went on the offensive in the Aleutians. Now reinforced with B-17 and B-24 heavy bombers as well as eleven newer Bell P-39 Airacobra fighters, the P-40s were joined by their Canadian counterparts, eleven Kittyhawks flown by a Royal Canadian Air Force squadron in an all-out attack on Kiska. In the first hours of the campaign, they knocked down two Mitsubishi fighters and destroyed eight float planes that had not had time to get airborne from the water. In the following months, P-40 pilots continued to harass the Japanese on Kiska, both with strafing attacks and, with planes equipped to carry a 500-pound bomb and six 20-pound fragmentation bombs, with hit-and-run bombing strikes. The strength of the P-40 squadrons

In far friendlier skies now, a Warhawk (bottom) flies escort for a C-47 transport. In the dark days of World War II, that upper craft—a Japanese replica flown by the CAF— would not be so innocently within range.

had increased to eighty planes by May 1943, and by August, the Japanese, having had enough, evacuated Kiska, never to return during the remainder of the war.

At the opposite extreme from bitter-cold Alaska, in both a geographic and climatic sense, P-40s achieved fame against the Germans and Italians in the Great Western Desert of North Africa. In June 1942, the fall of Tobruk to Rommel's Afrika Korps was a personally demoralizing and strategically costly defeat for the beleaguered infantry of British Army Commander General Bernard Montgomery. With Tobruk in German hands, the fate of most of North Africa lay in a precarious balance, and to decide that balance, a bolstering of air defenses was badly needed. It came in the familiar silhouette of the P-40. With the United States' role in the war now half a year old and P-40 production at Curtiss factories in high gear, the first squadrons of Kittyhawks with American pilots at their controls were ferried across the Atlantic aboard aircraft carriers and flown off their flight decks directly into combat. Before the Allied victory at El Alamein, which turned the tide of desert battle against Rommel, five fighter groups employing P-40s—the 33rd, 57th, 79th, 324th, and 325th—were pressed into battle as the Twelfth Air Force for the invasion of French North Africa. Allied losses were high at first, but as stepped-up strikes by Douglas A-20 Havocs and other light bombers continued to pound German bases daily, P-40s began to have a field day. The 57th Fighter Group alone produced at least fifteen aces in the African campaign, three of them in a single day's air combat, one of the most memorable of the war, which aviation historians aptly remember as the "Palm Sunday Massacre." Assigned to patrol the French North African coast to spot German transport airplanes crossing the Mediterranean to resupply Rommel's forces by air, three squadrons of the 57th along with the 314th Squadron of the 324th Fighter Group—a total of forty-six P-40s altogether—and twelve British RAF Spitfires—chanced upon a combat pilot's dream. Just before sunset, they spotted a huge formation of both German fighters and transports; later estimates of the transports alone placed the total at perhaps ninety Junkers Ju-52s. Supported by the Spitfires, the P-40 pilots jumped into the battle, and within twenty minutes, the North African coast line was a tangle of airplane wreckage. Statistics in an engagement of this magnitude tend to become distorted, but even allowing for acceptable error, the recorded claims give a fair idea of why the nickname of "massacre" is appropriate: fifty-seven Ju-52s, fourteen Messerschmitt Me-109s, and four Messerschmitt Me-110s were downed—seventy-five Luftwaffe combat planes in all. The Allied loss? Only six P-40s.

Although the Palm Sunday battle gave the 57th title to the greatest number of kills in a single day in North Africa, it was the later-arriving 325th that perhaps deserves the medal for the most effective unit all-around. The last P-40 group to see duty in the Great Western Desert, the 325th achieved the phenomenal kill ratio of seven German planes destroyed to each of its own lost. Further, 325th pilots could rightfully be proud of their record as bomber escorts; not a single plane they shepherded was lost to enemy action. Nicknamed the "Checkerboard Group" with their planes' tail surfaces painted in checks for identification, 325th pilots in one mission might as well have been decorated by the Navy; surprising a surfaced German submarine near the African coast, they launched a strafing attack so intense the U-boat sank before it could submerge to safety. It was the 325th, too, that first used the P-40 to tote a 1,000-pound bomb, a job the plane's manual said couldn't be done. Altogether, P-40s of the 325th officially knocked down 135 German planes in the relatively short period of the group's North African service against its own loss of 32 aircraft. (The 7–1 kill ratio of the 325th is accounted for by the fact that other, newer fighters were phased in, and the P-40 partially phased out, before Rommel was defeated in Africa.)

France, which at first had opposed the Allied landings in French North Africa, was the third nation to fly the P-40 in the Great Western Desert. For French pilots attached to the U. S. Army Air Corps's 33rd Fighter Group as the "Group Lafayette," the Warhawk, although new in their country's service, must have seemed vaguely familiar, as well it should have been; experienced fliers all, some of them aces, they had flown the P-40's Curtiss predecessor, the P-36, against the Germans before France fell to the Nazis. While enemy flak, fighters, and operational accidents took a heavy toll of Group Lafayette P-40s, their French pilots nevertheless managed to bag a number of enemy aircraft before the war ended. Only about thirty flyable P-40s were left by war's end, and these were used as trainers by France until 1946; there is no record of what happened to the few survivors since then.

Meanwhile, in the Pacific, the P-40 was the backbone of American fighter strength in the first years of the war. And even after the introduction there of faster, better-armed, better-performing twin-boomed P-38s, rear-engined P-39s, and massive P-47 fighters, they continued to perform various—and important—missions right up to V-J Day in August 1945. Japan's stunning surprise attack of Pearl Harbor wiped out most of the P-40s assigned by the Army Air Corps to defend Hawaii: The story of what happened in the Philippines, struck by the enemy only hours later, is not as clear. The Air Corps had four P-40 squadrons at three airfields on Luzon in late 1941; some, in fact, included small numbers of the even more antiquated Seversky P-35 pursuit fighters. On December 8 (December 7 east of the International Date Line, the same day as the Pearl Harbor attack) Japan launched a massive assault on the Philippines, as well as against other American outposts in the Pacific, which she hoped to seize quickly through her strategy of surprise. Unlike those at Pearl Harbor, the P-40s in the Philippines were scattered about in various phases of duty, but few were in any condition for combat. Some were in the air, returning from patrol, their fuel low. Others were on the ground, being refueled but not yet ready for takeoff. The fighter defense of the islands fell alone on the shoulders of the 20th Squadron, which quickly scrambled from Clark Field to bag their first Air Corps victories of the war against an enemy but hours old. Almost in their prop wash, other P-40s of the 3rd Pursuit Squadron were returning from patrol when they were jumped by a swarm of Japanese fighters bent on strafing their airfield at Iba. Although they were dangerously low on fuel and greatly outnumbered, they successfully beat off the enemy assault. Five of the 3rd's aircraft were sacrificed to Japanese fire and three others, their tanks empty, crash-landed.

In the first frantic weeks of the war when American forces were still reeling from the blow in Hawaii, valiant P-40 pilots flew what amounted to suicide missions all over the Pacific. Typical was what occurred in the Philippines in just one week after Pearl Harbor and one day after the co-ordinated enemy air attack against the airfields. On December 10, when American reconnaissance planes spotted a large Japanese naval force approaching Luzon, P-40s were scrambled in an attempt to turn it back. Heavily outnumbered by swarms of Japanese escort fighters, P-40 pilots of the 17th Pursuit Squadron from Nichols Field managed to sneak through to strafe several of the ships. Later the same day, they joined P-40s of the 21st and 34th Squadrons in an attempt to ward off an incoming raid of enemy fighters and bombers. This time they were not as successful;

Tender loving care is a constant requirement to keep the ancient war birds in flight readiness at Harlingen.

overwhelmed by the staggering Japanese force, only a handful survived the blistering aerial defense and the enemy attack itself continued without impairment. It became clear to Philippine defenders that continued use of P-40s in this role was useless; one more attack, perhaps, and no planes would be left at all. The surviving fighters instead were limited to reconnaissance missions from that point on, but even this order, a humiliating but necessary one to most of the P-40 fliers, could not limit their yearning for revenge for what had happened in Hawaii a few days before. On December 16, the restraints were lifted. Leading a flight of three Warhawks, Lieutenant Ray Wagner waded through a stiff barrage of antiaircraft fire at Vigan airfield, which the Japanese had taken; although one plane in his flight was shot down, Wagner and a wingman managed to damage or destroy twenty Japanese aircraft on the ground by strafing and puncturing the runway itself with fragmentation bombs before scooting safely back to their own base.

In the ensuing weeks, American and Filipino defenders drew into tighter and tighter pockets of retreat. Finally, they were ordered to evacuate their bases to begin their now-legendary last-ditch stand on the island of Corregidor. The supply of P-40s available for action had been reduced to less than a dozen; by March 4, 1942, two months before the Philippines' surrender, enemy action had cut the number to only four. In what may have amounted to the final fighting of any kind before General MacArthur's return to the islands, each of the four was loaded with a 500-pound bomb to pummel Japanese shipping in Subic Bay. Of the four, one was shot down by enemy fire, and the remaining three crashed upon returning to their own airfields. In what had become perhaps the darkest week of the fighting, for the P-40, in the Philippines at least, the war was over.

In other areas of the Pacific, the situation appeared as desperate, and as harried American forces continued to yield strategically valuable ground before the turnaround naval Battle of Midway in June 1942, P-40s often meant the difference between mere retreat and total catastrophe. Flown by Australian and New Zealand pilots as well as American, it was not at all unusual for a single Kittyhawk to take on fifteen or twenty superior Japanese fighters. That early in the war, however, when the Japanese had taken Rabaul and Lae and were poised to strike Port Moresby, the final jumping-off point for an assault on Australia, there was no choice; the Japanese were so confident of a quick victory, in fact, that they often flew bomber formations without any fighter escort at all, a cocky, nose-thumbing gesture of contempt, as it were. Yet as history so well records, the P-40s and their pilots, at tremendous self-sacrifice, bought the necessary time until newer, more adequate American fighters as well as pilots could arrive to turn the tide of battle.

That the P-40s were inferior to their Japanese fighter counterparts, despite sentimental but delusionary denials from most men who flew them, is perhaps best illustrated by an anecdote involving the enemy itself. Early in the war, the Japanese found themselves with a number of P-40Es in their possession after the fall of the Dutch East Indies. All were in good condition. Many, in fact, had never been flown, having been captured while still in their shipping crates. Since the P-40 was the United States' major land-based fighter at the time, the capture of not a single plane but several was manna from heaven. Not only did the P-40s give them the chance to flight-test their main adversary and thus assess both its strong points and failings, the Japanese reasoned, they might be used to replace interceptor defense planes in the home islands on a one-to-one basis, freeing their own fighters for combat use. First flight-tested on the spot and later shipped to Japan for further evaluation, the captured P-40s were then subjected to the kind of snub that not even the aircraft's most bitter detractor could later understand. Determining that the P-40 could not outperform the most obsolete of its own military aircraft, the Betty torpedo-bomber, the Japanese used the P-40s briefly to acquaint airmen of what they could expect in combat, then scrapped them all.

If there is any saving grace in this parable of war, it must, once again, be related in human terms, by the fact that it was the superior training, innate skill, and stubborn, iron-willed resolution of its pilots, and not merely the plane itself, that made the P-40 such an important weapon in spite of its many shortcomings.

Russian pilots flying the P-40, possessing no less determination or skill than their American counterparts, doubtless would agree. Although the Soviets favored the P-39 Bell Airacobra, which was shipped over later under the Lend-Lease program, they put the P-40 to good advantage in the earlier war years. The first shipment of Lend-Lease P-40s was convoyed to Archangel in early 1941. As an indicator of how desperately in need of fighters were the Russians, forty Soviet aviators—none of whom had even seen a P-40 or read its manual—were checked out and sent into combat in only ten days. P-40s were flown in many areas of Russia, but perhaps the most memorable missions were those in defense of Moscow; by the end of only two weeks of combat against German fighters and bombers raiding the Soviet capital, one P-40 squadron alone was credited with twenty-nine kills while losing only three P-40s.

In addition to their combat use, P-40s were used as trainers by the U. S. Air

Corps long after later fighters were delivered and phased into action. Wartime attrition accounted for losses numbering into the thousands. In Africa, the French, as reported earlier, used the P-40 in service until 1946–47. Two other air forces made both wartime and postwar use of them also; several were supplied to Brazil after that nation joined the Allies in a declaration of war on Germany and Italy, and others served, under American technical supervision, in the postwar Air Force of Chile.

Perhaps more than any other American-built World War II fighter, in other words, P-40s were scattered over a major portion of the world at war's end. Allowing for those also destroyed in combat, the final disposition of many of the almost 14,000 built can be accounted for. Yet when CAF founder Lloyd Nolen bought his first P-40 in 1951, only six years after the war ended, he was shocked to learn of its rarity; at the most, there were perhaps only two dozen that could be located anywhere in the world.

"At first I was merely surprised," he remembers. "Then, the more I thought about the situation, when I learned that the P-40 wasn't the only American World War II fighter that we had virtually consigned to oblivion, I wasn't just shocked and astonished, I was boiling mad."

Unlike many future CAF aircraft acquisitions, that Warhawk was in good condition, yet Nolen was able to buy it for a paltry $1,500; the figure doubtless is not as much an indicator of its true worth at that time but is a barometer of the disregard of most Americans for the historically important airplanes that had

Engines roaring, two restored Warhawks flying in formation as in yesteryear.

helped win the most momentous war in history. Nolen sold the P-40 in order to purchase the more powerful P-51 Mustang, but the P-40 was repurchased by the CAF eight years later, in 1960. Tragically, the plane and its pilot were lost in a fatal crash in 1964, one of only two to this writing in CAF history. By 1967, however, the CAF had honed the art of locating needed airplanes to a razor edge of perfection, and a second Warhawk, found in Phoenix, Arizona, was acquired at a cost of $11,500. Today, it bears the painted shark's jaws of Claire Chennault's Flying Tigers on its engine cowling and the insignia of Chiang Kai-shek's China on its wings. Insignia identification of any country or unit in which the P-40 saw service would doubtless be as appropriate since, virtually from pole to pole, it was an airplane that, as Flying Tiger ace Colonel Robert L. Scott, Jr., put it, was "damned by words but flown to glory."

THE P-51,
THE UNWANTED HERO

*If it looks good,
it'll fly good.*

> —Anonymous World War II
> aviators' saying

On the basis of aesthetics alone, the North American P-51 Mustang would have to rank as the finest single-engined fighter ever built. A trim, powerful, tough plane with the "lean and hungry look" that enchants model-builder and pilot alike, the *Mustang* just *looks* like what a fighter plane should look like, as opposed to some of its contemporaries that may have performed better in specific ways, yet were glaring abnormalities in appearance by comparison. If there is a single bump, bulge, roll, rivet, or other doodad on the P-51 that does not directly contribute to its basic function as a gun platform, it takes a mighty discerning eye to find it. The Mustang is probably the closest the aviation industry has ever come to perfection in aerodynamic design before the advent of the jet, when aerodynamic purity was not just desirable but, because of airframe punishment in ultra-high-speed flight, absolutely necessary.

An appropriate analogy between the P-51 and its World War II fighter contemporaries might be that between a racehorse and a plow horse. The plow horse is a fine animal in its own way; were it not for this faithful steed plodding tireless hours at the plow, agriculture in centuries past would have been a much more tedious undertaking. Yet few people, save perhaps the farmer whose livelihood depended upon his plow horse, would be as emotionally stirred as far as *appearance* is concerned as by a sleek, trim-boned, immaculately groomed thoroughbred that has just galloped off with top honors in the Preakness or the Kentucky Derby. Even looking at a P-51 parked on a runway, out of its true element with its huge propeller stilled and its tail drooping on the ground, one gets the feeling that here is an airplane that must have taken years of design and experimentation, more years of constant modification, the end result of winnowing out the faults and adding the best of its predecessors. Yet, almost unbelievably, the

There's only one word to describe the P-51 Mustang: streamlined. *Perhaps the hottest of all World War II fighters before the jet era dawned, the Mustang was one of the CAF's earliest restoration projects.*

P-51 is a plane that went from drawing board to test flight in an astonishing *117 days*—the shortest period of concept-to-flight of any airplane ever built in America. Moreover, although it went through many modifications, the P-51 was essentially the same airplane at the end of the war that it was when it first went into combat. A basic change was in the choice of engines—Merlins and Allisons of various horsepower ratings were used throughout the Mustang's lettered-model series—but in general, the mighty P-51 changed little. (An exception was the rare Twin Mustang, a marriage of two standard P-51 fuselages, but this hardly qualifies since it was an almost entirely different plane. The Confederate Air Force owns and flies a Twin Mustang, and it will be described briefly later in this chapter.)

As surprisingly, despite its superb combat record in World War II as well as in Korea, and its collection of trophies that made it a consistent winner in post-war sports aviation races, it was not until after another nation—Britain—proved the Mustang's worth in the air that the United States would even consider using it. The reason, some historians suggest, was purely a matter of ego. Though American-designed and American-built, the P-51 was originally built for the Royal Air Force in 1940; since it was never even proposed to the U. S. War Department and since it was designed for the RAF from the ground up to fill specific British war needs, the U. S. Army Air Corps apparently saw no reason to even evaluate it.

The demands of war, however, have a way of overruling even the most relentless ego, and when the Mustang finally joined American military service, it lost no time in finding acceptance and in becoming what many feel was perhaps the best all-around prop-driven fighter of all time.

P-38 Lightning pilots may disagree, but the Mustang was the fastest American propeller-driven fighter ever built. There's no question that it was the fastest *single-engined* fighter, as well as the most maneuverable. And, most important perhaps, it had the greatest cruising range of any fighter in the USAAF. It was this cruising capability, further extended by belly tanks, that gave the Mustang its fantastic absolute range exceeding 2,000 miles, and an endurance time of eight hours. This incredible range and endurance, plus the great mix of armament with which it could be equipped, finally led to a reduction in the staggering losses of B-24 Liberator and B-17 Flying Fortress bombers, which had plagued the Eighth Air Force over Europe. Strategic daylight bombing of targets well inside Germany, before the arrival of escort fighters with adequate range, was a highly controversial topic among European Theater military strategists, and the heavy aircraft losses did little to support the arguments of proponents of strategic bombing.

Until March 1944, when Mustangs were assigned to escort the "heavies" over *Festung Europa,* bomber losses were so prohibitive that for a period the Allied Command even considered bringing daylight raids to a halt. When long-range Mustangs finally entered the picture, however, the Nazis soon found their war machine exposed to continuous daylight attack, which even their best Luftwaffe fighter pilots seemed helpless to stop. With the American bombers escorted by fighters that were at least equal to, if not superior to, their own Messerschmitt and Focke-Wulf fighters, the vast industrial capability of Germany no longer was immune from damage. An extensive postwar strategic bombing study ordered by the White House concluded that, more than any other single factor, it was the constant day-to-day precision pounding of the German war industry that finally brought the Third Reich to its knees. The arrival of the P-51 as a bomber escort—belated though it was because of USAAF indifference —was therefore a critical factor in shortening the war in Europe, freeing vast amounts of manpower and matériel for ending the war in the Pacific.

The Mustang was the first single-engined fighter to reach Berlin. It was also the first to fly with heavy bombers over Ploesti, Rumania, whose refineries toward the end of the war had become Hitler's sole source of vital petroleum. And it was the Mustang, with its great range, that the USAAF assigned specifically for a full-scale, all-out, major effort over Germany to hunt down and destroy the dwindling Luftwaffe, thus giving Dwight Eisenhower's advancing armies a measure of respite from aerial harassment on their way to Berlin.

The inspiring genius for the P-51 was that of James H. "Dutch" Kindelberger, a shrewd, skilled, enterprising engineer who by 1934 had risen to the presidency of North American Aviation, Inc., after learning the airplane-building business with the Glenn L. Martin and Douglas Aircraft companies. When Kindelberger took over North American, the firm had a single airplane under contract, a passenger transport whose design, some say, Kindelberger had decided to try as a result of his earlier experience at Douglas with the DC-2 and its famed successor, the DC-3. For reasons still unknown, Dutch Kindelberger wasn't happy with his passenger plane, and he scrapped it in favor of trying out some new military designs. It was in the mid-thirties, it will be remembered, that America was at last beginning to shake off the complacent attitude that had

At rest, a CAF Mustang is mirrored in a Texas rain puddle.

delayed the welding of a strong and efficient military aviation capability.

Dutch Kindelberger was a hare, not a tortoise. His first military airplane venture, a trainer designated the BT-9, for which the Air Corps later placed an $82 million order, was conceived on a Saturday with actual work beginning only two days later, on Monday. Convinced that there was a lucrative market for trainers in Europe, where Hitler was already making his move, Kindelberger made an extended sales trip to the Continent in 1937–38. He sold very few ideas, but the European tour was by no means a waste of time; while visiting foreign aircraft plants, he watched various fighter plane designs moving from drawing board to assembly line. He was impressed with how far fighter design had advanced there compared with what he had seen in America. His engineer's brain constantly whirring in high gear, Kindelberger took copious notes of what he saw, and when he returned to North American's plant at Mines Field, near Los Angeles, a revolutionary new fighter was already being plotted in his mind.

Two years passed. By 1940, World War II had exploded in Europe, and by late fall of that year, having waged its valiant defense against a numerically superior Luftwaffe in the Battle of Britain, the Royal Air Force was, in terms of remaining Spitfire and Hurricane fighters, dangerously low in inventory. Britain badly needed a new fighter for the war years ahead, and it needed one quickly. The Spitfire was a top-rated combat ship, but, unlike America's, British industry simply was not geared for high-speed assembly line production. While waiting for more planes of its own to be built, the RAF began seeking fighters built by other friendly nations. America was the first logical choice.

The Curtiss P-40 Warhawk was at that time America's standard pursuit fighter. Even in 1940, it was an obsolete ship, though it was better than none at all. Hoping it could buy some P-40s to make up for its dwindling supply of Hurricanes and Spitfires, the RAF dispatched a delegation of purchasing agents across the Atlantic. Their disappointment was immediate. Curtiss was sympathetic, but at that time the company was hard-pressed even to meet its P-40 commitments for the U. S. Army Air Corps. The British next turned to Dutch Kindelberger and his company, whose reputation had become well known as a result of his earlier visit to Europe. At Mines Field, they presented Dutch with an unusual proposal. Under subcontract to Curtiss, they asked, could North American build a bunch of P-40s in a hurry?

A man of intense pride, Kindelberger was stung by the suggestion. "I will *not* build someone else's airplanes," he told the crestfallen British, "but I'll build you one of my own. And it will be even better than the P-40."

The British were nonplused. They knew that North American had no fighter in production, and they guessed—correctly--that none even existed on paper. Again, they stressed the need for acquiring fighters in a hurry.

"No problem," Kindelberger replied confidently. "I'll make you a firm commitment. Give me a contract, and I'll deliver a fighter in four months. One hundred twenty days. Not a day longer."

Four months! The British were aghast. Four months to design, build, test, and make operational a plane of entirely new design, a process that normally took up to three years? Had that statement come from anyone else, the speaker doubtless would have been written off either as a hopeless egomaniac or a raving lunatic. They knew Dutch to be neither, of course, and they were spellbound by his audacity. A handshake cinched the deal, a formal contract followed. Almost before its ink was dry—exactly 117 days later, three days earlier than the promised 120—the first completed P-51 rolled out of a hangar at Mines Field.

Years later, an engineer in the project described how Kindelberger had

The success of World War II Allied bombing raids over Europe is credited largely to the Mustang's role as an escort. Here, a P-51 re-creates that role with a B-25 Mitchell bomber over Harlingen.

pulled off his miracle. "First, Dutch put us on a sixteen-hour working day. The plant itself went on a twenty-four-hour-a-day basis. Sometimes, he'd even lock us in our rooms. There were constant conferences. We'd try one idea, decide it wouldn't work, throw it out, and try again. But from the very beginning, Dutch knew *exactly* what he wanted; all we were doing was transforming onto paper what he had already laid out in his mind."

Designated the NA-73X, the P-51 prototype first flew on October 26, 1940. It was the beginning of a long and illustrious line of 15,000 sister ships produced altogether. What Kindelberger had done to make it such a perfect airplane was to combine—first in his head, later on paper—the specific requirements that the early months of war in Europe had suggested were necessary. The P-51, in other words, was the first American fighter plane built entirely on the basis of combat experience, from lessons learned the hard way after Hitler's Luftwaffe had begun to overwhelm Europe.

The English had agreed to buy 320 Mustangs if Kindelberger met his 120-day concept-to-flight deadline. Even after the NA-73X crashed on November 20, 1940 (its pilot was forced to make a wheels-down landing on a plowed field due to a fuel malfunction), the British confidence in Kindelberger's plane held firm. In fact, when the first model was delivered to England and run through low-level demonstration tests, its performance seemed so unbelievable that the tests were repeated just to make sure the initial ones were not a fluke.

One of the basic features of the new fighter was its laminar flow wing, a type of design that was ideal for high speed, minimum drag, and long range. The disadvantage in the design was that the P-51 required a very high landing speed; however, the installation of large flaps helped considerably to solve this problem. Viewing its lines, the Mustang was one of the slimmest and trimmest of World War II fighters; maintaining that profile presented three related problems to its engineers: where to put the radiator, the cooling system, and the air scoop. The cooling system especially could not be minimized. By their very nature, liquid-cooled engines are extremely touchy beasts. In many planes with inadequate cooling systems for such engines, many a combat mission had to be scrubbed simply because the engine overheated while the planes were waiting in line for takeoff. It was for this reason that liquid-cooled-engine fighters normally were sent up after the bombers they were to escort had taken off and grouped.

North American solved the radiator problem by placing it behind the pilot. There, it delivered maximum performance without disturbing the plane's smooth lines. All the plumbing required for the cooling system was crammed into available nooks and crannies of the fuselage in such a way that the plane's slim silhouette was not disturbed either.

The air scoop was located under the fuselage, just aft of the cockpit. This worked well, too, except on those rare occasions when a Mustang jockey found

The CAF's famous "Gunfighter," flown in air shows by Colonel Ed Messick. Note the prominent air scoop below the cockpit, one of the Mustang's distinctive features.

himself forced to ditch at sea. Just as the B-24 Liberator bomber was a poor ditcher because of the high placement of its wing, P-51 pilots generally feared a water landing more than an encounter with an enemy, because the air scoop, hanging below the fuselage, tended to flip the plane over on its nose immediately upon contact. The P-51's manual perhaps best describes this hazard:

"Never attempt to ditch a P-51 except as a last resort," it cautions. "Fighter planes are not designed to float on water, and the P-51 has an even greater tendency to dive because of the airscoop underneath. It will go down in 1½ to 2 seconds." Not exactly the most reassuring words for Mustang pilots whose missions took them over water, but practical and realistic nevertheless.

The P-51 *could* be successfully ditched, however, although the number of pilots who opted for hitting the silk probably far exceeds those who decided to tough it out and belly in. The best way to abandon a doomed P-51 over water, the manual explains, is in the air. Standard procedure for that kind of a maneuver was to let the plane descend to about fifty feet over the water and then yank back on the stick to gain at least five hundred feet of altitude with the dwindling airspeed, then, as quickly as possible, jump out of the cockpit for a low-altitude parachute descent.

Ditching was extremely rare, however, especially since the P-51 flew the majority of its missions over land. It is mentioned here only to emphasize the fact that even in an airplane that approaches the zenith of perfection, some sacrifices must be made. In the case of the P-51, however, there were doubtless fewer sacrifices—and therefore fewer pilot complaints—than in most World War II era fighters.

Immensely impressed with the P-51, the RAF began working it overtime in the defense of Britain against Hermann Goering's vaunted Luftwaffe. U. S. Army officials continued to snub the fighter, however, apparently favoring the P-47 and P-38, until the Pentagon began receiving glowing letters of its RAF exploits from American airmen stationed in Britain. One of them came from no less illustrious a flier than Eddie Rickenbacker, who not only commended the Mustang in general, but offered a specific suggestion that, he believed, would make it the best fighter of them all. His proposal: remove the Allison engine and replace it with a Rolls-Royce Merlin high-altitude engine—the same power plant that helped the British Spitfire and Hurricane achieve their hard-won glory. The USAAF finally ended its long-standing boycott of the tough little Mustang, added it to its fighter inventory, and the rest is history.

Much has been said and written of the vulnerability of the Mustang's liquid-cooling system to enemy gunfire. It was this always-present risk, in fact, applied equally to *any* plane with a liquid-cooled engine, that split military airplane buyers into two quite vocal camps during the entire period when combat planes were powered with reciprocating engines. And the argument of the "cons" was irrefutable; even the P-51 manual admits that the tiniest rupture of the cooling system limits the life of that particular engine to a maximum of ten seconds. Yet while the merits and demerits of air-cooled versus liquid-cooled engines can be debated endlessly, much less has been recorded about the Mustang's almost uncanny ability to absorb enemy fire other than in its cooling system, yet return home safely. And certainly there can be no argument over the Mustang's ability to dish out punishment. During World War II, P-51 pilots of the 4th Fighter Group alone bagged more than 1,000 enemy planes, an all-time record for any American unit before or since.

Altogether in the European Theater of Operations, Mustangs were credited

Pride of the famed Flying Tigers, the Curtiss P-40 Warhawk is now also the pride of the Confederate Air Force.

Perhaps the hottest World War II fighter of them all, one of the CAF's North American P-51 Mustangs as seen from a Ghost Squadron B-24 Liberator.

OPPOSITE PAGE
ABOVE: A short-lived but effective phenomenon, the Twin Mustang, one of the CAF's rarest aircraft.

BELOW: A P-38 Lockheed twin-engined Lightning of the CAF fighter wing.

Its huge engine cowling is not so prominent at this angle, but the P-47 Thunderbolt is dynamite anyway. The CAF reached as far as Central America to find this "Jug" and others in its collection.

OPPOSITE PAGE
ABOVE: The CAF's P-39 Airacobra flies with Russian markings.

BELOW: The CAF's P-63 Kingcobra, basically the same plane as the Airacobra, but with a design much more advanced.

SIDE: Two Grumman TBF Avenger torpedo bombers in flight added substantially to the Ghost Squadron's "Navy arm."

BELOW: A valiant hero of the Battle of Midway, the CAF's Douglas SBD Dauntless dive bomber.

ABOVE: To many an enemy vessel, the Curtiss SB2C Helldiver was a blood-curdling sight. This one flies regularly in CAF air shows.

SIDE: Its design dating back to the mid-thirties, the CAF's Grumman F4F Wildcat was the Navy's standard carrier-borne fighter at the outbreak of World War II.

The Grumman F6F Hellcat, a marked advance over its immediate predecessor, the F4F Wildcat, was acquired by the CAF in 1961.

with destroying 9,081 enemy aircraft: 4,950 in the air and 4,131 on the ground, in 213,873 sorties. But it was not only as a fighter that the P-51 excelled. In later stages of the plane's development, North American built two greatly improved models, the P-51A and an attack version designated the A-36. The attack version was built with bomb-racks and diving brakes and given six .50-caliber machine guns instead of the standard four 20-millimeter cannon of the pursuit series. Thus, as the A-36, the Mustang became a triple threat to the Axis: fighter, strafer, and dive-bomber. The original P-51s were equipped with three-bladed propellers; when the USAAF switched to the supercharged British Merlin engine to improve performance at high altitude, the change also included a switch to a four-bladed prop, which remained throughout the development of all subsequent models.

The combat record of the P-51, particularly in the ETO, is legend, but a

The business end of a Mustang during a fly-by at Harlingen. The four-bladed propeller —added when the British Merlin engine replaced the original American Allison—is evident.

brief retelling of just two combat missions will help illustrate both the plane's great versatility, and the arm's-length respect it gained among Luftwaffe opponents.

The Germans began the war with fighter planes vastly superior to most of those the Allies were then flying, and at least equal to the latest models. But it wasn't long until American technology, particularly, began closing the gap. Hitler badly needed a first-rate Luftwaffe, and early in the war he gave top priority to the development of fighters that once again could give his Air Force a clear-cut advantage over the enemy. Long before American technology moved far into the field, it was learned through Allied intelligence that German engineers were accelerating efforts to build turbojet and pure-jet fighters. Had they proved successful in substantial numbers, the tide of the air war over Europe from 1942 onward might have been entirely different. Most of Hitler's jets came too late to help him. An exception, and a frightening exception it was to the Allies, was the twin-turbojet Messerschmitt Me-262, whose capability, it was feared, could outstrip any existing American or British fighter; it would thus become a devastating deterrent to Allied strategic bombing, which led to the eventual defeat of Germany.

The Me-262 was designed for a maximum speed of 600 miles an hour. At that blistering pace, no existing Allied fighter could come anywhere within gun range of it. The Mustang's top speed was 437 miles an hour; even at the plus-500 it could attain under certain conditions, it would have been as poorly matched against the 262 as the P-40 Warhawk had been against the Japanese Zero. The Me-262 was not just an image on the war horizon, however, it was already in production long before D-Day. But Hitler faced one disadvantage that American plane builders did not have to share; his factories were open targets for bombing raids. To offset this disadvantage (which applied as well to all German war-related industries), he developed a system of dispersing production over widely scattered areas of Germany. This meant that the various components had to be transported overland to be joined together, and to the Mustang fell the frequent task of making sure that the parts never reached their destination.

For instance, intelligence had disclosed that production of the Me-262 had been divided between a plant in Regensburg, where fuselages were assembled, and another at Augsburg, where further subassembly was done. Strategic bombing raids were ordered on both facilities, and heavy damage was reported. Worried about possible follow-up attacks, the Germans then moved production to Leipheim, but once again, on April 24, 1944, as the result of accurate intelligence, Eighth Air Force "heavies" moved in, wave after wave, seriously disrupting production. Despite such harassment, Germany managed to produce 1,300 of these turbojets in 1944 and 1945, and the Mustang must be at least partially given credit for the fact that only a handful got into actual combat.

One such successful mission, on April 17, 1945, was led by Lieutenant Colonel Joseph L. Thurty of the 339th Fighter Group stationed at Fowlmere, near Cambridge, England. Returning from a mission in southern Germany, Thurty and seven fellow P-51 pilots spotted a strange-looking conveyance moving along an autobahn 6,000 feet below. Truck traffic was small game for P-51s, hardly worth the risk of going down and shooting it out. But this truck was different, somehow; as it turned out, the bulky "package" concealed beneath a canvas canopy was an Me-262 being delivered to the Luftwaffe. It took about six minutes for Thurty's flight to reduce the enemy plane to scrap metal; based on this experience, later Mustang missions were ordered specifically to watch autobahn traffic, and the loss of an unconfirmed number of Me-262s resulted.

A very rare P-51C before its restoration by the CAF.

An even more unusual mission was one flown on April 11, 1944, which involved Captain Henry W. Brown of Fighter Squadron 354, 355th Fighter Group of the Eighth Air Force. Brown was in a flight of Mustangs that had escorted a group of heavy bombers on a raid at Sorau, near Berlin, a raid that, as it turned out, was extremely costly—sixty-four of the "heavies" failed to return. Brown's flight had run into heavy Me-109 opposition, and though the American fighters had used up most of their ammunition in protecting the bombers, they had a few rounds left each with which they managed to destroy a Messerschmitt spotted on the ground, and to pepper a few other small targets of opportunity. Then, their ammo completely gone, they pointed the needle-noses of their Mustangs west toward England.

Suddenly, still over Germany, Brown spotted four Me-109s closing in on his wingmen from behind. None of the Americans, apparently, were aware of their danger. To make matters worse, Brown's radio malfunctioned temporarily, and he could not broadcast a warning. His dilemma was, of course, further compounded by the fact that even if he decided to take on the enemy fighters, he had no ammo to take them on with. What he decided to do is something second nature to anyone who has played poker. He decided to bluff.

At this point, Brown realized that because he was flying somewhat apart from the other Mustangs, none of the Luftwaffe pilots had yet seen him. To make certain they did, he poured on emergency power and veered quickly in their direction, slipping quickly behind the trailing Me-109. By 1944, the Luftwaffe had become acutely aware of the great speed, fine performance, and lethal firepower of Dutch Kindelberger's 117-day miracle; instead of pursuing Brown's unaware wingmen, all four enemy fliers broke formation and began tactics to evade Brown himself. Doggedly, Brown kept on the trail of the

Messerschmitt he had picked out as his "target"—silently cursing his luck each time it fell within his gunsights. But he dared not linger too long within gunfire range, else the Me-109 pilot, seeing no fire from his pursuer and aware that Brown was returning from a mission rather than heading toward one, might have figured out the bluff. One by one, Brown jumped behind the other Me-109s, matching move for move until, tiring of the game, the Germans finally dove to gain additional speed and then disappeared over the horizon.

Back in England, Brown's wingmen were beginning to worry that something had happened to their leader, but less than thirty minutes after they landed their ships, Brown's finally showed up.

Later, in the base officers' club, Brown rounded up the others and angrily demanded to know why they had not been observant enough to spot the Messerschmitts. "Oh, we saw them all right," one replied. Brown was nonplused. "Then why in hell did you take off for home and leave me behind?" he demanded. "Because," came the answer, "we were all out of ammunition!"

Later, Brown, now promoted to lieutenant colonel, was awarded the Distinguished Flying Cross for his heroic action. It was probably the only time in Air Force history that a pilot was decorated for bravery in aerial combat in which he fired not a single round of ammunition.

Its combat days in Europe finished on V-E Day in 1945, the Mustang went on to achieve new glory in the Pacific Theater. As it had with B-17s and B-24s in Europe, it became the mainstay fighter escort for B-29 Superfortress raids on the Japanese mainland. When the war ended on August 14, 1945, several hundred P-51s, being then the first-line fighter in the Air Force's arsenal, were assigned to air national guard units for fighter pilot training. A very few were declared as surplus and sold to private owners. But hundreds of others were sent to

A Mustang undergoes restoration in Harlingen, 1964.

desert graveyards to await the smelter or the scrap dealer. The age of the jet had arrived, and there seemed simply no reason to hang on to a bunch of thirsty, costly-to-maintain prop fighters that had grown past their prime.

But the Mustang was to live to fight once more. When the Korean War exploded in June 1950, Air Force strategists were relieved to find that the P-51s ordered destroyed had not yet been scrapped. That helped them out of an unamusing dilemma. Although the combat jet fighter had indeed arrived on the aviation scene shortly after World War II ended, production had not yet caught up with demand; by 1950, only 2,500 operational jets of all types could be numbered throughout all Air Force commands throughout the world. Once again, the feisty little Mustang was drafted for war duty, as well as a handful of Corsairs and AD Skyraiders the Navy had thoughtfully kept around. A total of 750 Mustangs were "demothballed" from the desert bases, overhauled, and rushed to Asia. Another 700 were repossessed from the air national guard units, making a total of more than 1,400 available for duty in Korea, where they proved ideal for close air support operations. While the total may seem high, it was actually only about 10 per cent of all P-51s built by North American.

(Even rarer were the unique Twin Mustangs, of which only 270 were built. Designed in early 1944, and designated as the F-82, the prototype was flown in April 1945, too late for combat in World War II action, but early enough to score several air kills in Korea. The F-82 basically was two standard Mustangs "married" at wing and tail, but their design really wasn't quite that simple. The original P-51 fuselage had been lengthened, and many other modifications were made. Some termed the F-82 a "poor man's Lightning," because in appearance it vaguely resembled Lockheed's twin-boom, twin-engined fighter of the same period. But the derisive nickname quickly vanished when the Twin Mustang went

The perfect marriage: the very rare Twin Mustang F-82. Built too late for World War II, the Twin saw duty in Korea, and is a special prize of the CAF collection. This Twin is being readied for a ferry flight from Kelly Air Force Base to Harlingen.

into the air; its twin engines gave it a phenomenal top speed of 470 miles an hour and, with two fuselages instead of one where fuel could be stored, a range of 2,200 miles.)

After Korea, when peace arrived for the second time in less than ten years, the Mustang became an overnight darling of the aviation racing fraternity. With its tremendous speed, toughness, and reliability gained via wartime modifications, it became such a consistent trophy winner that many pilots flying other types of planes, learning that Mustangs were on the starting line, withdrew out of sheer hopelessness.

Mustangs won postwar races in the hands of many pilots. None, however, won as many or as consistently as the various Mustangs owned and flown by Albert Paul Mantz. A legend in his own time and one of the finest pilots since man first took to the skies, Paul Mantz shortly after the war had become the owner of one of the world's largest private air forces. In business as a flying stunt man ("precision flier," he preferred to call his trade), he owned at one time no less than seventy-five B-17 Flying Fortresses, twenty-eight B-24 Liberators, ten B-25 Mitchells, twenty-two twin-engined Marauders, six Bell P-39 Airacobras, ninety P-40 Warhawks, thirty-one P-47 Thunderbolts . . . and eight P-51 Mustangs. Whenever a moviemaker needed a World War II vintage plane for a flying sequence, Mantz invariably got the first phone call. However, although his business was stunt flying, his consuming passion was air racing, and with his highly modified Mustangs he soon became king of the hill among his competitors.

One of Mantz's favorite events was the Bendix Trophy Race, flown between California and Cleveland. Mantz won the Bendix race several times, usually establishing new speed records that he would later break himself. Many a jealous competitor wondered how he managed to win so often, especially those who flew similar planes, but Mantz was not one to divulge the secrets of his success as a racer. All he would admit was that it was not a single factor upon which winning counted, but a combination of factors. Mantz firmly believed in flying all-out, but he also knew that to exceed an engine's limits was to invite disaster. Perhaps that best sums up the secret of his success; he knew exactly where an engine's limit was and he flew just to that point, not a fraction further. To Paul Mantz, a plane's altimeter was just an ornamental gadget. "It doesn't mean a thing in racing," he was once quoted as saying. "In racing, what is more important is manifold pressure. You fly by wartime emergency power. You put your manifold pressure on sixty-seven inches of mercury and your rpms at 3,000, and leave them there. This might put you at 28,000 feet or 32,000 feet, but the altitude doesn't really matter."

Doubtless, Paul Mantz's most coveted Bendix victory was in 1946. What made that victory so especially sweet was the fact that he won over some top-rate competition, including three other Mustangs. Two of the P-51s were piloted by Bill Eddy of La Jolla, California, and Tommy Mayson, who happened to work for Mantz at the time. In the third was the famed aviatrix Jacqueline Cochran. Mantz might have settled for second place to Eddy or Mayson, but had Jackie Cochran come in first, it would have no doubt been the cruelest ego-crusher of Mantz's career, for it was no secret around Hollywood or anywhere else that Mantz and Cochran, for reasons never fully known, were more than competitors, they just plain didn't like each other.

Mantz was determined to win in 1946, come what may. For weeks, he planned and figured, replanned and refigured, working late into the night to figure such things as how much fuel he should carry, and how he could carry enough without the time-consuming fuel stop that many pilots were forced to

Not *a twin-tailed Lightning, which it closely resembles, but a rare Twin Mustang F-82.*

One of the CAF's Twin Mustang's engines is serviced.

make. Wing tanks were the obvious answer; it was their use that gave the P-51 its phenomenal range in wartime operations. Wing tanks, however, add drag. Even the tiniest amount of drag was too much for Paul Mantz. To beat his competitors, especially Jackie Cochran, whose P-51 was known to be modified to the hilt for ultimate speed, Mantz knew he had to come up with another solution. Suddenly, one night, it came to him like a lightning bolt. Instead of putting the extra fuel in tanks *outside* the wings, why not put it *inside?* That's easier than it sounds. The P-51, like most airplanes, was designed so that virtually every piece of the wing frame contributed directly to its structural integrity. But that, Mantz reasoned, was because it was designed as a combat plane, built to take exceptional stress, not as a straight-and-level air racer. If he could remove just enough internal wing gear for the exact amount of fuel he needed . . .

Paul Mantz's blood-red Mustang (named *Blaze of Noon* after a movie he had recently made) was the second plane off the starting line that year. It was a normal takeoff, but seconds later, Mantz knew he was in deep trouble; for some reason, the Mustang's landing gear had only partially retracted. Even the small amount of drag thus created, he knew, would knock him out of the running on a 2,000-mile cross-country flight. Mantz, however, refused to give up. Instead of landing, he headed for nearby Palmdale, a small, sparsely settled town in the Mojave Desert where there was plenty of uncongested air space above. Climbing to an altitude of 25,000 feet, he began a series of blood-draining outside loops. If Mantz worried about the fact that his fiddling with the wing interior might have led to the wing's collapse in such a maneuver, he certainly didn't show it. When the wide outside loops failed to shake loose the stubborn landing gear, he tightened the loops until they finally did; cranking the gear up by hand, he managed to pull the gear back into its normal retracted condition.

Despite the slight delay, Mantz zoomed for Cleveland in record time, flashing over the finish line at a sizzling 500 miles an hour. His average speed of 435 miles an hour was enough to win him the $10,000 top prize and a permanent niche in sports aviation history. As for his chief rival, Jacqueline Cochran, fate had placed her out of the running, unknown to Mantz. Perhaps pressing her Mustang too hard in hopes of besting her disliked rival, her engine quit dead over the Grand Canyon, forcing her to make a dead-stick landing in the nearby desert.

(Nineteen years later, at age sixty-one, Paul Mantz died tragically in an air crash while making the movie *Flight of the Phoenix* in the California desert. However, in a sense, he lives on, for his blood-red *Blaze of Noon* Mustang, which meant almost as much to him as life itself, is a permanent exhibit in the Movieland of the Air Museum, in Santa Ana, California.)

Fittingly, perhaps, a P-51 was the first formal acquisition of the Confederate Air Force. It was one of the many ironies of CAF history that its first combat plane was one that the USAAF long ignored. As noted in the previous chapters, CAF founder Lloyd Nolen had purchased a P-40 Warhawk earlier for his personal use, but since that was before the Ghost Squadron was formally chartered, the P-51 must be considered as the beginning of the collection itself.

Like most ex-World War II pilots, Nolen almost drooled every time he saw a P-51, whether parked or flying, and he was determined to own one. "I sold my beautiful P-40 Warhawk when I learned that the Air Force had a bunch of 51s for sale, as surplus, over in Arizona. But my timing couldn't have been worse.

When I got there, the Korean War had started, and the military had called off the sale."

It was five years later, following the end of the Korean War, when Mustangs would be available once again. When he first heard of a Mustang available in El Paso, Nolen headed west. When he got there and took a look at it, he understood why the price tag was a paltry, bargain-basement $2,500: although the plane was in generally good condition, its tail assembly had been chewed to pieces when a light plane taxied past too close. "I couldn't pass up the bargain no matter what," Nolen remembers, "so I plunked down the money and began looking for replacement parts. Replacing a rudder, fin, and elevators was not complicated and before long we had her in flying condition. And I can tell you one thing: the day I first flew the 51 and felt the power and responsiveness of that ship is one I'll never forget."

Double trouble (for the enemy). Two Mustangs, poetry in flight, as viewed from the window of a CAF bomber they are escorting.

4

THE FORKED-TAILED DEVIL

With one notable exception, the American fighters that flew multipurpose missions in World War II shared one common characteristic: they were single-engined. Most of the other warring nations—both Axis and Allied—brought twin-engined design to fighters considerably earlier and, in the case of some countries, had more than one available. As early as 1934, Germany conceived the highly effective Messerschmitt Me-110, a twin-engined, 340-mile-per-hour terror that first saw action against Poland and went on to serve on every German war front. The Junkers Ju-88 evolved in 1938 and the Heinkel He-219 was developed as a night fighter about the same time. Britain also developed a double punch. Manned by a crew of two or three was the Bristol Beaufighter, its nose bristling with six .303 guns and four 20-millimeter cannon. The Mosquito was originally intended to be a bomber, a role it filled admirably, but Royal Air Force strategists, aware that its unique, light construction of wood gave it a phenomenal top speed of 422 miles per hour, reconfigured it as a fighter; throughout the war, Mosquito pilots argued which job it did best, but agreed it did both superbly. Japan got into the twin-engined business early, too; designed as an unarmed, long-range (2,500-mile) reconnaissance plane, the Dinah was first produced in the mid-thirties and became both a night fighter and torpedo-bomber later on.

The United States' contribution to the wartime twin-engined fighter field was the Lockheed P-38 Lightning, and it racked up perhaps the greatest string of "firsts" of any prop-driven American fighter. (Northrop's 360-mile-per-hour P-61 Black Widow was also twin-engined but it did not become operational until much later; in fact, it was just being put to use exclusively as a fighter when the war ended.)

The Lightning was the first American fighter to shoot down a German plane. It was the first equipped with turbo-superchargers, the first fighter to fly the Atlantic nonstop. It was the first American plane to fly over Berlin, and first to provide air support for convoys bound for the invasion of France in 1944. It was in a P-38 that Medal of Honor holder Major Richard I. Bong shot down forty Japanese planes, ranking him as America's "ace of aces," and in which a friendly

America's noted contribution to the world's collection of twin-engined fighters was the Lockheed P-38 Lightning, here seen in a widely reproduced photograph from World War II.

rival, Army Major Thomas B. McGuire, Jr., bagged only two less and also won the Medal of Honor. It was in a Lightning, too, that Captain Thomas G. Lanphier, Jr., participated in the attack that shot down a Japanese Betty bomber carrying Admiral Isoroku Yamamoto, the naval architect of Pearl Harbor, who once bragged he would "dictate the terms of peace from the White House."

Although numerically outnumbered by P-51 Mustangs and P-47 Thunderbolts in most theaters, Lightnings boasted a higher "kill ratio" than their single-engined cousins, and in the Pacific, they shot down more enemy planes than any other American fighter. No single quality, but a balance of all qualities needed for a fine fighting plane, earned the Lightning an enviable place as perhaps the most versatile of all World War II planes.

After the Lightning's first successes in Africa and Europe, the Germans nicknamed it *"Der Gabelschwanz Teufel"*—"the forked-tailed devil." And in its Pearl Harbor to V-J Day service, a devil it was indeed, adapted with equal facility as a night fighter, photo-recon ship, low-level attack plane, smoke-screen layer, rocket carrier, troop and cargo carrier, flying ambulance, and high-altitude precision bomber.

The Lightning's history dates to 1937, the year that the Army Air Corps asked for bids on experimental pursuit plane designs that seem modest by today's standards but which approached the seemingly impossible at the time. What the Army wanted was a plane that could serve at high speed at high altitude: 360-mile-an-hour top speed, and a 20,000-foot ceiling that could be reached from sea level in only six minutes.

Lockheed designers Hal Hibbard and Clarence Johnson knew that even if a

A twin-tailed Lightning and a single-engined P-47 "Jug" perform over Harlingen.

plane could be built to meet those specifications, no engine was then available to provide enough power. So, logically, they designed a plane using *two* engines, each a twelve-cylinder liquid-cooled Allison that would crank out more than 1,000 horsepower. And rather than hang the engines on a single fuselage plane, they envisioned twin booms and twin stabilizers, with the wings joining the fuselage at midpoint. Though revolutionary at the time, the twin-boom arrangement not only provided plenty of storage room for the turbo-superchargers, radiators, main undercarriage wheels, and other equipment, it also gave the P-38 an amazing aerodynamic stability spread over a wide center of gravity about which pilots would sing praise throughout the war.

The Army liked what it saw on Hibbard's blueprints; Lockheed got the nod in the design competition, and a contract to build a single prototype to be designated the XP-38.

Lockheed's factory in Burbank, California, began building the prototype a year later, in July 1938. It was the company's first military aircraft venture, but it would certainly not be the last; by war's end, the California firm had built fully 200 million pounds of airplanes—9 per cent of all U.S. production. This was one of the reasons the San Fernando Valley community of Burbank was considered to be a high-priority military target, and why, after Pearl Harbor, the city was dotted with antiaircraft battery emplacements. Even in 1938—three years before Pearl Harbor—there was considerable secrecy surrounding the XP-38 project. Under supervision of Lieutenant Ben S. Kelsey, later to head the Air Force's research and development effort, the prototype was shipped by truck— tightly snugged within a tarpaulin—the following December 31 to March Field near Riverside, California. Clearly, big things were afoot for the revolutionary twin-engined fighter and to prove it, the Air Corps authorized Kelsey to attempt a nonstop coast-to-coast speed record. One morning the following February, with Kelsey at the controls, the XP-38 roared off the March Field runway and pointed its nose at Long Island, New York, nearly 3,000 miles away. Those who watched the takeoff were impressed first by the plane's sound. It was not the roaring, crackling staccato pitch they had been used to hearing in fighters, but a low-pitched muffled purr, a sound they could attribute to the twin turbo-superchargers. What they saw amazed them as much as what they heard. Holding the XP-38's nose down after lift-off, Kelsey flew the plane barely five feet off the runway until he had built up sufficient airspeed, then began to climb at an almost unheard-of angle until the plane disappeared out of sight and hearing in the clouds above. Racing at speeds of up to 420 miles an hour—speeds never before achieved in level flight—he reached Long Island seven hours and two minutes later. But on the final approach, both engines stammered momentarily, then lost power altogether. (Engine problems were to plague P-38 pilots throughout the entire war; as will be shown later, the possibility of losing an engine on takeoff especially haunted virtually every 38 jockey.)

Kelsey was a superb pilot, and managed to make a forced landing on a nearby golf course without injury to himself. The XP-38, however, was damaged beyond repair.

Although the Air Corps had enough faith in the plane to continue the project despite the crash, and order thirteen models for evaluation, it was a serious blow to Lockheed. The crashed airplane was the only XP-38 then built, and to Hibbard and his staff, it meant starting all over again. World events provided necessary impetus. In China, the Japanese were already demonstrating the superiority of their fighters over valiant but outranked defenders. Goering's Messerschmitts were raising hell over Europe. The United States badly needed a fighter as effective, and Lockheed crews pushed feverishly. Finally, in September 1940, the first test model—designated the YP-38—was ready for flight.

In most respects, the plane lived up to the most heady expectations; one Lockheed test pilot in fact flatly called it "the easiest plane I've ever flown." But in achieving speeds never before reached, even approaching the speed of sound, YP-38 pilots began to encounter a dangerous phenomenon that would take years to correct. Lockheed called the problem "compressibility" and it occurred at the worst possible time: during high-speed dives. Hal Hibbard explained the phenomenon this way: "In order to have the minimum possible drag, it is essential that air flow smoothly over any part of an aircraft structure. As the speed is increased, the air tends to be 'splashed' by the leading edge of the wing more or less like the prow of a boat at high speed in the water. As one approaches the compressibility range, the air is thrown so violently up and down by the leading edge that it does not have a chance to flow over the wing in the proper manner." The degree of compressibility increased with speed; it was "appreciable" at 425 miles an hour, "very serious" at 500 miles an hour and over. Even after later trial and error eliminated the worst of the phenomenon, the P-38 could not be flown beyond the vertical in a dive or it would virtually "flip over" and the pilot would lose all control. When that occurred, he had no choice but to punch open his canopy and bail out—assuming he wasn't already too low to do so. Enemy pilots soon knew about this inherent weakness of the P-38, too; all they had to do to escape a pursuing Lightning was to dive steeper than the P-38 could safely go.

Compressibility was not a surprise to Lockheed planners. Hibbard had, in fact, forewarned the company of it as early as December 1938, and even before the first test pilot encountered the phenomenon, remedies were being sought. Counterweights were first placed on the elevators, but proved of little value. On one model, the twin booms were designed to angle up, thus raising the tail. Finally, wind tunnel tests and later flight tests provided an answer that served in most situations. It was a flap or dive brake attached to the main wing spar. Whenever a P-38 neared the compressibility stage, the flaps immediately restored lift to the underside of the wing. The modifications were the first of many—nearly seven hundred altogether—that the Lightning was to undergo during its career. Some were due to the many purposes to which the ship would be put; others were meant to iron out the inevitable bugaboos that pilots would discover in a plane both so revolutionary and so fast.

Over all, however, the P-38 was soon to become a favorite with pilots, a plane that was not only among the fastest and most powerful of its time, and despite being outmaneuvered by lighter German and Japanese aircraft, a killer in the sky. In its initial battle configuration, the P-38's armament—concentrated in its nose—consisted of one 20-millimeter Madsen cannon, with fifty rounds of ammunition, and four 0.5-inch Colt machine guns, each with 1,000 rounds. This gave the Lightning a mighty effective wallop of 3,200 rounds per minute; because of this tremendously high concentration of firepower, P-38 pilots were constantly reminded to fire only in short bursts to conserve their ammunition.

In 1940, the P-38 was still designated just that; it had not yet been given the nickname that so appropriately described it in action. "Lightning" was a name favored by Lockheed President Robert Gross. Although the British had several candidates of their own—including Liverpool, which they later designated one of their own bombers—they accepted Gross's choice, along with a batch of planes, late in 1940. The first Lightnings ordered by the RAF arrived in 1941. However, since Lockheed and American aviation planners were skittish about having airplanes with still relatively untried turbo-superchargers used against German planes, the ones the British got were not equipped with them. In the American version, too, the Lightning had been designed with counter-rotating propellers. While this eliminated torque completely, this feature was also removed. With good reason, the British called the toned-down P-38 the "Castrated Lightning" (officially it was the Model 322-61) and found it vastly inefficient. Although a Lightning boosted its reputation by shooting down a German Focke-Wulf over the Atlantic minutes after war was declared on Germany (it was America's first German fighter kill of the war) the British relegated their P-38s to roles as trainers or to photo-reconnaissance missions, and canceled the balance of their order.

On the other side of the Atlantic, however, the popularity of the P-38 was skyrocketing. By June 1942, Lockheed was backlogged with 1,800 Lightning orders and in addition was doing frantic subassembly work on the B-17 bomber and several other military planes. The haste was of deadly necessity, since at the time of the Pearl Harbor attack, partly set back by the prototype's crash and early problems, the Air Corps had received but sixty-nine of this latest of first-line fighters. By the time Lockheed broke the log jam in 1943 (needing more production room, it had even commandeered a vacant winery near its main plant in Burbank), Lightnings were being turned out at a peak rate of fifteen per day.

In Europe, Africa, and the Pacific, meanwhile, the P-38 was writing aviation history. When Rommel's tanks were plowing their way across North Africa, a group of Lightnings with auxiliary fuel tanks flew nonstop across the Atlantic to lead the air attack that turned the Germans back at El Alamein. Other Lightnings rushed to Dutch Harbor in the Aleutians to protect Alaska against an expected Japanese invasion. Later, when the first American bombers began to blast Berlin, they were escorted by an advance guard of Lightnings—the only fighters up to that time with sufficient range to make the round trip from bases in England.

It was not only the P-38's firepower punch that gave it such a high reputation with those who flew it. With two engines, the Lightning gave pilots something else that no other first-line fighter could provide: an extra margin of safety. Many a pilot owed his safe return—and his life—to the fact that Lightnings could fly well on one engine; the record-setter doubtless was a P-38 that came home on one engine *five times*.

At a postwar reunion of P-38 pilots in San Diego, California, this feature probably was remembered best when the war exploits of a generation earlier were inevitably rehashed. Typical was the comment of Stan Lau, formerly a member of the 1st Fighter Group's 27th Squadron, who had piloted the P-38 in the European Theater. "The 38 seemed horribly big to us at first," he said, "but when you lost one of your engines in combat and had to fly 500 or 600 miles home, you became convinced that she was the most beautiful plane in the world."

At the same reunion, former P-38 pilot Hal Rigney recalled the affection for what all termed "the round-trip ticket"—the second engine—only his occasion to use it was singularly unique in Lightning history. A member of the 94th Squadron of the 1st Fighter Group, his was one of several P-38s escorting bombers to the Italian mainland when another P-38 joined the formation from behind.

"At first I thought it was a straggler," Rigney recalled with a sense of humor

Two Lightnings acquired by the CAF, one before and one after restoration.

that was undoubtedly missing at the time, "when it opened fire on me. A bullet
hit my left engine; when it caught fire, I knew I was in trouble. It turned out
later that the other 38 was piloted by a German; the plane had been captured.
My wingmen jumped in and worked him over and he got out of there in a hurry.
But I would have had to spend the rest of the war in a POW camp if it wasn't
for that second engine. Even though my plane was burning, I managed to get
fifty miles into the Mediterranean, off the island of Capri, where I ditched and
was later picked up."

Many accomplishments of Lightnings, especially those in assignments un-
orthodox for fighters and thus containing an element of surprise for the enemy,
were kept for months under unusually heavy secrecy wraps. The operation of the
now-famous "Droop-snoot Lightning," for example, was originally a highly secret tactic. Swift Droop-snooters with complete navigation and bombsight equipment installed in elongated noses led conventional Lightnings carrying heavy
bombloads far into Germany on regular bombing runs for almost a year before
the Luftwaffe discovered the deception. It was in spring 1945, almost at the end
of the war in Europe, that the Air Force first admitted its "secret weapon." The
Lightnings, units of the Fifteenth Air Force based in Italy, were employed this
way for the first time the previous August in a high-altitude bombing run over
Latisana in northern Italy. The formation flew at 15,000 feet, led by a Droop-
snooter with its target-locating gear. After dumping fifteen tons of bombs, the
P-38s swept in at low altitude, strafing and firing rockets that destroyed six locomotives, damaged three others, and put an end to thousands of pounds of related
equipment. Later, Air Force officials released details of the Lightning Pathfinder,
a radar-equipped P-38 that offered improvements over the Droop-snoot. With its
up-to-the-minute detection equipment, the Pathfinder could pin-point targets for
a bomber formation even on the blackest night or through dense fog and cloud
formations.

As the Lightning's reputation grew, stories of its rugged durability grew with it. Typical was the experience of two P-38 pilots in the Mediterranean Theater. Returning from a strafing mission in Italy, Lieutenant John M. Hurley was jumped from behind by a swarm of Luftwaffe fighters. Before he realized he was under attack, Hurley looked out to see that four feet of his right wing tip had been ripped off by a 40-millimeter shell. The flight leader, Lieutenant James A. Eddins, could offer no help; his own P-38 had been hit in the nose, wiping out the armament and exploding the ammunition. Chunks of debris had immobilized the left prop; other pieces had sieved the stabilizer. Even with the wing tip missing and loss of the auxiliary fuel tank it had carried, Hurley made it back to his base without too much difficulty. Eddins, however, had a struggle on his hands. With a mountain range looming between him and his base, both his altimeter and airspeed indicator suggested imminent disaster: he was practically on the ground and his speed had dropped to only 120 miles an hour. Even worse, the Lightning shuddered badly and tended to roll over and spin no matter what saving maneuver he tried. For almost an hour, Eddins worked his controls gingerly, coaxing the damaged plane to 11,000 feet—just barely the altitude he needed to clear the lowest pass in the mountain range and fly home.

In Europe, another P-38 pilot survived a head-on collision with a Luftwaffe Me-109, flying home on one engine and with one tail missing and a boom shredded. Another came home bearing holes of five 20-millimeter cannon and 100 machine-gun hits.

The ruggedness of P-38 design and the safety margin of an extra engine were reassuring to pilots for yet another reason: remembering the horizontal *empennage* directly behind them, none wanted to bail out unless it was absolutely necessary to do so. Called the "cheese knife" by many pilots, the danger of hitting the empennage on bailout probably was overrated, especially if the pilot was able to flip over and drop from the cockpit. "In reality," recalls Royal Frey, a

Its fuselage riddled by vandals' rocks, a Lightning awaits the CAF's magic touch.

member of the Confederate Air Force and ETO Lightning pilot who later became curator of the Air Force Museum in Dayton, Ohio, "the 'cheese knife' was less of a threat than the stabilizers on the P-47 and P-51, simply because it was located farther to the rear from the P-38 cockpit, thereby providing more chance for a pilot to clear it on bailout. In addition, the P-38 did not have a fin and rudder directly behind the cockpit which the pilot had to avoid."

Frey is well qualified to discuss bailing out of the P-38. He had to learn to do it the hard way, in February 1944, on a mission over Germany. Frey and four wingmen had taken on four Me-410s and two Me-110s, and, at the sight of the Lightnings, the German pilots scattered. "I decided that if I was going to have to chase one of the German planes," he recalls, "I might as well be heading toward England, so I selected a Me-110 scooting westward on top of the cloud deck." Frey had tangled with another twin-engined Me-110 two weeks earlier; having had an engine neatly dismembered by its rear gunner, he had acquired a respect for that enemy plane's tail sting. He slipped into a cloud for cover, dropped the P-38 to a lower altitude, and found the belly of the Me-110 neatly in his gunsights only 200 feet away when he cleared the cloud again. A short burst of the Lightning's clustered firepower vanquished the German, and Frey turned his thoughts—and his P-38—toward home.

Fifty-four inches of manifold pressure for fifteen minutes were the maximum allowable in the P-38's wartime flight manual. Frey intended to observe the rule, but three minutes later, the left Allison blew up. He quickly feathered the left prop, then just as quickly discovered a design feature that had annoyed other P-38 pilots. In 1944, the plane had only one generator, and it was on the left engine. With that engine dead, it was only a matter of time before the battery that cross-fed fuel from the left tanks to the right engine would be drained. Frey planned to stay on cross-feed until the battery went dead, then switch to the right tanks that, hopefully, would contain enough fuel to fly the remaining 300 miles back to England. He didn't have time to find out, however; about an hour later, emerging from a cloud cover, the P-38 flew into a wall of enemy flak. Within seconds, the remaining engine was smoking badly. Frey dove the plane toward the ground, hoping to avoid the gunners, but the smoke only grew heavier. It was time, he knew, to hit the silk. Using the dive to gain speed, he leveled off at treetop altitude and pointed the Lightning's nose up and over. Flames were licking into the cockpit as he released his seat belt, pulled the canopy release, and felt himself drop free. Frey spent the rest of the war in a POW camp.

Despite his close call in the Lightning and the many irritating deficiencies of the plane that confronted him throughout his brief career with the plane, Royal Frey holds a fond affection and high regard for it; he remembers almost begging for P-38 duty from the day Lockheed test pilot Jimmy Mattern landed one at the Air Corps Basic Flying School at Pecos, Texas, where Frey was then stationed. That desire is apparently no less today, as his description of flying the P-38 will attest:

"With its tricycle gear, counter-rotating props and inherent stability, the P-38 was extremely easy to fly. Once trimmed for straight and level flight, it was a hands-off airplane. If you put it into an unusual attitude (within reasonable limits) and then got off the controls, it would slowly waddle and oscillate around in the air and eventually return to straight and level flight. This was because its center of lift was above its center of gravity—i.e., most of the mass of the airplane was slung under a wing having a large amount of dihedral. Other fighters of the era with their low wings (and the consequential lower center of lift) tended to drop off on one wing or the other, since the center of lift would always tend to seek a position above the center of gravity. In the P-38 this feature was built in.

"Another excellent feature was the P-38's stall characteristic—it stalled from the center section outward to the tips. As a result, in a panic break with an enemy plane behind you, you could pull the P-38 into such a tight turn that it would begin to buffet, but you would still have remarkable aileron control.

"The P-38 was a sheer delight on takeoff. You would take the runway, line up and brake to a full stop, and advance the throttles to at least 44 inches of manifold pressure to where the turbos would cut in. The nose would gradually drop as the increasing pull of the props forced the nose strut to compress, and the whole plane would shake and vibrate, waiting to be released from the bonds that held it. A quick glance across the instrument panel and off the brakes. Up popped the nose and you bounded forward like a racehorse from the starting gate. As you gathered speed down the runway, the heavy weight of the plane deadened any bumps, and you felt as if you were in a Cadillac. At the same time the turbo exhausts made the engines sound extremely muffled as if you were in a high-powered pleasure boat: no loud crackling or roar so usual in those days of reciprocating engines. No torque to swing the nose, and beautiful visibility down the runway from the level attitude of the tricycle gear. At 70 mph you gently eased back on the control yoke, and at 95–100 mph the plane lifted softly into the air. What complete comfort for a combat plane!

"One of the greatest bugaboos of the P-38 was engine failure on takeoff. Consequently we had drilled into us critical single-engine speed on takeoff—130 mph. Even before God, Motherhood and Country came that 130 mph as soon as possible after your wheels left the runway. As a result, as soon as the plane broke ground, you dropped your nose to maintain level flight 5–10 feet off the runway. You always added 10 mph for next-of-kin and another 10 mph or so as a fudge factor. Then you gradually lifted the nose for optimum climb speed of 160 mph. If in a populated area, the tendency was to hold the plane on the deck and build up as much speed as possible before beginning your climb—it was much more impressive to the taxpayer who might be driving his auto down a street off the end of the runway when your props cut through the air within a hair of his head. We all knew it was legalized buzzing but defended it fervently; we had to get that safe single-engine speed or die!

"I do not personally recall anyone ever losing an engine or prop on takeoff. I do remember hearing of a runaway prop, but many of them might have been caused by the pilot taking off with one of his Curtiss electric props locked in fixed pitch.

"Landing the P-38 was as smooth and pleasant an operation as taking off. We would dive onto the field, buzz the runway at about 10 feet, and peel up into a steep climbing turn. With no torque there was no necessity for constantly cranking in rudder trim, and the nose did not wander all over the sky as airspeed dropped off. While on top of the peel-up, in a vertical bank almost on our back, we chopped throttles and moved the flap handle into half-flap position (maneuver flaps). With no power and so much increased lift, plus the great stability of the plane, we could pull it around onto the final approach as tightly as was required in order to line up with the runway. In fact, we soon got to be such 'hot pilots' that we would still be in a steep diving turn as we crossed the boundary of the field, as full flaps came down, rolling out just before the main wheels touched the ground.

"The P-38 was an excellent gun platform, although it was more difficult than in a P-47 or P-51 to get strikes on a target because the four .50-caliber

The CAF's first Lightning restoration was this plane, located in Sacramento, California. Not a standard P-38 in this configuration, this model sports a bubble nose to accommodate aerial cameras.

guns and 20-millimeter cannon were grouped so closely together in the nose. However, if we got any strikes at all, we had a much better chance of getting a victory; those five weapons cut out such a heavy column of projectiles that they bored a large hole in anything they hit.

"In addition to an agonizingly slow roll rate, the P-38s I flew in combat had two other very limiting features—restricted dive and cockpit temperature. It was suicide to put the P-38 in a near-vertical dive at high altitude; all we P-38 pilots knew it, and I believe all the Luftwaffe pilots knew it, for they usually used the vertical dive to escape from us. You could 'split-S' and do other vertical type maneuvers at high altitude; and as long as you continued to pull the nose through the vertical, you always held your airspeed within limits. But let the nose stay in the vertical position for more than a few seconds and you reached what was termed 'compressibility' in those days. The nose would actually 'tuck under' beyond the vertical position, and it would be impossible to recover the plane from its dive. The only salvation was to pop the canopy, release your seat belt, and hope you would clear the plane as you were sucked from the cockpit. The 20th Group lost two P-38s in vertical dives over England before we went operational, but both pilots bailed out successfully (although one of them almost killed himself when he popped his chute too soon).

"According to a Lockheed tech rep who once visited us, theoretically the air was sufficiently dense at 1,500 feet *below* sea level for the P-38 to *begin* pulling out of a high speed vertical dive. Such a statement did little to bolster my confidence. Later Lightnings had dive brakes under the wings to correct this problem, but they were too late to be of value to me.

"The other limiting factor, cockpit temperature, would be more correctly identified as 'paralyzing.' Cockpit heat from the manifolds was non-existent. When you were at 30,000 feet on a bomber escort and the air temperature was —55° F outside the cockpit, it was —55° F inside the cockpit. After 30 minutes or so at such a temperature, a pilot became so numb that he was too miserable to be of any real value; to make matters worse, he did not particularly care. Only his head and neck exposed to the direct rays of the sun retained any warmth.

"Admittedly the P-38 was outperformed by the P-47 and P-51 in the skies over Europe, but many of its difficulties were the result of unnecessary design deficiencies and the slow pace of both the AAF and Lockheed in correcting them. One can only ponder about how much more rapidly the troubles would have been remedied if the slide-rule types had been flying the plane in combat against the Luftwaffe. But I will always remember the P-38 with the greatest fondness. Even with all her idiosyncrasies, she was a real dream to fly."

Pilots who flew the P-38 in the Pacific would find little to quarrel over in Frey's assessment. Unloved by Britain, the P-38 nevertheless did its job well in Europe and the Mediterranean under American stewardship. But it was in the Pacific, where its great range easily conquered the added hazards of long over-water flights and where its second engine provided psychological assurance for the same reason, that it saw its greatest days of wartime glory.

Until the P-38 arrived in the Pacific near the end of 1942, Curtiss P-40s and Republic P-47s were the standard American fighters in action there. Both were tired, worn-out, practically obsolete ships compared to the light, highly maneuverable Japanese Zeros and other fighters that flew rings around the outclassed Americans. To Major General George C. Kenney, the tough, no-nonsense flier who was hand-picked by General Douglas MacArthur as air commander of the Southwest Pacific, the arrival of the first Lightnings was like manna from heaven. They were twin-boomed miracles with which he hoped to turn the tide of the air war. By late 1942, Kenney probably would have even accepted Jennies and Spads if they showed a whit of promise against the irritating Zeros; with the swift, high-altitude, long-distance Lightning, he at last had a plane that could adequately support Allied forces that had been driven into the southwest corner of the Pacific.

For weeks after the first batch of twenty-five Lightnings reached Australia, however, Kenney could only fidget and bite his fingernails; as they had been early in Europe, they were first grounded with mechanical defects and when these deficiencies were corrected, it was learned that most had arrived without feeds for their guns. Finally, in October, Kenney got his first operational sixteen P-38s and he promptly assigned them to the 49th Group of the Fifth Air Force. In the years that followed, the 49th was to become respected as *the* P-38 group. Flying P-38s, more than forty pilots became aces, including Medal of Honor winner Major Richard Bong.

Bong's amazing record can be attributed not only to his aggressiveness and skill as a pilot and his willingness to fly as part of a team, but to learning the superior traits of the P-38—its speed and firepower—and applying them well in action. In addition to its greater size, the P-38 carried armor plating to protect the pilot, as well as self-sealing gas tanks; these were features the Japanese fighters did not have, and the lack of which usually turned the enemy's ships into flaming torches the instant they were hit. Early in the Pacific action, however, Bong and his teammates learned that if P-38 pilots abided by a few hard-learned rules—if, for instance, they always flew in no less than pairs—their speed and firepower could offset the maneuverability of the enemy.

"Offensive measures go according to the number of the enemy, but they are always two to one," Bong once summed it up. "Any number of Nips can be safely attacked from above. Dive on the group, pick a definite plane as your target, and concentrate on him. Pull up in a shallow high-speed climb and come back for another pass. Single enemy planes or small groups can be surprised from the rear and slightly below, a large percentage of the time. He seems to be blind, or he does not look directly behind him enough to spot you and your first pass should knock him down."

Bong's friendly rival, ace Tom McGuire, stressed in his own tactical report that the best offense against Japanese pilots was to turn directly into their formation. "Try to make the Jap commit himself, then turn into his attack. If forced, go to their right if possible." (A tight right turn, which the P-38 could do handily because of its counter-rotating propellers and absolute absence of torque, proved a highly effective evasive tactic to which many a Lightning pilot owed his life. Japanese pilots generally could outmaneuver Lightnings, but never in a tight right turn.)

McGuire had another rule. "Go in close," he stressed, "and then when you think you are too close, *go on in closer.*"

The rivalry of the Lightning's two top pilots was to have a tragically similar and ironic ending. Major McGuire was killed in action January 7, 1945, while leading a fighter sweep over Los Negros Island; he died while violating several of his own rules to assist a fellow Lightning pilot who was in trouble. For his deed, McGuire was awarded the nation's highest decoration, the Medal of Honor.

Bong was to live another seven months. Also awarded the high medal, he returned home after completing more than 200 combat missions for more than 500 combat hours—30 of them voluntarily and all of them in P-38s. Remaining in the Air Force, he was assigned to the Lockheed plant in Burbank as a test and evaluation pilot. On August 6, 1945, the P-80 jet aircraft he was piloting lost power for a reason never explained, and Bong was killed in the crash that followed. What created the irony was the date: it was on August 6, 1945, that Hiroshima vanished under the atomic bomb dropped by the B-29 Superfortress *Enola Gay*. The end of the war—and the heyday of propeller-driven planes like the gallant Lightning—lay not far distant.

Throughout the arduous Pacific campaign that preceded Hiroshima, Lockheed tech reps flew to the battle area in a solid stream to work on the Lightning's persistent compressibility problem and to work out other "bugs." Their visits were not only to test various remedies for the problems, but to reassure worried pilots that they could be overcome. Compressibility problem or not, Charles Lindbergh was an outspoken champion of the Lightning, since he held a particular interest in twin-engined fighters. This was the same Lindbergh, of course, who soloed the Atlantic in a single-engine plane two decades before; after testflying the P-38 he argued that pilots might be able to squeeze as much as 600 miles per hour out of them with certain alterations. He was demonstrating his theory one day near the island of Ceram, where American bombers were on a mission, when he spotted a lone Japanese fighter which he assumed was a straggler. Even though he was a civilian, Lindbergh found the target too tempting to resist. Slipping in behind, he squeezed off a burst of cannon and machine guns that sent the enemy down in flames. Because of Lindbergh's status, the story was hushed up at the time, but an Army photographer snapped Lindbergh's return so that history might duly record the event later, after the war, when it did not matter.

Doubtless, the Lightning's finest hour began on the morning of April 18, 1943, on Guadalcanal, where a detachment of Lightnings had been assigned to support the U. S. Marines' stubborn defense of the island after it had been abandoned by the Japanese in their first major loss of the Pacific war. The previous day, the Army Air Forces command on Guadalcanal had received a top-secret message from Washington; a Mitsubishi Betty, carrying Admiral Isoroku Yamamoto, commander-in-chief of the Imperial Japanese Navy, was scheduled to arrive on an inspection tour of the Japanese-held section of the Solomons. Yamamoto was the strategist who planned the attack on Pearl Harbor, an attack that later historians described as an act of personal hatred against the United States. Yamamoto was a brilliant tactician and a man whose fist-shaking speeches could quickly rally demoralized troops after a loss in battle. His mission to the Solomons, Washington noted, was for exactly that purpose; if his Betty could be shot down, the psychology would be reversed. To the 339th Fighter Squadron based at Henderson Field went the order: "Destroy Admiral Yamamoto at all costs."

Eighteen P-38s were assigned to the mission. The pilots knew that Yamamoto's twin-engined plane doubtless would be heavily protected by well-armed fighters. They knew, too, that to achieve surprise, their mission, to be conducted at the extreme range of fuel-carrying capacity, must be timed to the minute if it was to succeed. The attack was led by Major John W. Mitchell; his second-in-command was Captain Thomas G. Lanphier. Both men were already aces, Mitchell with eight kills, and Lanphier with six, and they had flown hundreds of combat hours together.

The mission was pulled off superbly. Meeting Yamamoto's Betty precisely on schedule, Mitchell and Lanphier zeroed in on that plane while twelve wingmen (four of the eighteen P-38s had been forced to turn back with mechanical problems) took on six defending Mitsubishi and Zero fighters. Yamamoto's Betty dived to near treetop level, scooting at top speed toward the safety of

The Forked-tailed Devil

65

Even with one of its two engines out, the Lightning performs superbly, a fact the CAF proves dramatically in its popular air shows.

Bougainville Island. Lanphier dove his Lightning to meet him, squeezing off a long, steady burst. The Mitsubishi's right engine billowed with smoke; flames quickly spread toward the fuselage. At that altitude, bailing out was impossible. A loud explosion followed in the jungle below and the architect of Pearl Harbor joined his ancestors.

Because they were so popular with racing pilots, more Lightnings (as well as P-51 Mustangs) survived the smelter after World War II than most other fighters. Still, out of nearly 10,000 built, probably less than twenty were flying when the Confederate Air Force looked around for one to add to its collection. There were a handful in flying museums; one was in the Air Force Museum in Ohio, for instance. But rising operation and maintenance costs kept most of the others on the ground; flying a twin-engined plane means just about double the cost of flying a single-engined model.

The CAF's first P-38 acquisition was a photo-reconnaissance version, equipped with a bulbous Plexiglas nose. It was purchased in Sacramento, California, for $6,000 (P-38s bring five times that figure today) and ferried to Harlingen, Texas, by Lefty Gardner. The CAF has owned and flown three P-38s since then, and, minus battle armor, they're among the hottest and most popular ships flown by the Ghost Squadron in various air shows.

Specializing in the P-38, Lefty Gardner has developed one of the most spectacular and popular demonstrations of flying skill and aircraft performance in the world today, reminiscent of the legendary Tony LeVier's P-38 flying during the war years. One of the most popular shows of the CAF Lightning is a re-enactment of the mission that destroyed Isoroku Yamamoto. And well it should be, for it was that incident more than any other that fittingly avenged the sneak attack that ignited the costly Pacific war.

There is an interesting footnote to the Yamamoto story. For years after he left the Air Corps at the end of the war, Tom Lanphier steadfastly refused to discuss the mission in which he personally destroyed the plane carrying Japan's leading military strategist. Lanphier flew as a test pilot for Lockheed for a while, later joined the General Dynamics Corporation, and more recently held an executive job with the University of California. As the thirtieth anniversary of the Yamamoto mission neared, he finally agreed, for a BBC documentary, to talk about the flight for the first time. It was during a promotional around-the-world tour in behalf of the Air Force Association in the late forties, he recalled, that he met Yamamoto's widow. "The meeting occurred in Tokyo where my plane landing during the 4½ day trip," Lanphier remembered. "I was awakened about 1 A.M. to be told that a Tokyo newspaper had learned that I was due, and made a great promotion of it. Twenty-thousand Japanese were at the airport when we landed. There was no animosity. I simply had eliminated one of their leaders and was to be respected. Mrs. Yamamoto was there, and she brought me some flowers. She was very courteous and charming. By that time, I had learned that Yamamoto was a very decent fellow, contrary to our own wartime propaganda. You are not proud of having killed a man, but after all, he was leading the war against us. Eliminating him had a great effect in our favor. At the time, I didn't know that it was Yamamoto who was personally flying the plane in which he and others were traveling."

5

THE JOLTIN' "JUG"

To the Army Air Corps, which ordered her, she was the P-47. To the Republic Aviation Corporation, which built her, she was the Thunderbolt. But to thousands of enamored aviators who flew her, who found beauty in her fatness, elegance in her tonnage, and peace of mind in her ruggedness, she was, simply, the "Jug." There are other words that more accurately fit this heaviest and largest of all American single-engined World War II fighters, a plane that by war's end flew more than a half-million combat sorties, fired more than 135 million rounds of ammunition, dropped 132,000 tons of bombs, and destroyed more than 7,000 enemy planes. *Tough. Dependable. Indestructible.* But "Jug" was the name that stuck, and in every theater of the war where she operated—and that was everywhere but Alaska—it was uttered not as ridicule, but as an accolade of fond respect.

The P-47 was easily outclimbed by the P-38 Lightning. Until later models with increased fuel capacity became operational, she was as easily outranged by the P-51 Mustang. Certainly, she lacked the trim lines of her pencil-nosed sisters; squatting on an airstrip, her fat belly almost scraping the asphalt, she had as much aesthetic charm as a Sherman tank and the sex appeal of a Phyllis Diller. Yet by the end of the war, few would contest the "Jug" 's reputation as the roughest, toughest all-around fighter of them all, a plane that could do almost anything, go anywhere, take the worst the enemy had to offer . . . and come back begging for more.

A total of 15,684 Thunderbolts came off the production line, making them the most numerous American fighters built in World War II. Like the P-51 that superseded it, the "Jug" wasn't produced until after the war began, a barrel-chested heavyweight pushed quickly through prototype and testing stage to answer the Air Corps's demand, supported by wartime experience, for a faster, punchier, higher-performing fighter than those that already existed. By the end of the war, the six-ton P-47 had run the gamut of combat roles from fighter to

A portrait of sheer power, the Republic P-47 Thunderbolt —the "Jug" to those who flew it—was characterized by the huge engine and cowling. The largest and heaviest of all World War II American fighters, this P-47 is being serviced by a CAF crew.

rocket ship, from interceptor to single-engined bomber; by mid-1945, specially-configured "Jugs" were toting fully half the bombload carried by the long-range, four-engined B-17 Flying Fortress.

Statistics inevitably tend toward the monotonous, but in the case of the "Jug," they are nevertheless appropriate. In accomplishing the total effort against the enemy, according to Air Force records, P-47s flew 1,934,000 hours overseas, consuming 204,504,000 gallons of high-octane gasoline. This does not include 2,416,000 hours flown and 241,600,000 gallons burned in Continental training missions. After D-Day in Europe alone, "Jugs" destroyed 86,000 railroad cars, 9,000 locomotives, 68,000 motor transports, 6,000 armored vehicles, and 60,000 horse-drawn vehicles. Against enemy aircraft, their loss ratio was among the highest of American fighters; they shot down 4.6 enemy aircraft for each "Jug" destroyed by the enemy. Of the total of 7,067 enemy planes destroyed over all, more than half—3,752—were in the air.

"When I saw my first P-47," recalls Cass Hough, wartime commander of the Technical Operations Section of the 8th Fighter Command in England, typically, "it looked like a monster that would never fly. It was big, fat, and clumsy. But as soon as I climbed inside and got the feeling of its roominess and the solidness of its design and construction, I fell in love with it. It was a rough, tough airplane and the R-2800 engine was one of the most reliable ever put in a combat airplane. Few other planes could equal the 'Jug' as a stable, tough gun platform, and, after all, that's what counted."

Because of its 13,000-pound weight, the P-47 was not the most nimble of jack rabbits until Republic later added a water-injection system and better fuel was developed. But in a dive, it had no peer among fighters, Allied or Axis, and no one is better qualified to know this than Hough himself. In 1943, over Bovingdon, England, he was assigned to dive a P-47 to test its controllability at high speed and high altitude. Hough started the dive at 39,000 feet, pulled out at 18,000. Though the results were classified information at the time, USAAF headquarters later announced that Hough had exceeded 780 miles an hour, exceeding Mach I, or the speed of sound. In all fairness, it must be added that while the "Jug" could dive like a scalded gazelle, it was not agile in recovering from one. High-speed diving ability was pilot life insurance when under attack, but recovery took iron strength on the stick and a pilot's failure to remember to trim the elevator *immediately* to break descent was an invitation to disaster. Despite this irritating fact of life of the P-47 and other planes that were nearing or exceeding the speed of sound, the "Jug" probably brought more pilots home alive than any other World War II fighter.

A pilot's first glimpse of a "Jug" was always a startling experience, especially if he had been used to flying a smaller plane such as a P-40. Typical was the reaction of Lester L. Krause, a P-40 flier who converted to the P-47 while a member of the 324th Fighter Group of the Twelfth Air Force based in Corsica in mid-1944. "Alongside the P-40," Krause remembers, "the 'Jug' looked like a single-engined B-17. But when you flew it, the P-47 was certainly no B-17—it was one hell of a fighter, and just as capable a low-level bomber.

"The first thing that impressed me upon seeing my first P-47 was the wide-spaced landing gear. That gave it plenty of stability on the ground. The P-40 with its gear placed close together was a notorious ground-looper. In the P-47, you moved along the runway like you were in a groove. There were some problems with the 'Jug,' and it took a while to get used to them. For instance, the turbosupercharger wasn't instantly responsive; there was always a short delay before it cranked in, and you had to anticipate that. It was a great plane to fly,

Republic's P-47N, shown here warming up near its Farmingdale, New York, manufacturing plant, was a long-range version of the famous "Jug."

though a little 'heavy.' In the traffic pattern you couldn't yank it around 360 degrees like you could some other planes. If you tried that, you'd flip out. But in most respects, the 'Jug' was a tremendous plane to fly."

Landing the "Jug" was especially a snap. With its wide-spaced landing gear, it was a forgiving airplane on touchdown, even for green, inexperienced pilots. It was as forgiving in emergency landing situations, especially since its huge cowling and massive radial engine doubled as a battering ram, a fact which the P-47's pilot training manual missed no time in noting: "When making a forced landing, keep your speed up, even though the terrain is rough or wooded. A P-47, which is built like a bulldozer, will plough right through. If your safety harness is locked, you'll be all right. Stall out above the ground, and you'll have 13,500 pounds falling on you." The manual's assurance was justified more than once. One "Jug" flight instructor a few weeks after the war ended recalled how a student pilot, during an emergency landing, had been forced to barrel through a two-story brick factory when he undershot the runway. The engine divorced its mounts and joined the pilot in the cockpit, and both wings were sheared clean where they met the fuselage, but the pilot sustained only minor injuries and walked away.

The plane offered to the Air Corps by Republic in 1939 wasn't much different from an engineering and design standpoint from its contemporaries in the same stage of development. Conceived by Alexander Kartveli, Russian-born former military officer who had joined Republic as an engineer in 1931, it was to be designated the AP-10, would weigh a modest 4,900 pounds, and would be powered with a liquid-cooled Allison V-1710-29 engine. According to Kartveli's calculations, it would do 415 miles an hour and climb to 15,000 feet in only three and a half minutes. Even after the Air Corps requested an enlarged 6,570-pound design that would boost armament to two .50-caliber and four .30-caliber machine guns at a speed reduced to 400 miles an hour, the forerunner of the famous "Jug" followed the then-current trend toward slim-nosed planes utilizing in-line, liquid-cooled engines. But even as the Air Corps ordered two prototypes, an XP-47 and a stripped-down XP-47A, events were racing so fast in Europe that stiffer specifications were demanded. Not only must fighters of the future go faster, fly higher, and deliver more firepower, the Air Corps insisted, their internal design must be beefed up for additional pilot protection.

At Republic's plant in Farmingdale, Long Island, New York, Kartveli knew that no existing liquid-cooled, in-line engine would meet the requirements. Despite the fact that the earlier prototype was almost finished at a cost of nearly a million dollars, it was scrapped and Republic returned to the air-cooled, radial engine design with which it was vastly more familiar. In the mid-thirties, Republic's predecessor company, the Seversky Aircraft Corporation, had built a series of stubby little single-engined planes, capped by the popular but quickly obsolete P-35, all of which used radial, air-cooled engines. The new prototype designed by Kartveli looked quite similar to the P-35 but in size, weight, and expected performance, it reduced the trainer to Lilliputian scale. Republic's latest offering was 11,500 pounds, almost double the weight of the scrapped pencil-nosed prototype. It was designed to accommodate a 2,000-horsepower, Pratt and Whitney Wasp turbo-supercharged, eighteen-cylinder two-row radial engine—the most powerful engine then available in America. The Air Corps's new specifications were demanding enough—the end result must exceed 400 miles an hour, climb to 15,000 feet in five minutes, and carry eight guns—but designing a plane to handle the enormous radial engine was by far the most serious challenge Kartveli and Republic faced.

Kartveli's solution was simply to reverse normal design procedure. Instead of designing an airplane and then fitting in the engine and other internal equipment, he first mentally placed the turbo-supercharger and virtually built the plane around it. His first requirement was for an efficient supercharging system that would offer the least uninterrupted airflow; to accomplish this, he placed the large turbo-supercharger in the rear of the fuselage, with the large intake for the air duct mounted under the engine, along with the air coolers. Exhaust gases were piped back separately to the turbine and expelled through a gate at the bottom of the fuselage. Ducted air was fed to the centrifugal impeller and returned, via an intercooler, to the engine under pressure.

This required a lot of equipment, of course, and it was one reason why the "Jug" took on such a bulky, cumbersome appearance early in its design stage.

The mighty 2,000-horsepower engine, with its requirement for plenty of frontal space for cooling, was another problem, as was the need for increased fuel tankage that would meet long-range requirements. A third was the armament; with the mighty wallop the P-47 was designed to deliver, plenty of bracing was needed to absorb the expected recoil impact.

So powerful was the engine that no conventional three-bladed propeller would be efficient enough. Kartveli's design called for a four-bladed propeller, but its huge, twelve-foot diameter presented still another problem: ground clearance wasn't sufficient. Normally, this could be solved by installing longer landing gear but that would mean placing the undercarriage far out on the underside of the wings for the necessary stability. This wouldn't do in the case of the "Jug," however, since it would interfere with wing installation of the guns required by the Air Corps. So, telescoping landing gear were used; they were nine inches shorter when retracted into the wings (necessary because of the wing-mounted guns) than when extended. Early-day "Jug" pilots complained that the gear's telescoping system often didn't work well; for one thing, once pilots began to retract or extend their gear they could not reverse the procedure before the cycle was completed, and in emergency situations such as power loss on takeoff, this created some rather hair-raising experiences. Like most of the other "bugs" in the design of the "Jug," however, later modifications proved the answer.

It took only one flight of the P-47 prototype, on May 6, 1941, to convince the Air Corps that here was the rough, tough fighter it had called for, and among fighter pilots who would later fly it, there were ripples of shocked disbelief. The "Jug" towered over them, a plane twice as heavy and twice as powerful as the slim needle-nosed ships they'd been used to. But once they'd flown it, once they watched its airspeed indicator climb over the 400-mile-an-hour mark, once they'd felt the rugged stability its huge framework guaranteed them, they were hooked.

Naturally, the Air Corps was itching to try out the P-47 in combat, knowing that only under such realistic conditions could it begin to determine what modifications would be required for special purposes. A target delivery date of May 1942 was set, but it proved to be an overly optimistic one by more than a year. There were many annoying problems. Test pilots found that at altitudes above 30,000 feet, the ailerons of the "Jug" "snatched and froze," their cockpit canopies would not open, and control loads became excessive. Republic installed blunt-nosed ailerons, a jettisonable canopy, and balanced trim tabs to take care of these problems, but doing so delayed production on the P-47 until spring of 1942. Externally, it was only slightly modified from the prototype, with a redesigned antenna and a slightly larger R-2800 engine. But the addition of other internal equipment had beefed up its weight more than a half ton; the already hefty "Jug" now weighed an even heftier 13,356 pounds. Despite the extra poundage, the bigger engine had increased the P-47's maximum speed to 429 miles per hour.

Republic built 171 units of the P-47B. The first batch arrived in England in November 1942, and were phased in by the 56th Fighter Group. They tasted their first combat action the following April, assigned to high-altitude bomber escort and fighter sweeps. They were an immediate hit with pilots, especially with those who had German pursuers on their tail and had only to point the P-47's nose toward the deck to escape easily.

Fat as it was, the P-47 bore a faint resemblance to Germany's Focke-Wulf 190-A, the only radial-engined fighter flown by the Luftwaffe. At close range, the P-47 could hardly be mistaken for anything else, but to ground antiaircraft gunners, there was always the danger of the Thunderbolt being mistaken for its enemy opponent. To solve the problem, the Air Corps ordered all P-47 engine cowlings to be painted either plain white, or in a checkerboard pattern.

The early major shortcoming of the "Jug" was limited range. Republic told the Air Corps it would add fuel capacity to subsequent models that were shipped to the war front, but in Europe, what was being done at the Long Island plant wasn't solving the immediate problem, that of providing a capable high-altitude fighter escort for bombers on missions from England over the Continent. In the 8th Fighter Command, Cass Hough came up with a novel solution: *paper* drop tanks. Working with another pilot, Bob Shafer, Hough drew up a plan for a teardrop-shaped 110-gallon tank which would be made of several layers of heavy-duty, laminated paper, and got a company near London to begin manufacturing them. The tanks were affixed to the underbelly of the "Jug" by a self-designed shackle. With the additional 110 gallons of fuel, Hough's fliers could at last reach Germany itself, and return safely from their missions. By the time later-edition "Jugs" with greater fuel capacity arrived, more than 15,000 paper tanks had been used without incident.

The range problem at least partially solved, Republic turned next to solving another, the poor rear visibility many combat pilots had begun to complain about. The company was by now producing its "D" series, and at more than 12,000 copies, it became the most numerous subspecies of any American fighter built during the war. Republic's solution to poor rear visibility was a bubble canopy of a design adapted from Britain's Hawker Typhoon. Heavier armor plating was also added to this series as well as a water-injection system that gave the "Jug" a healthy boost from 2,000 to 2,300 horsepower. At 33,000 feet, this gave it a maximum top speed of 433 miles an hour; with additional fuel tankage also added, the P-47 at last had arrived as a first-line escort for B-17 and B-24 bombers over Germany. "Jug" pilots, flying the P-47D, began scoring victory after victory over the Luftwaffe, and aces began to emerge. Top-scoring was P-47 pilot Lieutenant Colonel F. S. Gabreski, with thirty-one kills; Captain Robert S. "Bob" Johnson, who was to join the Republic executive staff after the war, ran second with only three less.

About the same time, Air Corps strategists in England made the surprising discovery that although the "Jug" was designed as a high-altitude fighter, it doubled nicely "on the deck." Fitted with rocket- or bomb-racks, it began accruing a creditable record as a low-level attack plane, and it was this adaptation that was probably the P-47's most effective of the entire war. To outfit it for this purpose, later series were fitted with wing pylons which could carry either two 1,000-pound bombs or three 500-pound bombs. For missions of range longer than the standard fuel capacity could sustain, the armament could be quickly varied to accommodate additional drop tanks. With either six or eight .50-caliber machine guns spread wide on the forward edge of the wings for maximum firepower effectiveness, the joltin' "Jug" had become a tremendous weapon.

The P-47D was also the first "Jug" to see action in the Pacific, and its early successes there prompted Republic to subcontract Curtiss-Wright, even then hard-pressed to deliver P-40s, to build 354 two-seater "D" series "Jugs" for use as trainers.

Of special note was the P-47's combat record with the 348th Fighter Group of the Fifth Air Force in the Southwest Pacific Theater. Converting to "Jugs" in 1943, the 348th flew missions almost around the clock against Japanese targets in Borneo, Halmahera, and the southern part of the Philippines. They operated out of Nadzab and Gusap, New Guinea. The group received two Distinguished Unit Citations for its effort. The first was for covering Allied landings and furnishing ground support for the Allied invasion of New Britain. The second was for fending off a large enemy fighter force that was escorting Japanese bombers on a raid against Clark Field, Philippines, on December 24, 1944.

It was more than a year before the action that resulted in the second DUC that Colonel Neel E. Kearby, commanding officer of the 348th, began accumulating a string of kills that became perhaps the finest hour of the "Jug" in the Pacific. In September 1943, flying a P-47 he had named *Firey Ginger,* Kearby was leading a flight of four "Jug" pilots home from a reconnaissance mission over the island of Lea. Suddenly, he sighted a Japanese bomber with a Zero fighter escort 4,000 feet below him. Kearby signaled his wingman to follow him down. Closing in, he squeezed off a burst of machine-gun fire while his wingman flew close behind to watch for a possible ambush. Kearby meant his fire to be merely exploratory, but to his surprise, *both* enemy planes ripped apart and crashed. By the end of the month, Kearby's kill score stood at eight; not only had he become an ace, but he had racked up half the score of a P-38 rival, Major Richard Bong. On October 11, he narrowed the gap even further. During a fighter sweep over Wewak with three other P-47 pilots, Kearby spotted a lone Zero he assumed to be a straggler. He ordered an attack, pushed his stick forward, and seconds later the Zero was blown to bits.

Pulling out of his dive, Kearby suddenly realized the vanquished foe was not a straggler at all; ahead and above was a large formation of both fighters and bombers which he estimated to number more than forty planes in all. Noting that the formation was tightly clustered, Kearby and his three wingmen turned directly toward it. Apparently confident that no one would dare take on a formation that outnumbered the P-47s ten to one, the Japanese pilots were taken by surprise; three of the enemy were blown from the sky in as many minutes.

Kearby next noticed that two Zeros had worked their way behind one of his wingmen. Roaring to the rescue, he shot down both. Now, a second wingman was in trouble. Once again, Kearby went to the rescue, his machine guns downing the single Zero. Kearby called off the attack when he realized the fuel of the "Jugs" was running low, and the four scooted home. All told, Kearby's wingmen had bagged two enemy planes, and Kearby himself had gotten an astonishing seven, or two more than Navy Lieutenant Edward H. "Butch" O'Hare's five— the previous record for a single action. One of Kearby's kills could not be verified, however, and he was officially credited with six, a feat for which he was later awarded the Medal of Honor. Even with one official kill taken away from him, his total kill record now stood at three less than Bong's, whose total rose to twenty-one before he was shipped home for a much-needed rest. During Bong's absence, Kearby's total climbed to twenty. Now he had not only passed Bong's previous closest competitor, Major Tom McGuire, whose total was nineteen, flying a P-38, but found himself only one kill short of Bong's record.

On March 4, 1944, again leading a four-plane P-47 flight, Kearby sighted a fifteen-plane Japanese formation over Wewak, New Guinea. He bagged the first one himself, quickly followed this with a second victory. According to Kearby's calculations, that broke the tie, making him the nation's ace of aces. Kearby would never know, however, that Bong had returned to combat elsewhere the same day and had gotten two kills. Suddenly, Kearby found himself with three avenging Zeros on his tail. Wingmen destroyed two of them, but the third continued to bore in. Later at their base, the wingmen reported seeing Kearby's "Jug" crash in the jungle; none had seen a parachute, and it was assumed that Kearby was shot dead in his cockpit.

Later in the Pacific war, Thunderbolts were a mainstay of close air support in amphibious operations. During the costly taking of the Marianas, for example, they were shipped to the staging area aboard the aircraft carriers *Manila Bay* and *Natoma Bay* and catapulted into action. By July 1944, when the fighting ended on Saipan, they had become particularly useful in dropping hideous but militarily important "fire bombs"—canisters of napalm, diesel oil, and gasoline, which were the only means of routing diehard resisting Japanese troops from deeply dug caves.

P-51 Mustangs and P-38 Lightnings were by then considered the first-line fighters in the Pacific. But the reputation of the "Jug" for rugged durability kept it in action through V-J Day. The Lightning and Mustang were top performers upstairs. But "on the deck," providing close air support where it was badly needed, neither could touch the hardy Thunderbolt. Mustangs and Lightnings, of course, had liquid-cooled engines. A single sniper's bullet anywhere in the coolant system spelled certain doom for those planes. The "Jug," however, came home time after time bearing combat wounds that no other fighter could sustain. As an example, in Neel Kearby's 348th Group, one P-47 received a direct 20-millimeter cannon hit in its supercharger, located in mid-fuselage. The impact blew a gaping, three-foot hole in the plane but the pilot managed to land it without further damage.

Special credit for the durability of the "Jug" must go to the R-2800 engine, one of the most reliable ever put in an airplane. So designated because of its 2,800 cubic inches of displacement, the Pratt and Whitney R-2800 has eighteen cylinders arranged in two rows of nine. Each cylinder delivers about one horse-power for each pound of engine weight. Many R-2800s built thirty years ago are still in service today. They powered not only the P-47, but an imposing list of other World War II fighters, transports, and bombers, including the Navy's Corsair, Hellcat, Tigercat, and Bearcat, the Douglas Invader, and the Martin Marauder. Stories of the R-2800's virtual indestructibility are legion. A former P-47 pilot who flew combat missions in southern France once recalled coming home safely with one cylinder completely shot out and remnants of the piston hanging outside the cowling.

In Europe, meanwhile, the Thunderbolt was adding to its reputation of almost unstoppable versatility. As early as 1939, rumors reaching Allied intelligence from the Continent indicated that the Germans were accelerating production on a pilotless, rocket-propelled "flying bomb" against which there seemed almost no effective defense. Shortly after the Normandy landings in June 1944, the rumors were verified when a V-1 "buzz bomb" exploded in the center of London. Follow-up bombings had a tremendously demoralizing effect on British civilians as well as a highly destructive effect on defenders of military targets they randomly hit.

The new weapon had been anticipated, however, and the P-47, along with the Spitfire and P-51 Mustang, rallied to Britain's defense against it. In Long Island, Republic had produced a specially powerful "sprint" version of the P-47, designed to combat not only the high-speed V-1s and their successors, but also rocket- and turbojet-propelled fighters the Germans were known to be perfecting. Fitted with an R-2800-57(C) engine and a larger CH-4 turbo blower whipping up a war emergency horsepower rating of 2,800 at 32,500 feet altitude, the newest Thunderbolt was designated the YP-47M. With its underwing racks removed, it could reach a maximum speed of 470 miles an hour, even though the additional equipment had now boosted the plane's weight to nearly 15,000 pounds. Only 130 of this model were produced by Republic, but against the 400-mile-an-hour "buzz bombs," they proved to be a highly successful defense.

Launched from hidden bases in France, the V-1s were first picked up on radar screens along the English Channel coast of England. Because of the speed of the flying bombs, there wasn't time to scramble fighters against them; instead, Thunderbolts, Mustangs, and Spitfires flew twenty-four-hour patrols over England. When the arrival of a V-1 appeared imminent, the defending planes were ordered to a point of interception. The new water-injection system of the "Jug" gave it a tremendous burst of speed for the allowable few minutes. Pilots had to be exceptionally good marksmen, however; against a "buzz bomb," there was time for only a single pass from behind, a squeeze of the trigger, and, it was hoped, a hit. Altogether, the three Allied fighters were credited with destroying 1,847 "doodlers," as they were nicknamed, before V-E Day in May 1945.

Of the total of 15,660 Thunderbolts built, only one model did not have the familiar wide cowling required by the radial engine. In fact, from a distance, the XP-47H could easily have been mistaken for the P-51 Mustang. And with good reason: it, too, was powered with an in-line, liquid-cooled engine. Republic's radical departure from the traditional P-47 line was not an attempt to improve the breed, however, but was a framework for testing a new, potentially powerful engine. Prior to Pearl Harbor, most aircraft manufacturers were leaning more and more toward liquid-cooled engines. The P-47 was of course a notable exception. Chrysler wanted to join the trend, and had conceived a sixteen-cylinder, 60-degree inverted Vee configuration that, in static tests in early 1944, could turn up 2,500 horsepower. Both the Air Corps and Republic showed interest, and two P-47D-15 aircraft were chosen for conversion to handle the new power plant in flight tests.

This meant a complete rebuilding of the P-47. It meant a new design of the structure forward of the firewall, including a new cowling, engine controls, fuel and oil system, new exhaust manifold and shrouds, and engine mount. Its rear section remained virtually unchanged, but to those who saw the first conversion wheeled out for its flight test on July 26, 1945, the new pointed nose was somewhat startling. The plane took off without difficulty but once it became airborne, one problem followed another. Shortly after the XP-47H took off on its twenty-seventh flight at Evansville, Indiana, the propeller shaft broke. The pilot nursed the plane home to a successful dead-stick landing, but further tests were canceled. A second XP-47H was undergoing conversion inside Republic's plant in Evansville, but it was scrapped.

By the end of World War II, the Air Corps had thirty-one groups of P-47 fighters in operation and its peak inventory of the plane was 5,595—or about a third of all of them built. Britain ordered 830 P-47Ds, 590 with the later bubble canopy and 240 with the original cockpit design; they were used operationally mainly in the Southeast Asia Theater. Another 203 were Lend-Leased to Russia, and Brazil bought 88 for her postwar Air Force. Following the war, too, P-47s became popular with several nations whose air arms had not yet developed a jet capability. They included France, Italy, Turkey, Iran, and several Latin American countries. In addition, the P-47 was used by several air national guard units in the United States as a postwar trainer. Unlike some other fighters, in other words, a large percentage of Republic's production of 15,684 Thunderbolts were known to have survived the war. Subtracting the 8,000 or so that were known combat losses and operational accident victims, even eliminating the comparatively small number sold to other nations and used by American national guardsmen, there had to be a good number—perhaps as many as 4,000 or 5,000—*somewhere.*

Yet in 1961, a four-month search by Republic for P-47s that could be flown to Long Island for a twentieth-anniversary ceremony of the first flight of the "Jug," turned up only one. Just *one.* To be sure, a handful of others were located in various aviation museums, including that of the Smithsonian Institution in Washington, D.C., and the Air Force in Dayton, Ohio, but they were nonflyable static displays. Of "Jugs" that could be heard, smelled, felt, and flown, Republic could locate only one. It was privately owned by Bob Bean, operator of a flying service in Hawthorne, California. Republic wanted a P-47 for the reunion badly. It had invited well over 1,000 former "Jug" pilots to attend, including P-47 twenty-eight-kill ace Robert S. Johnson, who was now on the Republic payroll, and designer-engineer Alexander Kartveli, who had retired from the firm the previous year. The reunion was to be a full-blown affair, but without a P-47, a vital ingredient would be missing.

A former P-47 pilot himself, Bean had developed a sentimental attachment for his plane, but Republic executives, explaining the importance of their request, persuaded him to sell the plane back. Thus it was that a P-47 that had come into being two decades before was returned to the place of its creation. Bean delivered the P-47 to Long Island himself, making the cross-country trip in six leisurely legs.

What happened to the thousands of other P-47s that came home safely from the war, aside from those sold to other nations, has never been accurately determined. Doubtless, the majority were scrapped, along with those that served national guard units after their useful days were over. It is interesting to contemplate, however, what role they might have played during the Korean War, or perhaps even in the Vietnam War, had the leftover P-47s been "mothballed" instead of reduced to low-grade scrap ingots. The nation's production of jet aircraft was just getting into full swing when the Korean War began in mid-1950. Aircraft carriers assigned to duty there, in fact, were still mostly operating prop-driven World War II vintage Corsairs and Douglas AD Skyraiders. It wasn't until after the war that flattops like the *Essex* became fully operational with Panther, Banshee, and other early combat jets.

Because it could muster up only about 2,500 jets, the Pentagon reached back a generation and reactivated 750 P-51 Mustang fighters for duty in Korea, and recalled another 700 from air national guard units. At that time, only 1 out of 10 Mustangs that had been built were ready for service without extensive work. As we have seen, the Thunderbolt had virtually joined the dodo bird as an extinct species. Yet, ironically, there are many who claim that because of the nature of the Korean War, the P-47 would have been a far more effective fighter than the Mustang. As its experience in World War II proved, it was an extremely capable low-level attack plane, and in its role of providing close air support it had few if any peers. Boeing B-29 Superfortresses were tops as strategic bombers in Korea, but the day-to-day, low-level bridge-busting, troop-pounding, vehicle-smashing capability was as sorely needed by Allied commanders. Technically obsolete, Thunderbolts doubtless would have filled that need in spades.

In Mercedes, Texas, the Confederate Air Force was as astonished as Republic Aviation when it sought a restorable P-47 for its growing collection. Routine sources turned up completely blank. In 1963, the CAF located one in Nicaragua, where it was serving the Nicaraguan Air Force. It was in that Central American nation, in fact, that the Thunderbolt saw its last combat action during an internal revolution. The cost of $8,000, which the Nicaraguan government wanted for the old plane, seemed a steal, considering the rareness of the P-47, and a few months later, Colonel Dick Disney, the CAF's chief check pilot, personally flew it to CAF headquarters in Mercedes.

The CAF's original goal was to find, restore, and fly at least one example of every major combat aircraft of the 1939–45 period. But though it sought only one of each, there was no limit to the number it would agree to maintain and fly assuming that someone would agree to serve as a financial sponsor. In the P-47's case, considering how rare a plane it was, obtaining more than one model would mean a "backup" in case the first one could not be flown again. In Nyack, New York, where he operated his classic car and vintage aircraft business, CAF Colonel Ed Jurist decided he wanted a P-47. The most likely places to find them, he knew from the CAF's experience with its first acquisition, were the banana republics, which had purchased substantial numbers of "Jugs" as well as other World War II fighters after V-J Day.

Fortune smiled. Months after his search began, Jurist located not one but *six* "Jugs." Sold to Peru as surplus after the war, they had served the Peruvian Air Force; when Peru moved up to later-model fighters, the six were placed in storage. To Jurist's happy surprise, they were stored under excellent conditions, and except for some minor work, he decided that they could easily and safely be flown once again.

Months of sensitive negotiations followed. "The Peruvians thought I was nuts," Jurist recalls now. "Here was a group of worn-out planes that the United

Hardly an object of beauty, a P-47 Thunderbolt is off-loaded from the S. S. Rosalinda for restoration at Harlingen. This model was one of six located for CAF use in Latin America.

Hulks of P-47s are lifted by crane to a dock at Brownsville, Texas.

Disassembled Thunderbolt wings on dockside.

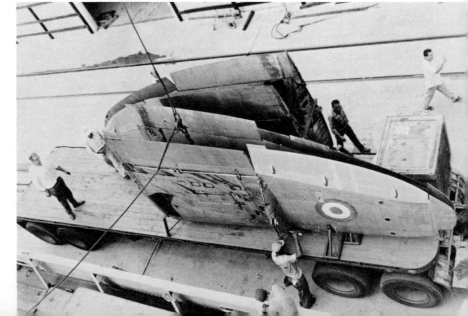

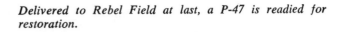

Delivered to Rebel Field at last, a P-47 is readied for restoration.

The big job of restoration lies just ahead. Six "Jugs" lined up in a hangar of the CAF at Rebel Field.

Alive and well once again, a restored P-47 wings its way over Harlingen in company with a CAF P-38 Lightning.

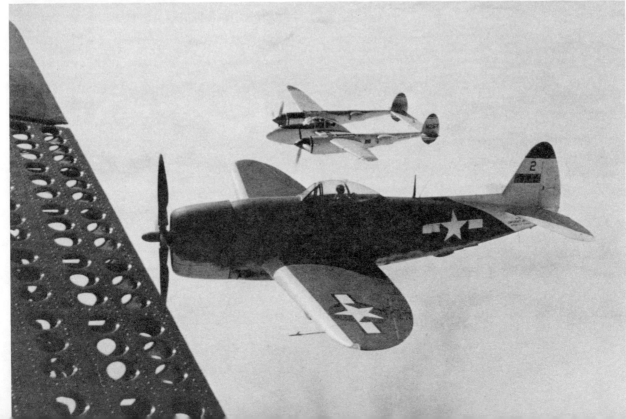

States had sold them for a song a generation earlier; now some oddball American was frantically trying to buy them back, even if it meant paying inflation rates."

Jurist is a persuasive man; by early 1969, Peru agreed to sell him the six "Jugs," stipulating only that it would maintain strict supervision over them until they were out of the country. At a cost that could hardly be considered modest, the planes were carefully disassembled, trucked to the port of Paita, and reloaded aboard the freighter S.S. *Rosalinda*. Back in Texas, Jurist and his fellow colonels, keeping track of the *Rosalinda*'s progress by radio, fidgeted nervously as the freighter reported encountering a hurricane shortly after transiting the Panama Canal. But on September 6, 1969, the battered but safe vessel steamed into Brownsville harbor, her historic cargo intact.

Later, by tracing their serial numbers, the CAF determined that the six "Jugs" had been stationed in Abilene, Texas, and later Independence, Kansas, before being sold to Peru in 1957. Their last Peruvian flight was on July 15, 1967. Now, thanks to the CAF, they're flying once again both as part of CAF air shows and with other organizations for patriotic and historical aviation events. It cannot be stated with accuracy that, as crowd-pleasers, the P-47 is as alluring as the twin-engined, needle-nosed Lightning or as coquettish as the trim Mustang. But to anyone who ever flew her, the fat, squat, obese "Jug" is probably the prettiest lady on earth.

THE FLYING CANNON

The shape was familiar, but only vaguely so. By no stretch of the imagination could it be called an airplane any longer. Lying in the parched dust of the New Mexico desert, it was but a hollowed-out, tangled skeleton of steel and aluminum. Its skin long ago had been stripped by souvenir hunters, its fuselage riddled by shotguns, most of its moving parts filched by vandals, its frame bleached by summer sun and rusted by winter rain.

To Confederate Air Force Colonel Joe Brown, however, the metallic ghost that sprawled before him was a challenge, not the piece of useless junk it appeared to be. Close examination verified the fact that the wreckage was that of a Bell P-39 Airacobra, which by 1962 had become one of the scarcest of remaining World War II American fighters, and a model the CAF had tried in vain to locate for restoration.

Closer inspection disclosed that it was not only a P-39, but a P-39-*Q*. The final letter, Brown knew, placed it near the end of the Bell Aircraft Company's wartime production of 9,589 units in the revolutionary, controversial P-39 series. It was the end result of fully twenty-one model changes, each an improvement over the preceding one, and therefore an extremely valuable plane, worth saving if at all possible. The P-39 lying on the New Mexico desert would indeed live to fly again, but not until seven years had passed and after an outlay of money exceeding $59,000, and a herculean, almost impossible salvage effort.

Not as well remembered, perhaps, as the P-38 Lightning, the P-51 Mustang, or the British Spitfire, the P-39 nevertheless filled a vital role in World War II combat, especially in the South Pacific in the frantic weeks after Pearl Harbor when the United States was literally fighting for her life.

Some had nicknamed the P-39 the "flying cannon." Others called it "a cannon on wings." Still others referred to it as "a cannon with an airframe built around it." It had other nicknames, too, but most referred to the fact that the revolutionary, rear-engined Airacobra was the first American fighter to carry a 37-millimeter cannon, and that its design from nose to tail was intended solely to support that lethal armor-busting sting in the nose.

Aviation historians still debate whether the P-39 was superior or inferior to

The Army Air Corps's powerful "flying cannon." This is the way the CAF's P-39 Airacobra looked when it was trucked to Harlingen for restoration. Note the unusual engine placement: it's behind the pilot.

the Curtiss P-40 and they agree she performed poorly at high altitude. Many pilots who flew her, remembering their feelings of sheer terror over the prospect of the rear engine crushing them to death should a wheels-up belly landing occur, still curse her. Others remember how the vibrations of the equally unique drive shaft between their legs began to fatigue them within minutes after takeoff. Despite the twenty-one modifications, the P-39 was never entirely free of "bugs," and flight reports are filled with tales of the wild behavior of the plane under certain conditions. Yet in terms of an aesthetically and aerodynamically smooth, pleasing design, of her combat record, and of pioneering radical thinking that was to soon become commonplace in the aviation industry, no World War II American fighter could surpass the cussed-and-loved 'Cobra. In a sense, too, it was the airplane whose success laid the groundwork for what has become one of the nation's major aerospace companies, and an important contributor to manned exploration of outer space.

Ironically, perhaps, the P-39 indirectly owed its existence to a decision of an aircraft company that later became a competitor of its designer and builder. In 1935, the Consolidated Aircraft Company, then a successful airplane builder located in Buffalo, New York, announced that it was moving to new quarters in San Diego, California. Though the company offered most of its employees the opportunity to move to secure jobs in the West, four of its executives decided to remain behind and, if they could raise the capital, start their own aircraft firm.

One of them was Lawrence Dale Bell, visionary son of a hardware store proprietor, who, from his grammar school days when history was being made at Kitty Hawk, North Carolina, had focused his dreams on the sky. First with the Glenn L. Martin Company in California and later with Consolidated in Buffalo, Bell had honed not only his skills as an administrator but his vision of the kinds of aircraft that the nation would need in the years ahead.

Raising $500,000 in capital from the sale of stock (plus $10,000 borrowed from a friend who owned a local retail store) Bell and three others launched the Bell Aircraft Company on July 10, 1935. Their first venture, the prototype of a radical, long-range twin pusher-engined fighter designated the YFM-1 Aircuda, drew enthusiastic response from the Army, which awarded Bell a $403,057 contract. But even more than the P-39 that was to follow, the Aircuda was too advanced for its time, and the project was reluctantly canceled after fourteen 'Cudas were produced. Only an $800,000 contract from the Navy to fabricate wing panels and other parts for Consolidated's PBY Catalina flying boats kept the infant company solvent in the months that followed. Despite its failure, Larry Bell couldn't get the Aircuda out of his head, however, and especially two features that made it truly unique for its time: a remote-control armament consisting of a 37-millimeter cannon located in each of the two engine nacelles, and tricycle landing gear. No one had ever mounted cannon on a fighter before. Nor had anyone yet designed a workable tricycle landing gear, which, though untested, suggested much easier handling on takeoffs and landings.

Meanwhile, as global war drew closer for the second time in one generation, farsighted military aviation planners realized that the United States was in a poor situation as far as its fighter aircraft were concerned. In 1939, the American fighter was grossly inferior to those of the Germans and the Japanese; some argued with good reason that even Italian fighters could outfly the aesthetically pleasing but underpowered, 200-mile-an-hour, open-cockpit Boeing P-26, which had been the Army's top-line fighter since 1933.

The Army Air Corps, recognizing that the fighter gap existed, called for bids on faster and more modern airplanes.

With typical foresight, Larry Bell was a jump ahead of the military airpower strategists. He had a plane in mind, but more than just a plane, it was a new, long-range philosophy of the tasks a combat fighter would face and how one should be designed to perform those tasks well.

Long before the formal organization of the company, the men responsible for the concept, design, and manufacture of Bell Aircraft studied the problems involved in fighter design and construction. Into their planning went considerable thought about the difference between fighters of World War I and those that would fight in the war that was certainly approaching.

They assumed, of course, that American fighters would have to be better than those of the enemy with respect to speed, ceiling, rate of climb, maneuverability, and general efficiency. They realized that others building airplanes—meaning Bell's competitors—had always thought in terms of the airplane as a vehicle, and they were aware that they were veering 180 degrees from conventional thought when they began to think primarily in terms of *firepower*.

As Bell's engineers saw it, three qualities were vital to a successful fighter; none then existing had any of the three, at least in the amounts that were considered necessary.

These qualities were sufficient firepower, improved landing and ground handling, and greater vision. In World War I, fighters were used primarily to kill unprotected individual men among the enemy forces, and to destroy enemy aircraft that were attempting to do the same thing. But in World War II, this would not be enough. What would be needed instead was an airplane that could fire an explosive shell powerful enough to cope with armored vehicles and fleets of mosquito boats, and to vanquish the biggest and most heavily protected bomber. In essence, a flying platform for a cannon.

Speed and the ability to land and takeoff on small fields formed the second important consideration. During World War I, even with their low top speeds of 120 miles an hour and landings at 50 miles an hour, dozens of airplanes were smashed during landings and takeoffs on jury-built wartime fields. What would happen when fighter pilots again had to operate from improvised fields, but at landing speeds of more than 100 miles an hour, and top speeds exceeding 400?

As for the third consideration—better pilot visibility—the race for more powerful engines to achieve higher speeds was having just the opposite effect. Increased engine power meant bigger engines, and as fighter nose design grew to accommodate them, pilot visibility was increasingly curtailed. Bell had to design some new arrangement of the equipment of the new fighter so that visibility forward, sideward, down, and aft would be guaranteed.

In the summer of 1937, Larry Bell at last felt his engineers had a fighter design that resolved these three problems. Answering the Air Corps's call for bids, he submitted a prototype design for the P-39 that drew on the ill-fated Aircuda's two novel features of tricycle gear and 37-millimeter cannon. To solve the visibility problem, and to accommodate the cannon as well, he proposed an engine mounted not in front of the pilot but *behind* and *below* him. In the Aircuda, the two cannon were accommodated in the engine nacelles by using pusher, or aft-facing, engines. That wouldn't work in a single-engined fighter, of course, and Bell wanted a craft capable of carrying an explosive shell firing cannon on the centerline. Even at that time, German manufacturers were installing 20-millimeter cannon on their specially designed Vee-type liquid-cooled engines so that they could be fired through hollow propeller hubs. The 20-millimeter cannon was not big enough to satisfy Bell requirements and Air Corps tests demonstrated convincingly the superiority of 37-millimeter projectiles over the destructive power of smaller-bore weapons.

Even if they wanted to make use of the plan adopted by the Germans, there was no engine in the United States or Great Britain which would accommodate *any* cannon, much less a 37-millimeter. Putting the engine behind the pilot made a cannon installation in the nose possible. The key to connecting engine to propeller was borrowed from a century before when ships switched from sail to engines in the age of steam: an extension drive shaft. Airplane manufacturers in 1937 probably were agreed that such a drive-shaft installation was possible, but they hesitated to risk the effort and expense of developing this method of power installation.

Consider what was gained by the rear-engined innovation. With respect to the cannon, the United States would put into the sky a weapon capable of coping with the most potent weapons that strategic planning for the coming war suggested: mechanized cavalry divisions, mosquito boats, heavy bombers. With the cannon, Bell proposed lifting antiaircraft and antitank guns into the air.

At the same time, the tricycle landing gear would give the United States a fighter that could be flown from and landed on small airfields, even highways if necessary. In the event of wartime conditions, when landing fields would be bombed, or for emergency landings, the tricycle-geared craft was still safe to bring to earth. This applied no less strongly to night conditions.

With the Airacobra, Bell stressed, it would be possible to land at speeds varying from 95 to 130 miles an hour. For the first time with respect to fighters, a plane would be developed in which the pilot did not have to run out of altitude and speed at the precise moment he reached the proper spot on his landing field.

Radical thought, all of it. But war, and the planning for it, welcomes, even necessitates radical thought, and in 1939 the Air Corps issued a contract to Bell for production of a single prototype of the P-39. A year later, on October 19, 1940, it flew before an Army Air Corps evaluation team at Boling Field, near Washington, D.C.

In February 1941, Bell wheeled out the same 'Cobra at Buffalo Airport to demonstrate its ability to another Army inspection team. With Captain George E. Price at the controls, the plane performed beautifully at first as it went through its paces in the sky above Buffalo. Suddenly, the February cold and high altitude joined forces; when Price tried to lower the landing gear, he discovered that it was frozen solid.

Watching from the ground, Larry Bell ordered Price to bail out, knowing full well that a crash would set the P-39 program back many months, or perhaps, because it was the only plane built so far, end it altogether. Price knew the penalty as well. Feeling perhaps the same apprehension that future 'Cobra pilots were to feel with an aircraft engine behind them, he bellied in instead, and walked away unhurt.

About the time that the Army had officially accepted the aircraft, Hitler's Panzer divisions were busily devouring country after country in Europe. One day, Bell Vice President Harry L. Collins returned to Buffalo with Bell's biggest contract so far: a $9 million order for 200 Airacobras from France; 2 million of it was in cash. For the first time in its brief history, Bell had a little fat in its bank account. Almost as the Buffalo plant began producing the ordered planes, however, France fell to the Nazis. Bell quickly persuaded England's Royal Air Force to take over the French contract; of 179 Cobras completed for Britain, the entire lot was repossessed by the United States shortly after Pearl Harbor in December 1941.

Thus lobbed about like an errant tennis ball by the vagaries of war, the P-39 finally tasted combat in February 1942, with heavy action against the Japanese at Port Moresby. Before that, squadrons of Airacobras had been deployed along the Pacific Coast from the Panama Canal Zone to the Aleutian Islands, an area believed to be under threat of imminent attack by the Japanese after Pearl Harbor.

Altogether, Bell produced 9,589 Airacobras, the last one rolling off the assembly line in 1944. More than half of them—about 5,000—went to the Soviet Union under the Lend-Lease program. They were considered of major value to the Russians during the defense of Stalingrad. Other P-39s served well in combat scattered around the globe, from the dripping heat of the South Pacific to the pea-soup fogs of the Aleutians, and from the scorching sands of the African desert to fifteen-hour winter nights protecting convoys headed for Murmansk.

Though designed with the cannon in mind, 'Cobras recorded machine-gun kills over Japanese Zeros, German Me-109s, and Fw-190s. They also downed Japanese Mitsubishi bombers, Italian Macchis, and German Junkers and Heinkels. Because the heaviest use of the P-39 was by the Russians, however, the model flown by the Confederate Air Force today bears the familiar red star of the Soviet Union on its fuselage.

Creditable though its combat record was, it was the unusual design of the P-39 that drew most of the attention of aviation buffs, even in the hectic early years of World War II when war achievements were grabbing headlines.

One of the first American fighters to achieve a speed exceeding 400 miles per hour, the 'Cobra was a streamlined, low-wing monoplane whose trim lines were often compared to the later P-51 Mustang. Its all-metal structure was covered with a flush-riveted stressed skin, except for movable control surfaces in the tail, which were fabric-covered. The fuselage was divided into two sections, which were bolted, this simplifying repairs or crating for shipment. The forward section consisted primarily of two longitudinal beams with a horizontal upper deck between and extended to the bulkhead aft of the engine. Detachable cowlings in the fuselage facilitated servicing of the engine, radio compartment, or armament.

That armament packed the heaviest wallop of any fighter up to that time. In addition to the nose-mounted, single 37-millimeter cannon, two .50-caliber machine guns fired through the arc of the propeller on standard models. The P-39 was adapted as a bomber, and some versions also carried rockets under their wings.

The power was provided by a liquid-cooled, 1,200-horsepower Allison inline engine, the same engine used in the Curtiss P-40. It was fueled by bullet-resisting, self-sealing gas tanks located in each wing directly adjacent to the fuselage.

The gross weight of the Airacobra as a fighter was approximately 7,400 pounds. Used as a bomber, it did not usually exceed the safety maximum of 8,400 pounds. It frequently carried either one 500-pound or 600-pound bomb and alternated as a fighter for increased range with a releasable belly tank.

The smallest of American World War II fighters, the P-39 had a wingspan of thirty-four feet, a length of twenty-nine feet nine inches, stood nine feet three inches high. Though many pilots had misgivings for other reasons, they could not fault the vastly improved visibility its design had provided. Locating the cockpit forward of the leading edge of the wings further increased the range of vision which the rear-mounted engine had provided by virtue of a smaller and more streamlined nose than other fighters. This feature proved especially popular with pilots flying night combat missions; wearily returning to darkened airfields, they needed every particle of vision that design could give them.

There is some confusion about the Airacobra's numerical designation due to the fact that it served the British and the Russians as well as the Americans. The original American number was XP-39. The British called it the Caribou, thus departing from the reptilian connotation of both the P-39 and its higher-powered successor, the P-63 Kingcobra. The American designation for the British planes was the P-400, but this reverted to P-39 after the first units were repossessed following Pearl Harbor. Many modifications were incorporated in the design, so many, in fact, the Air Corps later changed its contract to read P-45. But Air Corps planners found that Congress was far more generous with funds for tried-and-true products, those with traditional designations it could understand, so the P-45 reference was quietly dropped.

Because of the success it had with the Airacobra, the Soviet Union flew almost all of the more than 3,000 P-63 Kingcobras later produced by Bell. They were advanced, evolutionary "flying cannon" as beautiful, powerful, and graceful as their predecessors. The P-63 was first flown in 1942, the last rolling off Bell's production line in 1945. Ironically, not a single combat mission was flown by an American pilot in a P-63.

After the war, both 'Cobras appeared destined to oblivion . . . until CAF

Colonel Joe Brown made his chance discovery of the P-39 skeleton in the New Mexico desert one day in 1962.

His curiosity piqued, Brown located the plane's serial number and checked with the Air Force to determine how it had gotten there. After a long delay, the Pentagon found the answer in musty aircraft records going back seventeen years.

In 1945, the plane had served in a training squadron at the Army Air Corps's aviation gunnery school at Harlingen, Texas. When peace arrived and the base was closed and turned over to the city of Harlingen for use as a municipal airport, the plane and its companion P-39s were ordered to be air-ferried to the Arizona desert for storage or scrapping. Other P-39s in the squadron reached their destination; running out of fuel near Hobbs, New Mexico, the pilot of the remaining one chose a suitable open spot and made a perfect dead-stick, wheels-down landing. Routinely, an Air Corps crew arrived the next day and deactivated the plane by removing its nose gear retract screw. No one knows why the airplane itself was not refueled and flown away, a feat it was perfectly capable of performing, or at least why the military didn't haul it off in a truck. Possibly, it was theorized, the plane was destined to become scrap anyway, and by leaving it to the elements time and manpower could be saved all around. At any rate, the P-39 just sat where it had been landed, for seventeen years.

Could it be restored? Considering the plane's condition, Brown was doubtful, at least as far as flying it again was concerned. Gambling on an outside chance, however, he telephoned CAF headquarters in Mercedes to have someone come take a look at it. Since the P-39 was a much-needed type, the CAF immediately agreed to dispatch a member. A few days later, the wreckage arrived by truck at Mercedes.

For two years, the P-39 sat in an open field, exposed to the metal-withering elements of Texas' Lower Rio Grande Valley, as the CAF searched for sponsors and restoration money.

Colonel Don Hull, who owns an aircraft maintenance shop in Sugarland, Texas, became interested in rebuilding the neglected 'Cobra. "When I finally got it," Hull remembers now, "that plane was ready for the dump. It was nothing but a shell. You could stick your head in the door and see daylight out the nose. The skin was practically gone, and in what was left of it, I counted fifteen projectile holes of different caliber." To make matters worse, a hurricane that had fumed through the Rio Grande Valley scattered pieces of the plane's cockpit frame so far away that they couldn't even be found.

But since the aircraft was one of only two known existing P-39s in the world (the other was privately owned in Nevada) the CAF wanted a flying model badly, and Don Hull went to work.

The first priority was finding parts. A telephone call to Buffalo, where Bell was now turning out sophisticated birds of several generations later, offered qualified hope. Yes, there were a few P-39 parts lying around, but not many. By chance, Hull learned that Joe Engle, an astronaut and active CAF colonel, was at that moment visiting the Bell plant and planned afterward to return to the Manned Spaceflight Center outside Houston. Engle hand-carried Bell's entire P-39 parts inventory to Hull's doorstep. Regretfully, every one was either for a different model of the P-39 series or one that wasn't needed.

Hull next resorted to a restoration technique that had served well before: *when you can't find a part, make one*. Painstakingly, he went over the P-39 inch by inch, removing virtually every moving screw, bolt, nut, hinge, and brace. An

In a little better shape now (at least, it has wheels!) the Ghost Squadron's Airacobra is still a long way from flying status.

Almost ready to fly again, an Airacobra rests in a hangar at Rebel Field.

*Last of the Grumman "Cat" line designated and built for American carrier aviation,
this is one of two F8F Bearcats owned by the CAF.*

The workhorse of Leatherneck combat aviation in World War II, this gull-winged Chance-Vought F4U Corsair fighter required extensive work by the CAF after its acquisition in Arizona.

OPPOSITE PAGE
ABOVE: Serene in this post-rain pose at Harlingen's Rebel Field, the Messerschmitt Me-109 was a terror of the skies, its exploits dating back to the mid-thirties.

BELOW: The CAF's Royal Air Force Supermarine Spitfire, valiant defender of London in the Battle of Britain.

SIDE: "Iron Annie" was her nickname; the Junkers Ju-52 trimotor transport. The CAF found this rare bird in Spain.

BELOW: Who said wood was only for ships and houses? Proof to the contrary: Britain's high-speed, extremely maneuverable Mosquito fighter-bomber, ferried to Harlingen from England.

No light bomber saw more World War II service than the Douglas A-20 Havoc. The CAF located this one in Boise, Idaho, and restored it to flying condition.

A rapid climber despite its weight and size, the North American B-25 Billy Mitchell medium bomber, one of the hottest performers in the CAF Bomber Wing.

Mirrored in a rain pool left by a sudden Texas storm the C.A.F.'s B-24 is being readied for take-off.

Wheels retracting, the Ghost Squadron's B-24 Liberator thunders into the Texas skies wearing the insignia of the Ninth Air Force's 95th Bomb Group.

engineer was hired to draw exact duplicates on paper, a machinist to transform the penciled diagrams to reality. The cost of the P-39's restoration was skyrocketing, meanwhile, but CAF Colonel John Stokes of nearby San Marcos agreed to foot the bill, as official sponsor, to the tune of $59,000.

On November 19, 1974, with a red Russian star painted on its streamlined fuselage, the 'Cobra was landed at Harlingen, Texas, by CAF Colonel Ed Messick. It had literally come full circle: from a fully operational combat aircraft to desert graveyard and back again.

What is it like to fly the P-39? Though pilot opinions vary in detail, most agree that it is generally a smooth, trouble-free plane to handle, despite its radical design and that ever-present drive shaft rotating and rumbling between the legs, though constant attention to the controls is required. The CAF's Airacobra has been flown by several of its colonels. One of them is Patrick H. Murphy, of San Marcos, Texas, a member of the CAF's Cen-Tex Wing, who recorded his impressions as follows:

"The automobile-type door with which you gain entrance to the cockpit seems a bit strange at first, but you quickly grow accustomed to it. Upon squeezing into the cockpit, you realize right off that this aircraft was *not* designed to be flown by a large person. The rudder pedals, even adjusted full forward, and the seat height are a bit tight for a person of my stature, and I am only five feet eight.

"All switches and controls are placed in readily accessible locations, and it is, I believe, a well thought-out cockpit design in this respect. After the engine starts, you get the uncomfortable feeling that you are sitting on the end of a gigantic concrete mixer, what with that propeller drive making its high-pitched whine and with the associated vibration directly between your ankles. But, after a while, you soon get used to this, too.

"Takeoff presents no particular problems, but there is considerable torque which necessitates the use of light right braking intermittently. The aircraft flies off the ground with a smooth rotation at about 90 to 100 miles per hour. There is no particular pitch or yaw encountered upon gear retraction. However, the P-39 *is* sensitive in lateral control upon either the reduction or addition of engine power. (I spend a goodly part of each flight with my left hand on the rudder trim to keep these forces neutralized.)

"I think that flying the 39 throughout its flight envelope in well-coordinated flight is probably the toughest part of flying this airplane *well*. You really have to work at it, but then it leaves you with a great deal of self-satisfaction when you do it well, too. On pitch control, very positive results occur from any particular input, although there is a noticeable tendency to 'dig in' on accelerated turns, so this has to be watched fairly closely until you get the hang of it.

"Regarding aileron effect, the P-39 appears to have a fairly high roll rate. It is not a 'knife edge' roll control like on the F-86, but very good, nevertheless, with absolutely no slop in the ailerons.

"The CAF's P-39, at this writing, does not have the required fifty hours of flight time since its rebuilding, so aerobatics are prohibited, but we foresee no particular problems in this regard." (Rebuilder Don Hull notes an exception: because the P-39's manual calls for a maximum of six to nine seconds in inverted flight, sustained upside-down flying is definitely out; the CAF once lost a P-63 Kingcobra when the pilot inadvertently flew it inverted too long and a strained supercharger caught fire.)

After piling up considerable flight time in the P-39, Murphy discounts the oft-repeated horror stories of the 'Cobra in the air. "We've all heard stories of

Restoration completed, a P-39 Airacobra goes through its paces over Rebel Field.

'wild tumbling' in the air, flat spins, and other gyrations associated with this aircraft," he says with a grin. "From my own past experience, though, the bad habits of any airplane are about 90 per cent exaggeration, and the remaining 10 per cent seems to get hairier each time they are repeated, especially when the repeating is done with a touch of the grape added.

"Undoubtedly, one can get the 39 into some frightening maneuvers, if you work at it, like any other airplane. I personally believe that *recovery* from these maneuvers could indeed get a bit tense, and especially with an aft center of gravity loading, which is bad news in itself, not only for the P-39, but with any aircraft.

"Formation flying with the P-39 is a snap (except for some restricted pilot visibility from the upper part of the cockpit door jamb.) This type of flying will certainly point up an aircraft's handling ability, and the relative ease or difficulty of placing an aircraft exactly where you want it. Landings in the P-39 are a piece of cake; you just point the airplane where you want it to land, maintaining 110 miles an hour until you are over the fence. Then you grease it on beautifully, with plenty of elevator control, even after touchdown, to get maximum induced drag to slow the little bird down. Ground handling is no problem either, with differential braking.

"The major limiting factor of which I have become especially aware is the problem of keeping the engine coolant within limits. The normal operating temperature of 120 degrees C. and maximum of 125 degrees C. leaves a rather tight operating area. If you can't crank up and get off almost immediately, you might as well forget it as the coolant will exceed the red line in a hurry. Improved ducting and a large radiator would certainly ease this, and a water spray bar located in front of the radiator is also a very good modification.

"All in all, I think the P-39 Airacobra, even with its shortcomings, is a wonderful little bird; it is honest, has a very solid feel to it, and it is dependable. If you fly it correctly, it will make a much better pilot out of you."

The CAF later acquired a P-63 Kingcobra for its combat collection but it was destroyed by fire which occurred in flight. By tragic irony, pilot Dick Disney,

Even at rest, the P-39 is a study of aerodynamic perfection.

Bearing British insignia, a P-63 Kingcobra in its natural element over Texas.

one of the CAF's early founders and later its chief check pilot, managed to land the flaming aircraft safely, but later died in the fiery crash in Harlingen of the CAF's PBY Catalina flying boat.

Doubtless, those who flew the revolutionary P-39 Airacobra and P-63 King-cobra will long debate their merits and shortcomings. Admittedly, because it was not equipped with a supercharger, the P-39 performed well only below 17,000 feet and even with one, the P-63 was outranked at higher altitudes by newer fighters in the war. And although most 'Cobra pilots shrug it off as speculative nonsense, flying with a 1,200-horsepower engine practically in one's hip pocket can't exactly be considered as psychologically reassuring. Yet at a time when they were sorely needed, the 'Cobras performed their function adequately; except for the patience and perseverance of the CAF, they doubtless would have passed into oblivion.

7 THE CARRIERS' STING

With good reason, the Turk archipelago was feared as the "Gibraltar of the Pacific." Other descriptions were "invincible," "impregnable," "an impenetrable bastion." To Allied forces sweeping westward and northward across the Pacific in early 1944, the 40-mile-wide, 820-square-mile Truk lagoon in the Eastern Carolines was an ominous question mark on the road to Japan. Prewar Japan had sealed off the island stronghold from prying eyes. Intelligence nevertheless had managed to piece together a militarily frightening image: fully 40,000 Japanese troops and civilians, hundreds of aircraft, airfields, hangars, submarine pens, and in the lagoon itself—except for Ulithi, perhaps, the finest deepwater anchorage in the Pacific—the mighty battle fleet of the Imperial Japanese Navy. And all of it, to be sure, would be heavily protected with antiaircraft guns and long-range naval and coastal artillery.

But Truk's "invincible bastion" myth was convincingly shattered in one mighty thirty-six-hour naval air raid that began at dawn on February 16, 1944, which caught the defending Japanese totally by surprise. Swarming over Truk in thirty waves from elements of the Navy's Fast Carrier Forces ninety miles away, American fighters and bombers left devastation in their wake. When the din of battle cleared, the loss to the Japanese Navy was catastrophic: more than sixty ships, including fifteen naval vessels, seventeen cargo ships, and six tankers had been sunk or damaged beyond repair. Two hundred fifty aircraft had been destroyed. Bombs had devastated countless shore facilities. In all, 200,000 tons of Japanese naval might were gone.

True, most of the Imperial Navy's warships had left Truk several days before (though for operational reasons, and not in anticipation of the American air raid). Nevertheless, the ships that were sunk were critical in a logistics sense, and the fact that not one managed to flee the lagoon was a stunning setback for the Japanese. In total, the ships lost at Truk represent the largest fleet of vessels sunk at one time anywhere in the history of the world. Pearl Harbor was avenged, and in an air attack fifteen times more powerful than that the Japanese had pulled by surprise more than three years earlier.

Tarawa . . . Iwo . . . Léyte Gulf . . . Midway. Lined up an airport apron at Harlingen, these are examples of the fighting Navy planes that helped to lift those names from obscurity and make them an indelible part of American history after Pearl Harbor.

The naval air raid at Truk was not the turning point of the Pacific war; that had been reached in June 1942—two years earlier—in the stunning American victory in the Battle of Midway. But Truk was convincing proof positive, if anyone needed it at that point, that it was the military airplane and its mobile airfield, the carrier, not the battleship, that was the decisive tactical weapon in the battle of the Pacific.

By all odds, the Pacific war should have been decided on the basis of traditional sea power—great fleets of warships meeting on its vast expanse to slug it out toe to toe. The Pacific, after all, sprawls across more than one third of the earth's surface, and long range was something that airplanes had yet to achieve when the Japanese sneak attack on Pearl Harbor drew the United States into the global conflict. The aircraft carrier had come into its own, of course, but for the United States, at least, its concept and value had not yet been tested in battle. The attack on Oahu changed that; in the Western Hemisphere, the Imperial Navy's surprise attack was the first use of the carrier in combat. Before V-J Day three and a half years later, fully five major Pacific naval battles would be fought without any ship sighting an enemy vessel, the entire burden of combat being borne by aircraft.

Ironically, while the United States Navy had twenty-six aircraft carriers operational in 1941—seventeen of the *Essex* class and nine of the lighter *Independence* class—it would be years later, much nearer the end of the war, in fact, that they would be equipped with fighters, dive-bombers, and torpedo-bombers that were any match for those of the enemy. At the time of Pearl Harbor, the Douglas TBD Devastator, for example, was the United States's only carrier-borne torpedo plane. Though it was a rugged, durable plane that pilots found a joy to fly, it could barely reach 150 miles an hour top speed with a full load, and it was, inadvertently, the nearest American equivalent to the Japanese *kamikaze*. Its far-superior successor, the Grumman TBF Avenger, saw no action until mid 1942. Even then, in its blistering baptism of fire in the Battle of Midway, only a single Avenger of Torpedo Squadron 8 survived, and it was months later before the supply of replacements finally caught up with demand.

Among carrier fighters, the single-engined Grumman F4F Wildcat was the standard plane in 1941, yet the Zero could fly rings around it. The Wildcat's successor, the F6F Hellcat, wasn't operational until January 1943, and the 450-mile-an-hour F8F Bearcat, which could climb to 10,000 feet from a standing takeoff in eighty-one seconds, arrived so late it saw no combat at all. Less than a thousand were delivered before the American victory and the arrival of jets. It was only in the Vought F4U Corsair, a plane so hot it was flown mainly by land-based Marine units before it could be adapted to carrier duty, that the Navy was able to throw the fear of God into smug, superior-planed Japanese pilots in the war of the flattop.

For dive-bombing, a tactic the Army Air Corps had discarded in favor of level-bombing light and medium planes, but which the Navy developed to near perfection, the SBD Dauntless, a Douglas-built close cousin to the TBD, was all the Navy had when the war began. Technically obsolete long before Pearl Harbor, the SBD was thrown into action as a stopgap device; Curtiss was rushing production on its heavier, faster, more powerful SB2C Helldiver, but so many problems plagued the replacement it did not arrive until late 1943—more than halfway through the Pacific war.

Yet despite the so-little-so-late aircraft position that the American Navy found itself in during the frantic weeks and months after Pearl Harbor, its gallant fighter and bomber pilots managed to write one of the most stirring chapters in military aviation history. Often outnumbered, their aircraft outmoded compared to those of the Japanese, their superior flying skill was credited with turning the Pacific air war in their favor especially after the Battle of Midway put a stunned Japan on the defensive for the first time.

The Confederate Air Force's earliest acquisitions were Army Air Corps planes. It was land-based planes and a handful of Air Corps veterans, not ex-Navy pilots, that provided the early impetus. It was evident from the beginning, however, that if the Ghost Squadron was to be truly representative of *all* major types of World War II combat planes, the contribution of the flattop fliers could hardly be ignored. Not only was the Navy *not* ignored, nearly half of the American war planes flown today by the CAF, not counting the trainers that were used by all three flying services, are shipboard types. And the Navy's many historic Pacific air battles are ably recalled in the CAF's annual air show in Harlingen, Texas, in full-fledged re-enactments: the Battle of Midway, the defense against the attack on Pearl Harbor, the Battle of the Coral Sea, the "Marianas Turkey Shoot," and Jimmy Doolittle's famous carrier-launched B-25 raid over Tokyo.

American carrier aviation, whose tactical value the Pacific war so effectively proved, dates to the 1920s, first with smaller ships such as the ex-collier *Jupiter* (renamed the *Langley*) and later with larger vessels such as the *Lexington* and *Saratoga,* both originally cruisers whose superstructures were altered to permit installation of 880-foot landing decks for airplanes. Later, in the thirties, the Navy began building carriers as such from the keel up. At the same time, it began to experiment with a series of fighter and attack plane designs that could adapt to the special rigors of carrier duty. To accomplish their unique tasks, carrier planes required far more airframe stressing than their land-based cousins, because of the impact of arresting gear upon landing and the shock of catapult on takeoff. For the long overwater flights to which they would be subjected, they also needed improved radio communications equipment, and flotation gear to permit pilot escape if a ditching became necessary. Space is at a premium aboard ship; while early carrier aircraft were simply standard land planes beefed up for sea duty, later models were designed with folding wings for more compact storage. By necessity, the training of carrier pilots was far more exacting and rigorous than that of land plane aviators. Not only does landing on a carrier's flight deck require a far greater degree of skill than touching down on a stable, unmoving airfield, but Navy pilots flying long stretches over ocean expanses also had no landmarks to refer to; they had to be top-notch navigators.

Early in the evolution of carriers, those of the United States as well as other nations, it became evident that naval planes would have to be developed that were capable of delivering torpedoes in battle. One of the United States Navy's first contributions in this field was the Martin T4M-1 biplane, a relatively frail and underpowered ship that had difficulty finding 120 miles an hour even with a good tail wind. Despite its limited speed and short range, it was nevertheless a revolutionary and remarkable advance in the burgeoning field of carrier technology. Much faster was the Navy's leading fighter of the era, the Boeing F4B-1, powered with a R-1340-17 Pratt and Whitney engine that could drive it at 187 miles an hour.

And as we have seen, the Douglas SBD Dauntless—which emerged from the Navy's 1934 design competition, which produced the Northrop BT-1—became

Wings that can be folded to conserve valuable space aboard aircraft carriers are a special requirement of all Navy fighting aircraft. Normally, the operation can be accomplished by the pilot. Occasionally, however, as the photographic sequence (left) from the Harlingen flight line demonstrates, the best method is one dating back to caveman days: human muscle power. A CAF P-38 Lightning is in the background. This is the CAF's Curtiss SB2C Helldiver, believed to be the only one of its type still flying.

the first effective monoplane dive-bomber, though Germany's Junkers Ju-87 had already been tested in battle, in the Spanish Civil War of 1936–39, and was already combat-experienced when Hitler invaded Poland in 1939. A variety of other fighters, dive-bombers, and torpedo planes came and went during the thirties, but despite the fact that aviation technology was greatly accelerated in the last half of that decade, the Navy was still scrambling for really effective carrier planes in all categories when Pearl Harbor plunged the nation into war in December 1941.

The slow but deadly SBD dive-bomber was one of the major aircraft victims of the Pearl Harbor attack. Conversely, it was the SBD that was credited with downing the first Japanese plane of the Pacific war. The first Dauntlesses were delivered to the Marine Corps in late 1940, and by December 1941, the SBD was the standard carrier-borne dive-bomber with the U.S. fleet. For two years, it fulfilled the Navy's entire scout dive-bomber requirements. Carrying a crew of two, the SBD had a rated top speed of 252 miles per hour, a range of 1,400 miles, and a service ceiling of 25,200 feet. Its combat weight was 9,000 pounds. By shifting its bomb-racks, various ordnance loads could be carried, and the Navy put the SBD to limited use as a smoke-screen layer as well. Standard machine-gun armament was four .50-caliber guns.

Dive-bombing itself was a tactic employed to some extent in World War I,

The Douglas SBD Dauntless dive-bomber, one of the hardest-hit casualties of Pearl Harbor. History also credits this prewar "relic," now at Harlingen, with the first Japanese "kill" of the Pacific war.

but it was not until the between-war period that American tacticians, realizing its value, began to fully develop its potential. Although the Army Air Corps was involved in some early tests, the major development of dive-bombing was conducted by the Navy. As early as 1926, the Navy demonstrated the effectiveness of dive-bombing in mock runs against battleships off the California coast. Three years later, Martin Aircraft was awarded a contract by the Navy for the first airplane designed strictly for such missions and the result was the Martin XT5M-1; powered with a 525-horsepower Pratt and Whitney radial engine, it could carry a 1,000-pound bomb in addition to the single, fixed .30-caliber machine gun in its nose.

Word that Hitler was developing the Junkers Ju-87 Stuka spurred American dive-bomber development, and production was accelerated even further when the Stuka was tested in battle in the Spanish Civil War. The SBD was considerably more sophisticated than the Martin dive-bomber, but even it was intended only as a stopgap weapon until a plane could be produced that would be more in keeping with expected demands of the next conflict.

Only a day before the sneak attack, the carrier *Enterprise* was steaming back to Pearl Harbor from Wake Island where it had delivered six Grumman F4F fighters to the island's Marine garrison. On board also were eighteen SBD Dauntlesses, which, in addition to their bombing capacity, were used for scouting and patrol missions in the ocean area west of Hawaii. Aware that touchy negotiations were then in progress between American officials and the Japanese envoy in Washington, Vice Admiral W. F. Halsey, flying his task force flag aboard the

An SBD Dauntless at rest. Note the prominent perforated flaps beneath the wings; highly effective as air brakes, they were necessary to slow the dauntless in a dive position to ensure bombing accuracy.

Enterprise, ordered all SBDs aloft. They were under the command of Commander Howard Young, who flew the lead plane with his destination intended to be the naval air station at Ford Island, Pearl Harbor. About 8 A.M. on Sunday, December 7, Young had the island of Oahu in sight when a plane he assumed to be an American fighter approached his formation. Young paid little attention, since the Army frequently used patrolling Navy planes as practice targets in the Hawaiian area. Suddenly, however, he realized this was no practice—he felt the SBD shudder violently as the "friendly" fighter slipped behind him and opened fire. There was no time to warn pilots of the other SBDs, who had been assigned their own patrol sectors as they sped toward Hawaii, out of sight of one another. Nor did Young realize at the time that almost at that moment, World War II had begun for the United States, and that a few miles ahead, a substantial part of the Pacific fleet lay in smoking ruin at Pearl Harbor. Young made a fast retreat for Pearl Harbor's Ford Island, but he had no time to warn other American planes behind him that enemy craft were near. When all arrived, they found Pearl Harbor under full-scale attack.

Of the *Enterprise*'s eighteen SBDs, seven were lost to Japanese fighters that morning; in addition, of twenty-nine others operated by Marine Air Group 21 on Oahu, all were either destroyed on the ground or badly damaged. The Navy, however, enjoyed a small measure of revenge; of twenty-nine Japanese aircraft shot down in the surprise attack, at least two kills were credited to the *Enterprise*'s Dauntless pilots. This was followed up three days later by the sinking of the first Japanese warship of the war. Credit for the victory went to Lieutenant

C. E. Dickinson, who had shot down a Zero with his Dauntless after being surprised on Sunday; following up the report of the sighting of a surfaced Japanese submarine 180 miles northeast of Pearl Harbor, he dove through a wall of antiaircraft fire to lay a single 500-pound bomb in the water alongside the enemy craft. Later identified as the I-70, the sub, its sides ruptured by concussion, sank in less than one minute.

The days and weeks that followed Pearl Harbor were frantic, desperate ones for the American Pacific Fleet, and Dauntless pilots did an admirable job in buying the time the Navy needed to recover from the wounds inflicted at Pearl Harbor and reverse the direction of the war in the Battle of Midway. In February, SBDs carried out a dawn attack on Kwajalein Atoll in the Marshalls; in the following weeks, their bombs wreaked havoc on such scattered Japanese outposts as the Gilberts, Marcus Island, Rabaul, and New Guinea, as well as Wake Island, whose valiant Marine garrison had surrendered to the Japanese shortly after Pearl Harbor.

In an airplane designed for dive-bombing, incredible airframe strength is required to withstand the loads of diving. Ideally, dive-bombing is conducted at an angle of between 60 and 90 degrees, with the plane pointed directly toward its target. Because of the requirement for dead-on accuracy, the SBD was built with special large, perforated diving brakes to reduce speed. Glide-bombing, a variant of dive-bombing, is done with the plane pointed down at an angle of attack of between 30 and 55 degrees. Because the angle is less than that in dive-bombing, the air brakes are not necessary.

The value of the design was proved many times between Pearl Harbor and the Battle of Midway the following June. In early May, Dauntless pilots were ordered to sweep the Japanese base at Tulagi, Solomons, where, intelligence had indicated, the enemy was marshaling its forces for an attack on Port Moresby, New Guinea. There were fifteen Japanese vessels in the Tulagi anchorage; carrier-borne SBDs sank seven of them. But the boats were small fry—patrol craft, barges, mine sweepers. Three fatter targets, Japanese aircraft carriers, were steaming miles away, moving south from the heavily defended anchorage at Truk toward the expected invasion of New Guinea. To SBD pilots aboard the American flattops *Lexington* and *Yorktown* went an order from the task force commander, Rear Admiral Frank J. "Jack" Fletcher: *"Get those carriers!"*

The Battle of the Coral Sea, which began three days later, was a milestone in the history of naval warfare. Fought entirely with aircraft carriers of the opposing nations, not one combat vessel approached within sight of an opponent, and the only naval gunfire exchanged was that of attached vessels against airborne attackers. And Dauntlesses led the way.

The first sighting of the Japanese fleet was reported at 8:15 A.M. on May 7 by a *Yorktown* scout plane. From high altitude, the two Japanese ships appeared to be heavy carriers; actually they were cruisers, and at 9:15 A.M., twenty-eight Dauntlesses began roaring off the flight deck of the two American flattops. Identification of the enemy ships was soon corrected, and although no heavy enemy carriers could be found, a smaller carrier, the 11,000-ton *Shoho,* was spotted. Sixteen SBDs of the *Lexington*'s Bombing Squadron 2 moved in for the attack.

Led by Lieutenant Commander W. L. Hamilton, the SBDs rendezvoused with a flight of Navy TBD Devastator torpedo-bombers; the plan was for the

SBDs to move in from above to draw the fire of the *Shoho* and her escort vessels away from the exposed low-level torpedo planes. About 200 miles away from his own task force, Hamilton watched the *Shoho* making frantic turns as it attempted to escape. At 11:10 A.M., the SBDs swept down in 70-degree dives. Fortunately, the *Shoho's* cruiser and destroyer escorts had been forced to move five miles away because of the carrier's twisting path, and antiaircraft fire was light. The Dauntlesses scored five hits; with the *Shoho* knocked dead in the water, the flight of TBD Devastators moved in at low level to administer the *coupe de grâce* with their torpedoes. To seal the victory, SBDs of the *Yorktown's* Air Group 2 arrived fifteen minutes later to achieve six more hits. The *Shoho* slid under the Pacific's surface at 11:35 A.M., the first of six carriers to be sunk by American naval aircraft during the Pacific war.

Because the American carriers early in the war were not sufficiently equipped with fighters, Dauntless pilots were pressed into service as a patrol screen around the flattops, as well as fulfilling their role as offensive bombers. In the action against the *Shoho,* the pilot-gunner team of Lieutenants John Leppla and John Liska began to build their now-famous reputation as Zero-killers; they bagged four enemy planes that day alone. Lieutenant Stanley "Swede" Vejtasa of the *Yorktown's* air group did nearly as well the following day, splashing three attacking Japanese fighters unassisted. For the American task force, however, the sinking of the *Shoho* drew only brief celebration; before the Battle of the Coral Sea was over, the U. S. Navy lost the *Lexington,* with a costly toll in life and scores of vitally needed SBDs.

Like the SBD Dauntless, with which it worked so well as a double-punch combat team, the TBD Devastator was also a product of the Douglas Aircraft Company in Southern California. A three-man airplane, it replaced the obsolete Martin torpedo plane when it joined the fleet in 1937. Its two major deficiencies were a woefully short range and lack of power. In one sense—it had folding wings—it was a more advanced plane than its fixed-wing dive-bombing cousin, but in other departments it ran a poor second. Its radial Pratt and Whitney R-1830 engine delivered only 900 horsepower, and although its top speed was officially rated at 200 miles an hour, it reportedly could reach less than two thirds of that with a full load of ordnance. Nor, according to the pilots who flew the TBD, did the Devastator have the light, agile control response of the SBD, although in level flight and without a heavy load it was considered a rugged, reliable plane.

Typical of the opinion of the plane by pilots who flew it is that of Admiral Robert Laub, now retired, who was the senior surviving torpedo plane pilot from the *Enterprise* after the Battle of Midway, which followed on the heels of the Battle of the Coral Sea. Laub remembers the TBD as a docile, beautifully finished, comfortable plane, but absolutely frustrating in speed, climb, and maneuverability. "The XTBD may have flown at 200 knots," he recalled in an interview after the war, "but I never flew an operational type that did better than 150 knots and that was downhill, with all the right conditions. You were doing well to make 120 knots in the TBD with a torpedo, and since the protruding 'fish' didn't create a great deal of drag, 130 knots clean was normal. The TBD took all day to climb to altitude and if you went to 15,000 feet in it, you just about used up all your fuel. Twelve thousand feet was maximum bombing altitude, and because we never went higher, we carried no oxygen, although the aircraft was equipped to handle it. The TBD-1 was very stable and landed with full flaps at 60, even though the flaps didn't change its handling characteristics much. It had a good solid feel and was rock steady when coming aboard. The maneuvers we did with it were very limited. Basically, the TBD-1 was a straight and level airplane. It would perform moderately short turns, but I wouldn't roll or spin it. Its glide ratio was rather short and although we thought it was modern in 1937, it was very obsolete by 1942, and we knew it."

Like the Dauntless, the Devastator at the war's outbreak had a successor being rushed through design and production stage. It was the sleeker, faster Grumman TBF Avenger, fully 100 miles an hour faster than the TBD, designed to carry its "fish" internally instead of hanging below the fuselage, and, more importantly, a range expanded to 1,130 miles. The powerful Avenger would relieve the TBD earlier in the war than the Curtiss SB2C Helldiver would relieve the antiquated but hard-working Dauntless. In both cases, the fact that two obsolete planes performed so valiantly is, once again, a tribute to the courage and flying skill of their pilots. Without the teamwork developed in combat by Devastator and Dauntless squadrons, the effectiveness of either doubtless would have been substantially reduced. Consider, for instance, the peril of the torpedo-bomber pilots in a standard attack situation and the potential uselessness of their mission had there not been dive-bomber or fighter teammates to divert at least a part of the enemy's defense. Modified from a standard destroyer torpedo, the TBD's "tin fish" was both slow and unreliable. At best, World War II torpedoes moved along at only 33 knots after being released into the water. As often as not, they veered off the mark. Add to this the fact that they were launched at a moving target. Overcoming these difficulties meant that a TBD pilot had to slow to 100 miles an hour, drop to only 50 feet off the water, and move to within 800 yards

The Battle of Midway provided a baptism of fire for the Grumman TBF carrier-based torpedo-bomber, the Avenger. This was the Navy's standard torpedo-bomber from mid-1942 until the end of World War II.

if he was to stand any chance at all of scoring a hit. Further, he could not take evasive action, no matter how heavy the antiaircraft fire against him or the fire of the enemy's defensive fighters, if he was to aim with any degree of accuracy. Considering all these factors, plus the chilling reality that flying only 50 feet off the water meant certain death if enemy flak did its job, the Navy's gallant torpedo pilots must rank among the bravest fliers in the history of combat aviation. In a single day—June 6, 1942—they were to prove it beyond all doubt in the Battle of Midway. Because it was an engagement that not only turned the tide of the Pacific war but naval history as well, Midway has been the subject of infinite description before, including entire books, and repeating the story at length would be redundant. However, viewed as historical backdrop for the Ghost Squadron's urgency in later seeking flying models of both the Dauntless and Avenger for its collection, a brief summary is appropriate.

Because the loss of Midway Island to the Japanese would place enemy forces only 1,100 miles from Hawaii, and thus perhaps force an American military withdrawal to the United States mainland, defense of the island was given top priority after the Battle of the Coral Sea, an engagement which gave the U. S. Navy a psychological victory but one which Japan rightfully could regard as merely an irritating delay in sweeping through the entire Pacific. Midway was to be the showdown battle of the Pacific war, with victory in the war itself hanging in the balance for either side.

To defend Midway, the U. S. Navy could muster but three carriers: the *Yorktown,* damaged in the Coral Sea but now back in action; the *Enterprise,* with her battle-hardened Air Group 6; and the *Hornet,* with her less-experienced Air Group 8. Aboard these three carriers were 112 SBD Dauntless dive-bombers, 42 TBD Devastators, and 79 F4F Wildcat fighters. Aboard the *Hornet,* also, Torpedo Squadron 8 had been selected to put the TBF Avenger into battle for the first time. The new planes arrived too late from Hawaii to be phased in to shipboard duty aboard the carrier, however, and only 6 were ready in time for the engagement; all 6 were flown from the airfield on Midway.

Against the three American carriers was pitted the largest fleet of ships the Imperial Japanese Navy had ever assembled in one place. It included 4 heavy carriers, *Akagi, Kaga, Soryu,* and *Hiryu,* comprising essentially the same strike force that had crippled Pearl Harbor half a year earlier. Supporting the 4 carriers was a large force of battleships and cruisers; the Americans' 3 carriers, in contrast, were protected only by light cruiser and destroyer escort. In all, the American fleet, with 28 ships of the line and 230 aircraft, faced a formidable force of nearly 200 ships and 700 aircraft.

Although naval histories of the battle vary in detail, they agree on the essentials, and certainly on the outcome. In a single day of blistering give-and-take, Admiral Chuichi Nagumo's superior striking force was convincingly routed; in the follow-up phase, the U. S. Navy delivered to the Japanese their first major naval defeat in more than three hundred years, a defeat that confirmed carrier-borne aviation as the critical element of modern naval warfare.

Nagumo was unaware of the presence of the American carriers when he launched an all-out attack on Midway at dawn on June 6. A prowling Navy PBY Catalina patrol plane had spotted the Japanese fleet, however, and although they were vastly outnumbered, the Midway defenders were ready for the assault. The six TBF Avengers freshly delivered from Hawaii scrambled aloft, along with every other available aircraft of the Navy, Marine Corps, and Army on the island, including four Army B-26 Marauders converted to torpedo-bombers, four

B-17 Flying Fortresses, and a handful of Marine Vought SB2U Scouts, the latter being planes that had been obsolete for years. Five minutes later, the Avengers ran into a swarm of Japanese fighters at 4,000 feet, which they mistakenly reported later as "German Me-109s." Of the six TBFs, only one, piloted by Ensign A. K. Earnest, made it back to Midway. To a man, the crews of the other five died in action; aboard Earnest's TBF, his radioman had been wounded and the gunner killed.

At sea, Rear Admirals R. A. Spruance and F. J. Fletcher learned of Nagumo's attack on Midway. Shortly after 7 A.M. the *Enterprise* and *Hornet* launched their air groups for a strike against the invaders. It was to be a tragically unsuccessful morning for the torpedo squadrons. Unknown to the American pilots, Nagumo had become aware of the presence of the American carriers, after the Japanese original attack on Midway, and had changed his course at 9:15 A.M. Many of the TBDs, SBDs, and escorting F4F Wildcat fighters ran out of fuel trying to locate the rerouted Japanese, and had to ditch before reaching their own carriers. The *Hornet*'s Torpedo Squadron 8, relying on instinct, guessed what had happened and found their target; in the ensuing battle, however, hampered by a low cloud cover in which the fighters lost sight of the planes they were assigned to escort, all fifteen TBDs were shot down.

Not far behind Torpedo 8 was a flight of fourteen Devastators from Torpedo 6 of the *Enterprise,* led by Lieutenant Gene Lindsay. Of his fourteen planes, only three survived Nagumo's antiaircraft fire and the savage attack of the defending fighters. No sooner had Lindsay's attack been rebuffed at such terrible cost, the *Yorktown*'s torpedo squadron, led by Lieutenant Commander Lance E. Massey, waded in against the carrier *Soryu.* Seven Devastators, including Massey's, were destroyed. Only five were able to launch their torpedoes and three of those were shot down. Not a single torpedo hit was scored. For the Devastators, the morning had been a slaughter. Out of forty-one planes launched by the three American carriers, only six had returned; not a single torpedo hit had been scored on the Japanese. Naval historians have noted, however, that in their tragic loss, a victory of great importance nevertheless was scored. By keeping Nagumo constantly on the defense, the Americans forced the Japanese fleet to maneuver radically; thus the number of planes the Japanese carriers could launch was minimized. Further, they kept the defending "Zekes" and "Zeros" nearly at water level, thereby giving the late-arriving SBDs a clear sky from which to launch their attack on the Japanese carriers. At a staggering price, the Devastator pilots had bought time for the American Dauntless dive-bombers, and it was by this sacrifice that the Battle of Midway was decided.

As the battle neared its end, Nagumo had lost three of his four carriers; only the *Hiryu* was left. Seeking revenge, he launched a strike from the *Hiryu* against the *Yorktown* and obtained two hits. A second attack against the American carrier brought her to a dead halt in the water. That evening, however, twenty-four SBDs from the *Enterprise* and fourteen others "orphaned" from the wounded *Yorktown* plunged out of the setting sun and battered Nagumo's remaining flattop so badly that her crew finally scuttled her. In addition to the four carriers, Japan had lost thirty-five hundred seamen, including one hundred first-line pilots, and more than three hundred aircraft. From that point on, Japan was driven inevitably to her defeat in the Pacific.

The airplanes that succeeded the Douglas TBD and SBD were infinitely better designed to fly the kinds of missions demanded by the Pacific war, and by the end of 1942, when the aerial offensive was regained by the Americans, one was already a combat veteran and the other was being rushed through its final testing and production process.

At 18,000 pounds, the Grumman TBF Avenger scout torpedo-bomber was the heaviest single-engined American combat aircraft of World War II. Conceived in 1939 to replace the antiquated Douglas TBD, it was a three-man plane, the same as the TBD, its crew consisting of a pilot, torpedo officer or bombardier, and rear gunner, who also functioned as radio operator. The Avenger had a top speed of 261 miles per hour and a range of 1,200 miles, which could be extended to 1,500 miles when flown as a scout; this gave it a range three times that of the TBD. The first prototype flew on August 7, 1941, and testing continued until November 28 of that year when a bomb bay fire forced the crew to bail out. The prototype was destroyed in the crash that followed.

A second prototype was rushed into production. Ironically, it was on display during an open house in Grumman's Long Island plant on December 7, 1941, when the Pearl Harbor attack was announced over the public address system. The outbreak of war accelerated the Navy's demand for the plane and the first production models were delivered for testing only a month later, in January 1942. Grumman geared up to a twenty-four-hour-a-day wartime production footing, and by May, eighty-five TBF-1s were ready for service. (TBF was the Grumman-built designation, the "F" indicating the manufacturer; actually, General Motors built the majority of Avengers—more than 7,000 out of a total of 10,000—so the majority were designated TBM, although TBF was the more common description.)

One major advance of the TBF over other carrier designs was its hydraulic wing-folding system. On most carrier planes, wings folded in one direction only: up from mid-wing. Grumman designed the Avenger so that its wings would first fold up, then could be "tucked" by a second fold toward the fuselage. Furthermore, the hydraulic system allowed the pilot to do this quickly, even while taxiing; this saved valuable time in carrier air operations and doubtless prevented injury to many deck crewmen. Because the procedure reminded so many of a bird

The Grumman Avenger acquired by the CAF served after World War II as a fire-fighting ship. Here it is at rest with wings folded.

tucking its wings, the Avenger soon earned a second nickname—"Turkey"—which aptly described its bulky but rugged appearance as well.

After the Avenger's inauspicious debut in the Battle of Midway, it quickly began to pile up a creditable combat record in the Pacific. In August 1942, two months after Midway, forty-one Avengers from the carriers *Enterprise, Wasp,* and *Saratoga* were flown in support of the amphibious assault on Guadalcanal. For many Japanese who had not previously seen a TBF, the plane often was mistaken for another Grumman aircraft, the F4F Wildcat, at that time still the Navy's front-line fighter. Among the Japanese pilots making this error was Saburo Sakai, the famed ace, who moved in from the rear of an Avenger for what he thought was a sure kill. He had not reckoned on the TBF's .30-caliber tail machine gun, however. Sakai learned of his blunder rather painfully; though seriously wounded, he managed to fly his plane home 800 miles and went on to score a total of sixty-four kills against Allied planes, mostly American, to become Japan's second-highest-scoring ace.

By the end of 1942, Avengers had helped sink the Japanese carrier *Ryujo* in the Battle of the Eastern Solomons, and, by war's end, they had added the *Yamato* and *Musashi,* twin queens of the Imperial Navy's super-battleship fleet. Avengers caught the *Yamato* in April 1945, as she tried to break up the invasion of Okinawa. The previous October, they had nailed the *Musashi* out of Singapore, sinking her with three solid hits. Although their planes had more speed and range than their predecessors, the life of TBF torpedo plane pilots was no less harrowing; closing time in making a torpedo run was shorter, and, since the enemy had less time to turn stern-on as an evasive maneuver, generally more effective. However, Avenger pilots deserve no less credit than those who flew TBDs in the courage department, and the bottom of the Pacific is strewn with evidence of that courage.

Following World War II, the TBF was pressed into civilian service as a fire fighter. Because of its relatively stable attitude in the air, the huge capacity of its torpedo/bomb bay, and the flight duration made possible by its long range, it became a favorite of the fire-bombers who dropped chemical borate from extremely low altitude on countless brush fires, particularly along the West Coast. TBFs were active in the Korean War, too. There were no enemy ships to torpedo, of course, but in their cargo-carrying capacity, the Navy found them ideal for ferrying personnel, mail and supplies from bases in Japan to the Seventh Fleet steaming off the coast of Korea.

As badly as the Navy needed the TBF to replace the Devastator, it needed the Curtiss SB2C Helldiver even more to phase out the SBD Dauntless. This was especially true in the latter years of the war when a top-rated dive-bomber was essential in supporting the amphibious landings that were picking up momentum.

Although the Helldiver was first flown in 1940, it was not until Armistice Day, 1943, in a strike against Rabaul, that it saw combat action. It had been agonizingly long in arriving, this 14,000-pound, 294-mile-an-hour giant that was the last pure dive-bomber ever produced for the U. S. Navy. Rough and tough, the Helldiver could, in addition to carrying a heavy bombload, effectively double as a strafing platform, being equipped with either six .50-caliber machine guns, or two .50-caliber guns and two 20-millimeter cannon. But it took fully 880 major design changes from prototype to the last-delivered combat plane before the Navy could consider the SB2C "bug-proof." Nevertheless, it was a widely used and powerful addition to the fleet's sting during the latter part of the war; during the famous "Marianas Turkey Shoot," by which time the Helldiver had completely retired the war-worn Dauntless, it was the star of the show. With

The Curtiss SB2C Helldiver, last pure dive-bomber to see service in the U. S. Navy. This model is the CAF's best camera ship, owing to the wide view afforded by its cockpit.

The CAF's Helldiver in flight, bomb bay doors extended.

its mighty Pratt and Whitney fourteen-cylinder R-2600 engine churning up tremendous horsepower, the SB2C was assigned many other jobs where power was a necessity; the Army's version, for instance, designated the A-25, was even used as a glider tow, a function usually reserved for multiengine planes.

Among World War II carrier fighters, Grumman dominated the field until the introduction of the Chance-Vought F4U Corsair. Grumman fighters were, in succession, the F4F Wildcat, the F6F Hellcat, and the F8F Bearcat, all of them generally similar in appearance but vastly different in performance.

The F4F Wildcat was the only fighter serving with the U.S. fleet at the beginning of the war, and continuing in service in 1945. It saw action in every major battle in the Pacific. The slowest of all Navy fighters and outperformed by the Zero, its success was attributed to its rugged construction and the superior skill of its pilots. During the two-week siege of Wake Island, beginning December 9, 1941, Marine pilot Major Paul Putnam and his men broke up many Japanese air attacks, and managed to sink an enemy destroyer with a 100-pound bomb. On December 22, the last two Wildcats were finally destroyed and the island overwhelmed. On the following February 20, Lieutenant E. H. "Butch" O'Hare, flying a Wildcat from the carrier *Lexington,* destroyed five enemy bombers within six minutes. Until P-38 Lightnings later began dominating fighter action in the Pacific, this was the greatest number of "kills" scored by an American pilot in a single mission. (Much later in the war, O'Hare, who had been awarded the Medal of Honor, was lost in action while flying an F6F Hellcat from the *Enterprise.* He was leading the first attempt at carrier-based night interception, a tactic the Navy considered necessary because of the ease with which Japanese torpedo pilots had conducted nighttime attacks. O'Hare and his wingman, Warren Skon, both flying F6Fs, were to be guided to their targets by a radar-equipped TBF Avenger. The F6F pilots somehow got separated from John Phillips, piloting the TBF, who shot down two attacking Japanese fighters on his own. O'Hare, apparently shot down, was never seen again.)

In addition to being the slowest of World War II fighters, the F4F was also the poorest in rate of climb, maneuverability, ceiling, and firepower. First produced for the Navy in 1940, it also served the British, who named it the Martlet. Actually designated as a "pursuit fighter," the F4F evolved from the 1936 Grumman F3F biplane; even as a monoplane, the F4F retained the traditional stubby appearance of the single-engined Grumman line. Early model Wildcats

First of the Grumman "Cat" series of shipboard fighters was the stubby F4F Wildcat. It was the Navy's sole carrier-based fighter at the start of World War II.

A CAF Wildcat in flight; almost five thousand were built before 1945.

Wake Island was the first World War II battle after Pearl Harbor in which Wildcats participated. Marine pilots were at the controls. Now this rebuilt F4F flies the Texas skies.

were powered with Wright Model 1800 engines, later ones with Pratt and Whitney Wasps. They weighed but 6,000 pounds but even so their top speed was limited to 306 miles an hour.

In the F6F Hellcat, which began rolling off the assembly lines in late 1942, Grumman had boosted horsepower to 2,000 via a Pratt and Whitney R-2800 engine, top speed to 371 miles an hour, and gross weight to 13,190. The Wildcat had been conceived and designed in the thirties, before the agility of the Japanese Zero was well known; its successor was built specifically with Japan's famous fighter directly in mind. The Hellcat made its combat debut in August 1943 when Air Groups 5 and 9 from the *Essex* and *Yorktown* participated in an attack on Marcus Island. Later, in what was probably the greatest dogfight of the Pacific, some seventy-two Hellcats from Task Force 58 attacked Truk in the raid described earlier. More than fifty Zeros rose to meet them, plus an equal number launched from Rabaul to bolster the stricken "Gibraltar of the Pacific." Hellcat pilots bagged half of the Zeros, while losing only four of their own number. In other F6F strikes that day, fifty more enemy aircraft were shot down and another hundred and fifty destroyed on the ground. On the night of the February 16, 1944, attack, several Japanese Kates attempted to avenge their losses with torpedo attacks on the American task force. Antiaircraft fire kept most of them at a

The CAF's F6F Hellcat at Rebel Field, in 1961, before its new paint job.

harmless distance. Flying an F6F from the *Yorktown,* Russ Reiserer of Fighter Squadron 76 attempted the first combat night interception mission without benefit of radar against one that managed to penetrate the flak. He failed to find the Kate, however, and the enemy plane made a successful, though not fatal, torpedo run on the *Intrepid.*

Moving westward into the Marianas, Hellcats had another field day five days later. Their pilots knocked down sixty-seven of seventy-four Japanese planes that rose to challenge them, and destroyed another hundred on the ground. Only four Hellcats were lost. Throughout the following months of the war the story was much the same: tremendous Hellcat victories in Palau, Ulithi, in the Battle of the Philippine Sea, the famous "Marianas Turkey Shoot," and in the campaigns leading closer to Tokyo at Iwo Jima and Okinawa. Statistics tell the story even better; during the Pacific war, Hellcat pilots were officially credited with shooting down 5,155 Japanese planes, well over half of the total of 9,258 "kills" by all American Navy aircraft. The F4U Corsair was second, with 2,141 kills.

In the Okinawa campaign, particularly, Hellcat pilots were thrown into the combat against the dreaded, highly damaging Japanese *kamikaze* suicide planes. By the time of this operation, Japan knew that she was perilously close to defeat and withdrew most of her remaining fighters and attack planes to the homeland islands for a last-ditch stand. Japan anticipated an invasion by fall; that, of course, was made unnecessary by the two B-29 atomic bombings of Hiroshima and Nagasaki, which brought the war to an end in August. *Kamikazes* did considerable damage to American ships, particularly the carriers, whose decks could be suicide-bombed and made inoperable for aircraft. Because of the *kamikaze* menace, many American carriers kept F6F Hellcats aloft on constant patrol. Typical of these defense tactics was that on March 21, 1945. Eighteen Japanese Betty bombers, each of them a suicide bomb, and thirty Zekes were intercepted that day by Hellcats; within twenty minutes, all the Bettys and twelve Zekes were shot down, with the loss of a single F4F. Later, as the war entered its final weeks, Hellcats performed as attack planes over targets on the Japanese home islands.

By this time, fortunately, the remnants of the Japanese Air Force were a ragtag lot, the cream of the pilot crop having been sacrificed in the campaigns following Midway. Although a new plane had been developed by Grumman specifically to combat the *kamikazes*—the 450-mile-an-hour, 7,690-pound Bearcat—it arrived too late for its intended mission, even though the Navy ordered its production from Grumman as early as 1943. The Bearcat, possibly the only American propeller-driven plane that could compete with the P-51 Mustang in the speed department, was the last prop-driven Navy fighter ever built, yet it never fired its guns in anger in World War II. Bearcats served with the Navy until 1950, though production beyond the 1,000 planes delivered in 1945 stopped when the Navy canceled the contract at war's end.

Both the F4F and F6F faded quickly into obscurity after V-J Day. Although the Navy retained a handful of F4Fs for special purpose roles after the war, most were sent to training duty, or to the smelter. Some Hellcats were used as targets, guided missiles, or research aircraft. In the latter capacity, several pilotless F6F-3Ks were flown through the mushroom clouds of the Eniwetok and Bikini nuclear tests in the late forties to measure radioactive levels. In its last combat mission (like the bomb-test drones, pilotless) the Hellcat was flown as a

Horsepower was boosted to 2,000 in the Grumman F6F Hellcat, which first flew in June 1942 and joined the fleet the following year. Here is the CAF's Forget Hell *in her new, spic and span color scheme.*

The Zero was Japan's No. 1 fighter menace in the Pacific war; the Hellcat was the first American fighter that could outmaneuver this frequent opponent.

guided missile against North Korean targets in 1952; radio-controlled guidance was directed from Douglas AD Skyraiders, which flew at a safe distance.

The Wildcat proved itself a capable fighter despite the fact that it was far outclassed by the Zero. The Hellcat's combat record speaks for itself. The Bearcat came too late for World War II combat, though it would have been interesting to see what it could have done against the Zero. But without question the best all-around prop-driven Navy fighter of all time was the Chance-Vought F4U Corsair. Produced and kept in service longer than any American fighter, it was still being flown in combat by the Navy as late as 1953, the same year that the last of its total of 12,571 copies was built. Some flew in peacetime service as late as 1965. The first American fighter to exceed 400 miles an hour in level flight, the Corsair was found to be superior to the Zero in all respects—speed, rate of climb, firepower, and ceiling. That was proven in a flight test against a captured Zero in May 1944. A plane that could rightfully claim the adjective "versatile," it also served as a night fighter, high-altitude bomber escort, dive-bomber, skip-bomber, and attack-bomber. Designed to carry a bombload of 1,000 pounds, Corsairs proved capable of improving that by an incredible margin; they routinely flew with 2,000 pounds of bombs and, after a demonstration by Charles Lindbergh in the Pacific, F4Us lumbered aloft with an astonishing 4,000 pounds of bombs each, dumping a total of 200,000 pounds in a seven-week campaign in the Marshall Islands. Against enemy aircraft, their "kill rate" was phenomenal, losing only 185 of their own number against 2,140 enemy planes downed.

Two anecdotes, perhaps better than any, illustrate the uniqueness and ability of the Corsair among fighters of its time or before. During the Okinawa campaign, Lieutenant R. R. Klingman discovered one afternoon that his Corsair's guns were jammed, just when a fat Japanese photo-reconnaissance plane loomed in his sights. Klingman wanted his kill. He got it by moving in close, so close in

In production too late for World War II service, the Grumman F8F Bearcat was nevertheless the Navy's hottest fighter before jets arrived. In terms of performance, many still rate the F8F on a par with North American's land-based Mustang.

fact, that the F4U's huge propeller sawed off the rudder and elevator of the enemy ship, causing it to crash. Damage to Klingman's plane was so slight he was able to return safely to his base. And during the Korean War, when Corsairs in the first ten months of the campaign flew 82 per cent of all Marine and Navy close air support missions, an F4U was credited with shooting down a MIG-15 jet fighter. So far as is known, this was the only time in combat that a jet was knocked down by a propeller-driven aircraft.

Its design approved by the Navy in 1938, a prototype of the Corsair, designated the XF4U-1, was ready for Navy inspection the following year. The Navy wanted it equipped with the most powerful radial engine then available: the Pratt and Whitney R-2800. Chance-Vought agreed, but to install it in the slim fuselage it had envisioned for single-seat fighter use, and to accept the huge propeller needed for top speed, engineers had to resort to the unusual inverted gull-wing "U" design. For obvious reasons, the Corsair was frequently nicknamed the "U-Bird." The experimental Corsair's maiden flight was on May 29, 1940.

The first flight of a production Corsair occurred in June 1942 and the Navy accepted delivery of the plane the following month. Its inventory of carrier fighters in critical short supply, the Navy pressed for delivery of the Corsair for shipboard use in the Pacific. A number of problems delayed delivery, however, and it was as a land-based aircraft instead, with the Marines on Guadalcanal in February 1943, that the F4U first saw action. One obvious early shortcoming of the Corsair that delayed shipboard use was its impaired pilot visibility, attributed to the inverted gull-wing design that placed the cockpit so far off the deck. Good visibility is a must on a carrier, where maneuvering space is in short supply and where there is constant danger by taxiing aircraft to deck crews. Another problem was "aileron flutter," which in fact had caused the prototype F4U to crash. These problems and others were corrected by reconfiguration and constant testing, however, and the F4U went on to acquit itself gallantly throughout the Pacific war.

For the Confederate Air Force's Ghost Squadron, building a "Texas navy" from scratch was no mean feat. World War II Navy planes, like most land-based

The standard fighter of Marine Corps World War II air wings, the Chance-Vought F4U Corsair was noted for its unusual gull-wing design. More than 12,500 were produced. The Corsair (designated the FG-1D by Goodyear, which subcontracted to build many of them) was still flying combat missions in the Korean War.

The CAF Corsairs at idle, and warming up for takeoff. These planes each had an astonishing bomb-load capacity of 4,000 pounds in wartime configuration.

military aircraft, had virtually disappeared by the mid-fifties. At the Navy's main surplus aircraft disposal depot at Litchfield Park, Arizona, near Phoenix, hundreds had been tossed in the smelter or chopped up for scrap by the bulldozer. Some planes—particularly the TBF Avenger, which had ably been adapted as a forest-fire bomber—had been sold to private individuals and firms, but the majority were simply dumped or scrapped. However, in line with various military assistance programs of the United States in the late forties and early fifties, many circa 1939–45 aircraft, particularly fighters, were shipped to various Central and South American nations. Three of the most popular planes sent south were the P-51 Mustang, the P-47 Thunderbolt, and the Navy's F4U Corsair. The reason is obvious: they were the latest of the World War II vintage fighters and fighter-bombers, and thus could be considered not only as the most capable of prop-driven planes, but were generally in better condition than their predecessors.

What had happened to all of the American-donated "South American air force" after the merging nations began switching to newer jets was not known by the Ghost Squadron. Even before the transition to jets was made, it was known, however, that many of the fighters had crashed and, because parts for World War II era planes were even then practically nonexistent, many others had been "cannibalized" to repair the ones that had broken down. The Ghost Squadron therefore considered South America as a last source for building its flying collection, mainly on the basis of cost; the logistics price tag for disassembling, shipping, and reassembling a five-ton airplane half a hemisphere away is, obviously, hellishly high.

The F8F Bearcat, the first Navy plane acquired by the CAF, proved to be an easy matter. The Bearcat had still been in service not long before, and the smelter had not had time to wreak its havoc. Several surplus F8Fs were available at Litchfield Park, although after lying in a field for eleven years they were not in top shape in 1959. "Still, we considered ourselves lucky," remembers CAF founder Lloyd Nolen, "especially when our bid of $805 each proved to be the highest bid in the lot of thirty-two Bearcats. We bought two, and the other thirty were bought by the scrap dealer and went to the smelter. We picked our two, spent some time restoring them, then flew them down to the Rio Grande Valley." Later, one of the Bearcats was sold, but the other is regularly flown in CAF air shows today. It bears the colors and markings of the Navy's Fighter Squadron 19.

The F4U Corsair was the CAF's second Navy acquisition. It was found parked on a dirt airstrip in Buckeye, Arizona, in 1960, and its owner agreed to part with it for $1,800. Planes are like antique autos; as they grow older, it seems their value goes up. More than ten years later, CAF Colonel John Stokes was responsible for adding a second Corsair. Unlike the first, for which no combat history could be traced, Stokes's F4U had indeed been in battle . . . with other Corsairs. One of approximately 4,000 F4Us built by Goodyear under license from Vought (and, therefore, correctly designated the FG-1D), it had been transferred to the Air Force of El Salvador in the 1950s. Unlike some Latin nations, El Salvador had found the means to maintain its planes in top condition. In 1969, this vigilance paid off, when a squadron of Salvadorian Corsairs met in dogfight battle with Corsairs of neighboring Honduras during a brief and inconclusive border skirmish. When El Salvador began buying jet fighters, the FG-1D was sold to a Texas aircraft collector, who in turn sold it to Stokes. Painted with the insignia of Fighter Squadron 84 of the carrier *Bunker Hill,* circa 1944, it made its CAF air show debut in 1975.

The CAF added the F4F Wildcat and F6F Hellcat in 1961. Ironically, the

The Corsair in static display at Rebel Field.

Wildcat, the oldest of the three Grumman fighters, which was obsolete even as World War II began, brought more than twice the price of the newer Hellcat: $4,000. The CAF's Navy fighter collection was now complete, but it would be another ten years before the "heavy stuff"—the dive-bombers and torpedo-bombers—would be added. The Ghost Squadron was fortunate to find these aircraft for two of them—the SBD Dauntless and the SB2C Helldiver—are among the rarest flying aircraft in the world.

In early 1971, the CAF acquired its TBF Avenger. It was located in California where it had been used as a fire-bomber for the previous decade. Of the six thousand Dauntless dive-bombers produced by Douglas, the one flown by the CAF is believed to be only one of two flying in the world. It was acquired later in 1971 from a private owner in Los Angeles. The Helldiver is even rarer; according to the CAF, which searched for years to locate one it could restore and fly, it is a "one of a kind" as far as being in flying condition is concerned. Purchased by Colonel Bob Griffin at a cost of $25,000, it was fully restored to combat configuration. In addition to performing in air shows, it is considered the best camera plane of the entire Ghost Squadron, because of its great cockpit visibility.

Of all the important World War II Navy combat aircraft, only the TBD Devastator, which figured so importantly in the Battle of Midway, is conspicuous by its absence. Although the CAF has sought a restorable model for years, that search has been without success.

Although there is no connection with the CAF, another museum's acquisition of an F6F Hellcat for display purposes emphasizes once again the lengths to which aircraft restorers must go these days to find aircraft that, over the range of aviation history, can still be considered recent models. On January 12, 1944,

Navy Ensign Robert F. Thomas, took off from the North Island Naval Air Station in San Diego, California, in an F6F-3 Hellcat for a test flight following overhaul of the plane's engine. About twelve miles out in the Pacific, flying at 20,000 feet, he spotted a training flight 13,000 feet below him; following accepted procedure, he decided to "attack" the trainers . . . with empty guns, of course. He pushed the Hellcat's nose over, but as he began to pull out at 7,000 feet, the newly overhauled engine went dead. Thomas rode the stricken plane down, splashing into a neat but watery dead-stick landing. The plane sank almost immediately; it was all Thomas could do, as a matter of fact, to free himself of the cockpit and avoid being dragged down with it. Fortunately, the trainers had seen the Hellcat plunge in, radioed the Coast Guard, and a cruising cutter soon rescued Thomas.

The incident was forgotten. Ordered to duty in the South Pacific, Thomas continued to fly F6Fs, and before V-J Day he had four enemy kills to his credit. The Navy, meanwhile, wrote off the sunken F6F as a loss; its exact location and depth were not known, and besides, even if it could be located, the cost of salvage would far exceed the plane's worth.

For twenty-six years, the Hellcat lay in its watery tomb.

Then, on March 17, 1970, the instruments of the Lockheed research submarine *Deep Quest,* diving off the coast of San Diego, picked up a metallic object on the ocean floor at a depth of 3,400 feet. The *Deep Quest* moved closer to the spot so that its crew could see the object through an exterior scanner. What they saw was, of course, Ensign Thomas' Hellcat. Under other circumstances, the Navy would have left the plane where it was, especially with deepwater salvage costs skyrocketing as they had been for more than a quarter century. The *Deep Quest,* however, had reported that the plane appeared to be in amazingly good condition even after that period of time; its instrument panel was intact, for instance, and there were no barnacles or other marine growth on the entire airframe. Puzzled, the Navy decided to bring the F6F to the surface to determine how and why it had survived so well.

The salvage was done on October 9 and 10, 1970, using both the *Deep Quest* and the submarine tender *White Sands.* Even in nearly seven miles of water, retrieval was not difficult, and the wreckage was soon in a dry land hangar undergoing intensive study. Some corrosion was found, but not nearly as much as would be expected for twenty-six years of saltwater submersion. Most of the cockpit instruments appeared to be salvageable; there was some corrosion on their faces, but their working parts were intact. One of the Hellcat's .50-caliber machine guns was removed for a checkout. It was ultrasonically cleaned and lubricated; although no parts were replaced, it fired thirty rounds with no difficulty.

Following the Navy's research, the Hellcat was deeded to the San Diego Aerospace Museum, whose staff placed it on static display after an extensive restoration. Unlike the Ghost Squadron's F6F, it will never fly again. But as a memorial, perhaps, to the thousands of gallant Navy airmen who paid for victory in the Pacific with their lives, it serves a purpose just as important.

THE CAF'S "FOREIGN SQUADRON"

8

To Winston Churchill it was "cruel, wanton, indiscriminating blackmail by murder and terrorism." For sixty-six consecutive days and nights in the grim summer and fall of 1940, the Nazi bombs rained their death and destruction on a helpless Britain. They fell first on military targets in coastal towns, later on larger cities, including the largest of them all, imperial London. In Berlin, Adolf Hitler beamed with glee as his aides brought him daily, glowing reports, inflated though they were for his benefit, of the Luftwaffe's aerial exploits. Flushed with recent victories in France, in the Low Countries, and in Poland, his hopes for world domination spinning higher by the minute, his vaunted *Blitzkrieg* having pulverized whole chunks of mainland Europe, he had turned at last on Great Britain, and its defeat, he honestly believed, lay only days or weeks away. In French ports like Boulogne, British intelligence confirmed to Whitehall, the Fuehrer's fleets of landing barges, protected by gunboats and other warships, were even then gathering by the hour, to be used perhaps only days hence in Operation Sea Lion—the invasion of the British Isles which lay but twenty-one miles from Fortress Europe. The Luftwaffe's daily pummeling of Britian was but a prelude to that growing certainty.

In the long run of the nation's history, it was the moment of England's greatest agony. For the doughty British people themselves, however, it was to become what Churchill called on June 18, "their finest hour." It was the Battle of Britain, perhaps the most significant, history-turning engagement of the Allies' defense against and defeat of German forces in World War II. It was a battle upon which, quoting the Prime Minister at the time, "depends the survival of Christian civilization." And for Hitler, an overconfident, power-mad tyrant who was to grossly misread both the military strength of Britain and the resolve of its people, it was the beginning of the end of the "thousand-year Reich."

The Luftwaffe's attacks against British soil ordered by the portly German air marshal, Hermann Goering, had begun in July. The attacks at first were concentrated strictly against military targets: harbors, military shipping in the English Channel, radar and antiaircraft defenses, and, particularly, installations and aircraft of Britain's Royal Air Force. Defeat of the RAF was critical, Goering and Hitler knew. Although their own Luftwaffe numerically outnumbered both pilots and planes available to the British, the RAF's Fighter Command was nevertheless an invasion deterrent; it must be pulverized if Operation Sea Lion stood a chance of succeeding. What followed—the saturation bombing of English cities, with their stunning loss of life and property—was an act that simply could not be justified by even the most liberal interpretation of the rules of warfare. In later writings, Hitler himself admitted that the aerial Blitz against England's cities—particularly London, for its repetitiveness, and Coventry, for its singular intensiveness—was a "terror war," a tactic by which he expected to demoralize the British, perhaps even to force a surrender without the necessity of a costly invasion. After all, the defeat of England's major ally in Europe, France, was accomplished with scarcely a fight. The Low Countries had succumbed even more easily. And from Britain's major remaining hope across the Atlantic, the United States, drifted only sympathetic silence.

Outnumbered in aircraft and pilots almost three to one, the RAF totaled up its losses in the first weeks of the Battle of Britain with growing anxiety. In June and July alone, it had lost more than 100 of its Spitfire and Hurricane fighters, and nearly as many of their pilots. This was close to one sixth of the then-available fighter strength and a severe drain on desperately needed manpower. It was not only the statistics that agonized Whitehall but also the realization that in terms of both aircraft and pilots, the loss far exceeded England's capacity at the time to replace either.

Smugly confident that the RAF had been reduced to a ragtag, second-rate shadow of its former self, Goering, at Hitler's command, had turned the Blitz to the cities on August 15. Though the British people were to pay dearly for it, the decision was a major blunder on Germany's part, for it gave the badly mauled RAF a much-needed breathing spell to regroup and replenish for the full-scale air war that was to follow. The Blitz on London began less than a month later, on September 7. Nightly, without fail, the great city felt the full weight of saturation bombing by Goering's Dornier and Heinkel bombers, while beleaguered RAF fighter pilots doggedly fought off attacks by *Schwärme** of their escorting Messerschmitt Me-109s. Hitler's purpose in pounding what had been the political, cultural, and philosophical capital of the Empire for nearly eighteen centuries hardly escaped Churchill or his embattled fellow Britons. "The bombings are of course a part of Hitler's invasion plans," the Prime Minister warned in a speech on September 11, "by which he hopes [that] by killing large numbers of civilians . . . that he will terrorize and cow the people of a mighty imperial city . . . and thus distract our attention from the ferocious onslaught he is preparing."

But as history so well records, the British refused to be cowed; they faced up to the terror. In the stirring two-month Battle of Britain, which many historians feel was of greater significance than Drake's defeat of the Spanish Armada and Napoleon's defeat at Waterloo—landmarks in British history—an underdog Britain fought gamely back . . . and won. And in no small measure, it was the combat airplane, supported by the will of the people who built it and flew it, and their unswerving courage, that turned the tide of battle.

Almost the full weight of the air war over Britain was carried by three sin-

---

* The basic combat flying formation developed by the Luftwaffe and later adapted by almost every other nation, a *Schwarm* is two pairs of fighters flying together—four in all—with three *Schwärme* comprising a twelve-plane *Staffel*.

gle-engined fighter planes, two of them British, the other German. In the British defense arsenal were the Hawker Hurricane and the Supermarine Spitfire. The attacking Germans flew the Messerschmitt Me-109, which in terms of length of service, performance, and combat record must rank as perhaps the most famous fighter plane of all time. Had any of these three planes been missing, had any not been developed, had any not met in aerial combat over Britain in those dark days of 1940, the course of World War II doubtless would have taken an entirely different turn. Who can say, for instance, what might have happened had Goering's squadrons of Me-109s continued to enjoy the same mastery of the skies later in the Battle of Britain that they had at the beginning? Had they managed to destroy the RAF's fighter capacity, or even seriously weaken it, would Hitler have pushed ahead with Operation Sea Lion? And if he had, could Britain have survived the invasion without adequate air defense? No one can state the answers with assurance, of course, but of another fact there can be no doubt. The Battle of Britain was the first time in history that such a bombing action— Germany's—was attempted against a first-rate nationwide air force. It is doubtful that Hitler was unaware of the RAF's fighter strength, but it is highly probable that he underestimated the skill, courage, and resolution of the RAF's pilots, a painful surprise that led him to first postpone, then cancel, Operation Sea Lion, which might have kept the war going much longer in Germany's favor. As the Battle of Midway proved to be the turning point in the Pacific war against Japan, it was the Battle of Britain that became the "hinge" on which the tide of war shifted from Hitler's grasp and turned the momentum toward the inevitable defeat of the Third Reich. And in both battles, victory and defeat hinged on air power.

Significantly, then, it was a movie re-creation of the famous Battle of Britain, in 1967–68, that inspired the Confederate Air Force to begin adding *foreign* combat examples—of both enemy and friendly nations—to its growing collection of flyable, historically significant airplanes. Today that collection, changing constantly as it does with new acquisitions and deletions, includes a venerable Spitfire, an entire *Schwarm* of Messerschmitt Me-109s, a squadron of mocked-up

One of four Me-109s purchased by the CAF for the movie The Battle of Britain *in straight and level flight over Texas.*

Japanese Zeros, Kates, Zekes, and Vals (acquired for use in the movie *Tora! Tora! Tora!* which re-created the Japanese attack on Pearl Harbor), and assorted transports, observation planes, and special-purpose aircraft of the German Luftwaffe, as well as one of the only all-wood flying British twin-engined Mosquito fighter-bombers in the world today. In the history of these individual planes, squatting wing tip to wing tip at Harlingen with the fighters and bombers their kind once fought with and against, can be traced much of the aviation technology and development from which the combat airplane emerged as a war weapon in its own right in World War II. There is nostalgia, too, especially among the post-fifty generation of visitors to CAF headquarters who once flew, fueled, or maintained the now-obsolete aircraft of both sides and who have found in Harlingen the only place in the world where so many fighters and bombers in flying condition are gathered. Old animosities quickly vanish here; even airmen who once found themselves pitted against each other in personal, deadly combat find a camaraderie, their hostility softened by years of separation from the reality of war, in comparing notes on their respective airplanes, and in remembering the momentous days of 1939–45, when military aviation, after a quarter century of indifference and stagnation, emerged as a critical influence in warfare.

The post-World War I indifference toward aviation was mostly on the Allied side. Even as war clouds gathered over Europe, even as Japan clandestinely fortified the South Pacific islands turned over to her care following World War I by the League of Nations, the isolationist policies and general indifference to military aviation of administrations in the United States, and of her later World War II allies, kept a tight lid on aircraft development. As an example, the U. S. Army Air Corps could assemble less than 500 fighter aircraft—and most of those were already years obsolete—when Hitler invaded Poland on September 1, 1939. In Nazi Germany, there had been no parallel lack of interest. Despite the fact that the Treaty of Versailles forbade Germany, in the wake of her defeat in World War II, from building military airplanes, she had become a leading nation in aviation technology in the twenties and thirties. The treaty did permit building planes for peaceful, nonmilitary purposes. Threading themselves neatly through this loophole, German aeronautical engineers made great strides in this period in the development of "commercial" and "civil" airplanes. Through the simple expedient of reconfiguration, they designed airplanes that could be quickly converted to birds of prey. Overnight, civil transports became bombers, "sports" planes became fighters. Flying clubs and aviation contests became the rage, and who could prove that the "sports plane" that set a new speed or altitude record would in just a few years rain death and destruction on country after country of Europe?

By 1933, as time continued to dim memories of the "war to end all wars," Nazi Germany dropped all pretense that her mushrooming aviation capability had dovish intentions. In April of that year, Hitler appointed Hermann Goering as his national air minister; two years later, in 1935, the Fuehrer openly admitted the existence of the Luftwaffe itself. The word is generally taken to mean air *force.* Literally translated, however, Luftwaffe means air *weapon,* and by 1935, Germany had put real teeth into the definition. By that year, even as farsighted military strategists in Washington were vainly trying to build an Air Corps of a meager 500 planes, Germany openly admitted possessing nearly 2,000, manned and supported by a force of 20,000 men.

The Spanish Civil War, which broke out in July 1936, gave Germany a chance to combat-test both the planes and pilots of its growing Luftwaffe. The first German ships—twenty Junkers Ju-52 bomber-transports and six Heinkel He-51 fighters—arrived the following month as Germany and Italy sided with General Franco's Nationalist Forces to oppose the Republicans, backed by technicians from the Soviet Union. The resulting dogfights and bombings over Spain became the world's first test in actual combat of air power as a distinct and separate tactic from ground operations. By early 1937, when some of the Heinkels were replaced with newer Messerschmitt Me-109s,† the German aviation contingent had evolved into the famed Condor Legion, which saw wide action throughout the Civil War. From this first taste of air battle, an experience which gave Hitler and Goering an opportunity not only to combat-test their growing fleet of airplanes but to perfect the flying tactics of their pilots as well, came the later onslaught—covered by military planes—against Poland, Czechoslovakia, the Low Countries, and finally Britain and armed forces of the United States. The rest, as they say, is history.

Hitler was no advocate of strategic bombing (a policy that, some historians feel, may have cost him the war). Yet, he nevertheless was a strong proponent of the attack-bomber, the dive-bomber, and especially the fighter plane. The latter drew Germany, starting in the early thirties, to the development of what even its enemies will agree was probably the best all-around fighter ever built anywhere. Conceived in 1934, the Messerschmitt Me-109 was the standard Luftwaffe single-seat fighter for nearly a decade and, totaling up its broader lifetime from prototype to final version, it covered nearly a quarter century of active duty. More Me-109s were built than any other type of airplane—33,000 altogether—and Me-109s accounted for more enemy "kills" than any aircraft in history. Aviation buffs may argue that the British Spitfire was truly a greater airplane, but when all the statistics are added up, the title of "best all-around" must go to the trim, spartan, no-nonsense brainchild of Willy Messerschmitt.

To fighter pilots, the Me-109 was the epitome of what a fighter plane should look like. Nothing was put on it that was not absolutely necessary to its basic function, and a lot of pilot conveniences (in early models, hydraulic-operated flaps, for instance) were conspicuous by their absence. Me-109 pilots may have grumbled over their lack, but most agreed, after only brief periods of combat, that the savings in weight and space was a worthwhile swap. The Me-109 is a small airplane. Unless it is pictured in photographs alongside its fighter contemporaries, its compactness is not apparent, yet it was indeed one of the smallest prop-driven fighters ever built, only about half the size, for instance, of the North American P-51 Mustang, which came along later in World War II.

The Me-109 was the result of prewar design competition in which Willy Messerschmitt nosed out such illustrious competitors as Heinkel and Focke-Wulf and several others, all of which, unlike Messerschmitt, had previous experience in fighter design. The prototype, bearing the same lean, hungry, sharklike look that would later strike fear in the hearts of many an Allied pilot, first appeared in 1935. A far cry in terms of performance from its later, highly modified cousins, it was powered with a Jumo service engine turning up only 900 horsepower, giving it a top speed of 295 miles per hour. A second prototype, designated the Me-109-V1, had even less power; ironically, its 695-horsepower engine was one imported from Britain, a Rolls-Royce Kestrel. It was this version that

---

† The designation Me-109 derives from Willy Messerschmitt, who designed these airplanes for Bayerische-Flugzeugwerke A.G., which built them. Technically, the term Bf-109 is therefore more correct. Since the prefix Me was so widely used in identifying this aircraft, however, it is employed throughout this book.

Lanky pilots complained about its cramped cockpit and limited range, but Germany's famed Messerschmitt Me-109 was one of the truly classic fighter planes of all time.

won the 1935 fighter trials at Travemünde, on the Baltic coast of Germany. Unlike the four-place Messerschmitt Me-108B *Taifun* (Typhoon), which Germany had mass-produced for commercial use in the mid-thirties, the 109 was a very small, low-wing monoplane with sharp, angular lines that would remain throughout later development. While sitting idle on the ground, it looked quite awkward and unstable due to its narrow underpinning, but once airborne, it seemed by design to be ideally suited to its element, as if it belonged nowhere else. (The narrow undercarriage was a much-debated failing of the Me-109 throughout its career; it has been estimated that about 5 per cent of the 33,000 built were lost in ground accidents due to this engineering characteristic.) Structurally, the Me-109 was all metal, with fabric-covered control surfaces. Its skin gained a smooth appearance due to Messerschmitt's insistence on flush rivets, and in addition to the large slotted flaps and ailerons that dropped 10 degrees when the flaps were lowered, it was also mounted with Handley-Page automatic slats in the leading edges of the wings; these greatly aided in low-speed aileron control.

As fighter cockpits of the era went, that of the Me-109 seemed almost unbearably cramped, even to pilots of small stature, yet many of them insisted on remaining in Me-109 duty later in the war when more comfortable Luftwaffe fighters were produced. The reason was that, despite its small size, the Me-109 was a pure joy to fly and once they got the hang of its few eccentricities, most Me-109 pilots felt inherently safer and more effective in it than in its more sophisticated followers. Because the engine seemed to overpower the fuselage due to the small size of the plane, pilot visibility on the ground was poor, yet, once in the air, pilots could enjoy a kick of power that felt like an army of mules. Pilots agreed that the Me-109 was extremely sensitive on the controls, yet it climbed like a rocket, had tremendous maneuverability, and, flown by a skilled pilot, would generally outperform any of its enemy contemporaries.

Given these glowing endorsements, then, how was it that the highly rated Me-109, numbering more than twice its opposition, came out second best in the fabled Battle of Britain? In a single word, *range*. Even operating from the westernmost airfields in occupied France, Me-109 pilots had but ten or twenty minutes of remaining combat flight time available to them when they reached the coast of England before they had to turn and run for home. Pilots of the RAF's Spitfires and Hurricanes, on the other hand, were performing in their own skies, within gliding distance of friendly airfields, a tremendous psychological as well as technical advantage.

The earliest Me-109s—about a quarter of the total production—were designed with squared-off wing tips. This is the version most familiar in combat in the early years of the war, including the Battle of Britain. Although, starting about 1941, eight factories scattered about Germany began producing round-tipped models, the Me-109 was even by then past its prime; only the fact that Germany, hard-pressed after her aerial defeat over Britain in 1940, could not afford the long delays in developing better fighters, kept the Me-109 in production as long as it was.

A glance at the specifications of the earliest and latest Me-109s amply demonstrates how radically it was modified during its long service. By the time of the Battle of Britain, when it was fitted with a Mercedes-Benz fuel-injected engine, the fighter had seen its top speed beefed up to 354 miles per hour at 16,000 feet, or fully 59 miles an hour faster than the first service model flown five years before. The Battle of Britain version was armed with two fuselage-mounted 7.90-millimeter machine guns and two wing-mounted 20-millimeter cannon, a very potent punch. Only a year later, switching to a 1,475-horsepower Daimler-Benz

If pure function is beauty, the "no-frills" classic from Willy Messerschmitt's drawing board would win hands down. CAF pilots find it still "a joy to fly."

power plant boosted the 109's maximum speed over 400 miles per hour for the first time, to 403. And by the time the Me-109K arrived, horsepower had been increased to a sizzling 1,800, which gave it a top speed of 450 miles an hour; armament by this time had been boosted as well. It now had a 30-millimeter Mark 108 cannon, fired through its propeller spinner, as well as two 13-millimeter machine guns.

Volumes have been written about the comparative merits of the Messerschmitt, Hurricane, and Spitfire in the Battle of Britain, in which the Me-109 finally lost its superiority, and its pilots, a bit of their rightly earned smugness. In June 1940, the Luftwaffe pilots were supremely confident. Aware that the valuable battle experience they had acquired in Spain in the mid-thirties gave them a psychological edge over their British opponents, who had scarcely tasted combat at all, the German pilots often broke formation to engage the enemy many times their number. It may be argued that this smugness led to complacency, and thus to lack of efficiency. At times, their confidence spilled over. In Berlin, for instance, American correspondent William Shirer interviewed a young Luftwaffe officer, just returned from a raid on the Isle of Sheppey early in the summer of 1940, who calmly bragged, "The British are through. I'm already making plans to go to South America [after the war] and get into the airplane business."

But the Luftwaffe's failure to win the Battle of Britain cannot be blamed on overconfidence alone, nor the British advantage in range alone, nor the fact that the RAF also had the advantage of radar and was able to predict the Luftwaffe's arrival with considerable accuracy. Much of the responsibility must be placed on Hitler himself, and, particularly, on strategic decisions of Hermann Goering. An important one was the order to bomb British cities, which committed great numbers of Luftwaffe fighters as bomber screen. In the early stages of the battle, when only coastal ports were involved in bombing attacks, the Messerschmitts, in tremendous numbers, were free to engage with the RAF's Spitfires and Hurricanes at will. When the city bombings began, however, much of the German fighter strength was committed to escorting the bombers, which had become easy targets for defending RAF fighters. With the added disadvantage of limited range, the Luftwaffe simply lost the initiative . . . and the battle itself. Statistics covering the final outcome of the Battle of Britain will long be a subject of debate, inflated as they were on both sides. Best estimates place the Luftwaffe's aircraft loss at about 1,733, the RAF's about 915, or a little more than half. At any rate, the invasion of England never occurred, and although the Messerschmitt performed long and gallantly after 1940, its heyday was clearly over even by the time the United States entered the war a year later.

Britain's Hurricane and Spitfire were both aircraft that, like the Me-109, were technically "over the hill" by 1942 but which nonetheless went on to perform well throughout the war. Less glamorous than the Spitfire, perhaps, the Hurricane actually saw more action than its better-publicized cousin by the time of the Battle of Britain if for no other reason than the fact that it had been produced in greater numbers. It was designed by Sydney Camm for Hawker Aircraft Ltd., which had come into being following a merger in 1920 with the T. O. P. Sopwith Aviation Company, producer of World War I's famous Sopwith Camel biplane and other noted airplanes of the twenties and thirties. A total of 14,231 Hurricanes were built (1,451 of them in Canada) although by the end of the war the production of Spitfires (22,000 of them altogether) placed them second only to the Messerschmitt Me-109 in total numbers built. The Hurricane Mk. I was of conventional (for its time) construction, fabric-covered, and powered with a 1,030-horsepower Rolls-Royce Merlin engine that gave it a top speed of

340 miles an hour. By mid-1943, horsepower had been increased to 1,650, but speed had been cut to 294 miles per hour because its wing had been redesigned to handle a variety of ordnance loads. In various configurations, the Hurricane could carry two Browning .303-inch machine guns and eight 60-pound rockets, or two 40-millimeter cannon plus a bombload.

Over all, the Hurricane proved to be Britain's most versatile fighter. It was the first foreign fighter received for war use in Russia, where it served in both the Stalingrad and Leningrad battles. One Hurricane model was designed with folding wings and served briefly in aircraft carrier operations.

The Supermarine Spitfire was the more-publicized half of England's one-two punch in the Battle of Britain, owing in part, in the United States at least, to the exploits of the Eagle Squadrons—contingents of volunteer American aviators who flew the Spitfire against Germany before their own country entered the war.

In the Battle of Britain, it did not matter that the Spitfire and Hurricane were inequals in opposing the Me-109, because in tandem they made a most effective team. After early engagements with the Luftwaffe, it became apparent that the Hurricane was no match for the speedy, high-performing Messerschmitt Me-109, whereas the Spitfire was its equal. To reduce losses, the RAF began flying the two fighters together, sending the Hurricanes in to engage the attacking Luftwaffe bombers, and assigning the Spitfires to meet the escorting Me-109s. It was an ideal tactic; in its own skies, the Spitfire accounted for major defeats against the Me-109, while the sturdy, tough Hurricane, being an ideal gun platform, kept the bombers on the run. Of the two fighters, the Hurricane was considered far more capable of being able to withstand considerable damage from return fire, and still make it home safely. Since both were at the time powered with the same Rolls-Royce Merlin engine, what made the difference was purely design.

Its prototype first flown in 1936, the Spitfire evolved from a series of Schneider Trophy seaplane racers built during the twenties and early thirties, culminating in the Supermarine S6B of 1931, which reached a phenomenal speed (for the time) of 431 miles an hour. About the same time, Rolls-Royce was rushing development on a V-12 aircraft engine. The marriage of the two resulted in one of the best all-around fighter planes of World War II. Early versions of the Spitfire were powered with a 1,230-horsepower Merlin engine turning a two-blade, fixed-pitch wooden propeller that gave it a top speed of 360 miles an hour. That, however, was only the beginning. By war's end, the fighter had undergone no less than forty major modifications. There were almost as many changes in its armament, although in standard configuration the Spit carried *eight* wing-mounted Browning .303-inch machine guns. Some aviation historians have written that it was Goering's lack of knowledge of the Spitfire's considerable firepower that made him overconfident when he developed the strategy for the Luftwaffe's role in the Battle of Britain. It is well known that as early as the mid-thirties, German intelligence kept a close eye on the development of both the Hurricane and the Spitfire, and modifications of the Me-109 were, as a result of that information, made almost in tandem. Later in the war on the other side of the English Channel, it was intelligence data gathered by the RAF on the Luftwaffe's Me-109, and its successor, the Focke-Wulf Fw-190, that prompted many of the later modifications of the Spitfire. By 1942, for instance, most RAF fighter squadrons had been equipped with the Mk. IX version, whose 415-mile-an-hour top speed owed to a two-stage, two-speed supercharger aiding a Merlin engine beefed up to 1,650 horsepower. With this engine, the Spitfire could gallop to 20,000 feet in less than five minutes. By the end of the war, the Spitfire's top speed had gone to 450 miles an hour with horsepower increased to 2,375, making it perhaps the fastest of all World War II fighters, Allied or enemy, with the exception of the American P-38 Lightning and the P-51 Mustang.

The Spitfire, the Hurricane, and the Me-109 were to meet in anger many times until the end of World War II. After that, they seemed destined to separate forever. What brought them together once again was the Confederate Air Force. Today, with CAF pilots at their controls, the one-time antagonists fly often, wing tip to wing tip, in air shows and special events, to remind those watching of a time when the world did not enjoy a relative peace, of an age when combat aviation was considerably more of a personal, wind-in-the-face adventure than it is in today's era of jets and air-to-air missiles.

The catalyst for bringing the wartime opponents together was the announcement of a movie, appropriately titled *The Battle of Britain,* which was to be filmed in Spain in 1967–68 by a British company, Spitfire Productions, Limited. The CAF had, prior to that year, already acquired a Spitfire, its first of two, although after paying $11,500 for it the aircraft was still in England. But it had no Messerschmitts. Those, everyone in the vintage-aircraft-buying business knew, would most likely be found in Spain, where great numbers of Me-109s wound up in the latter years of World War II and in the few years following Germany's defeat. (The Me-109, powered with a Spanish Hispano engine, had become the mainstay of Franco's air force until jet fighters were phased in.) In Harlingen, Texas, following purchase of the Spitfire, which was the CAF's first

Exceptional maneuverability was a hallmark of Britain's Spitfire Mk. IX Supermarine interceptor fighter. Nearly four decades later it still demonstrates its amazing agility in the hands of CAF pilots.

One of the CAF's first two Spitfires, photographed here at Rebel Field.

A ground's-eye view of a Spitfire over Texas.

venture into the foreign airplane field, there was considerable support for adding at least one flyable model of Germany's most famous fighter, a plane for which many CAF veterans had gained considerable respect during the war years. A series of telephone calls and cables between Texas and Madrid determined that Franco was willing to part with several Me-109s, and after considerable negotiation, the CAF agreed to buy four.

The purchase coincided neatly with Spitfire Productions' shooting schedule; the film company, however, had neither Messerschmitts nor Spitfires of its own. Would the CAF be willing to lease its new acquisitions? From Texas came an affirmative answer, but with one major stipulation: only if they could be piloted in the movie by CAF pilots. Spitfire Productions agreed, doubtless a bit skittishly since it was common knowledge that no CAF fighter jockey had ever *sat* in a Spitfire or Me-109, let alone flown one.

Swapping their lofty Stetsons for Luftwaffe caps, their Rebel-gray flight suits for medal-dripping, Swastika-emblazoned tunics, and their Texas prairie saddle boots for the stiff, knee-high black leather boots of the Third Reich, the first contingent of the CAF's pilots-turned-matinee-idols arrived at Tablada Air Base in Spain, where Spitfire had chosen to film its location shots, one balmy spring day in 1968. Looking around, the irony of the situation suddenly struck the pilots. Here, on a spring day in Spain in 1968, was a group of Texas pilots about to fly German and British combat planes in formation—and against each other—in company with Spanish pilots in other planes, to re-create one of history's greatest battles, which occurred in the skies over England almost thirty years earlier!

For the American pilots who might have seen an Me-109 only in the air or on the ground from a distance during World War II, the aircraft close up was a startling surprise. The shock was especially apparent to those who had flown the P-51, which, though considered tiny by 1968 standards, was a veritable barn compared to Willy Messerschmitt's creation. And, spoiled by the pilot conveniences American aviation technology had made standard in its airplanes, the Me-109 seemed a creature out of the Dark Ages once they climbed inside. Lacking a hydraulic system, its flaps were to be rolled down by hand with a wheel operated by a bicycle chain. The master switch was an unmarked piece of wire on the right of the pilot's seat, which was to be pulled to actuate. There was no aileron or rudder trim control. In planes they were familiar with, the pilot placed his heels on the floor and operated the rudder pedals with his toes, with action by flexing the ankles. In the Me-109, however, the pilot's feet were to be placed in stirrups with straps across the toes which would operate a rudder bar, bicycle-fashion, by action from the knees. To make matters more confusing, the altimeter registered in meters, the airspeed in kilometers, the fuel quantity in liters, and the manifold pressure in strange decimal figures. More complexing were the instructions on metal placards mounted about the cockpit. Though carrying vital information, they were printed in *Spanish!*

But they were experienced pilots, seat-of-the-pants veterans all, these CAF fliers, and although they had managed to wring wonders out of American World War II aircraft types with which they were vastly more familiar, none was naïve enough to believe he could fly an Me-109, or even a Spitfire, especially in formation, without an extended check-out. To do so, they enlisted the aid of knowledgeable advisers. One was Major Pedro Santa Cruz, a skilled and experienced combat pilot, who had piloted Me-109s with the Spanish Air Force since 1950. Further help came from General Adolf Galland, former commander of the Luftwaffe's fighter forces, who had come to Spain from Germany as much to relieve his pangs of nostalgia as for the pounds sterling Spitfire Productions had agreed to pay him as a consultant. (It was Galland, incidentally, who once was widely quoted for his description of the Spitfire prior to the Battle of Britain: "It's a good plane, but good only for shooting down," a remark which, after September–October 1940, he studiously avoided repeating.) RAF Group Captain Robert Stanford-Tuck, who was Britain's counterpart of Galland in World War II, served as adviser for the Spitfire flying sequences.

By Wednesday, May 1, following three months of filming in ME-109s and Spitfires, the CAF pilots completed the aerial sequences needed over Spain: formation flying, dogfights, mock attacks on several venerable Heinkel bombers that were still serving on active duty with the Spanish Air Force. Accompanied by several Spanish pilots, they then flew the Me-109s, the Spitfires, and Heinkels across Europe to London, where another six months of filming, mostly of close-ups, followed. Never again, it seems certain, will as many aircraft that were involved in the history-making Battle of Britain be flown together. Yet, thanks to the CAF, a scaled-down re-enactment each autumn in the skies over Harlingen, Texas, inevitably evokes a tug of wistful nostalgia from even the most hardened antiwar cynics. The Battle of Britain was not pretty history, for no battle is, yet it happened; as a clash of giants upon which the fate of the world hung in the balance, it was important history, and as a part of the CAF's motto reminds us, it is history "we must never forget."

Through the years, the CAF's "foreign wing" has continued to expand. One of its rarest acquisitions was a vintage German single-seat Focke-Wulf Fw-44J primary trainer, one of the many aircraft first developed by Germany as a "sports plane" and later converted to military use. Ranked, powerwise, about midway between the J-3 Cub and Stearman PT-17 of American manufacture, it was originally fitted with a Bramo engine whose 150 horsepower refused it more than 110 miles an hour, even with a stiff tail wind. Located in Europe by Ed Jurist, an inveterate plane-swapper, active CAF "colonel," and founder-owner of Vintage Aircraft International in Nyack, New York, one of the nation's best privately owned collections of old planes, it is believed to be the only flying model of its type in the world.

That honor may also be claimed by one of the CAF's most recent foreign acquisitions, a Junkers Ju-52 trimotor transport first mass-produced in Germany in 1935. An exceptionally strong airplane, which facilitated its conversion for limited use as a bomber, the CAF's Ju-52 was purchased from the Spanish Air Force.

Three other foreign combat aircraft now in CAF service deserve specific mention. The first is a Fieseler Fi-156C Storch, a single-engined observation plane developed in the mid-thirties by the noted German aviation firm of Fieseler. In German, "Storch" means stork, which is what this awkward-looking but highly efficient single-engined airplane, rising as it does above a long and wobbly-looking undercarriage, resembles. Powered with a 240-horsepower engine, the Storch has a top speed of only 109 miles an hour. Speed, however, is the enemy of observation flying, not its friend, and the Storch's usefulness was enhanced by the fact that because of the combination of a very short (thirty-two

"Iron Annie"— that's the nickname given Germany's Junkers Ju-52 trimotor transport, a plane that began service as a civilian airliner and which was later pressed into military duty. The Junkers flown by the CAF is one of the few remaining models of its type in the world.

An awkward-looking plane, the Luftwaffe's Fieseler F1-156C Storch was a real performer nonetheless; it could take off or land almost anywhere. Here is the CAF's Storch on the Harlingen flight line.

feet) fuselage and very long (forty-seven feet) wingspan, it could fly as slow as 40 miles an hour and take off and land in the handiest cow pasture.

Second is one of the world's few remaining flyable single-engined Messerschmitt Me-108B *Taifuns,* forerunner of the famed Me-109. Winner of many prewar international flying contests, it is a four-place plane, and was used widely by the Luftwaffe as a trainer. Because of its close resemblance to the Me-109, the *Taifun* often doubled for its faster, better-performing successor in postwar combat films. The model flown by the CAF was acquired by members of the CAF's New Mexico Wing, which is responsible for its upkeep and mainte-nance.

Finally, the CAF's foreign contingent includes one of the fastest, most ver-satile, and most unusual light bombers built for World War II or any other war, the twin-engined DeHavilland Mosquito. On most missions, the lightning-like "Mossie" flew without guns . . . it could outrun and outmaneuver most enemy fighters. With such armament being unnecessary, it could tote a powerful bombload; although the Mosquito was designed for 1,000 pounds of bombs, it flew many World War II missions with as much as 4,000 pounds.

Like many World War II designs, the effective, beloved "Mossie" had its

A highly acrobatic airplane, the Messerschmitt Me-108 was the predecessor of the bet-ter-known Me-109 Taifun. *With lines very much resembling its more illustrious succes-sor, it was used by Germany both as a courier plane and trainer. It is shown here with the CAF's P-38 flying escort.*

failings. A major one was that, due to its all-wood construction any large openings would have fatally weakened its framework; for this reason its crew escape hatch was literally a widowmaker. Cut from the after floor, it was by necessity simply too small for a large man wearing a parachute to drop through easily. "In a 'Mossie,'" one Mosquito crewman remembers, "you had three choices if you got hit. You could drop out *without* a parachute. You could ride it down to a belly landing. The first choice meant a pretty sudden stop. The second, because of the plane's wooden construction, almost certainly meant a fire. The third choice was the one most of us took. We crossed our fingers . . . and prayed a lot."

Because of its blistering speed (422 miles an hour) the Mosquito was ideal for low-level dam busting, pin-point bombing missions, and high-altitude flights. It was first used on a raid on Oslo, Norway, in September 1942, and served throughout the war. One of its most valuable assignments was as a pathfinder, used to lead large formations of Lancasters and other "heavies" to the target, which it marked with extreme accuracy. Its speed was due, of course, to its lightness. Designed to satisfy a requirement for a multipurpose plane that could be built anywhere in the British Empire from nonstrategic materials and by semi-skilled labor, it had a molded plywood fuselage covering a balsa core, and wings made of wooden spars and plywood ribs covered by a rigid outer skin. It was powered by a pair of Merlin V-12 engines, had a service ceiling of 34,000 feet, and a range of 1,750 miles.

A description of just one of the Mosquito's many special purpose World War II missions will help underscore the extreme value that the RAF—and its allies—placed on this versatile little bomber. In the weeks following the fall of Holland to Hitler's *Blitzkrieg,* intelligence reaching the Netherlands' government-in-exile in London began piecing together a rather frightening, ominous pattern. In The Hague, Holland's seat of government, the reports confirmed, Hitler's Gestapo had moved its headquarters into the five-story Kleykamp art gallery, from which valuable paintings and sculptures had been removed. In place of the art treasures now reposed row after row of Gestapo file cabinets, each containing growing dossiers of loyal Dutch who had gone "underground" to serve the Dutch Resistance. For weeks, jack-booted Gestapo agents had been sifting through bits of their own intelligence, and within days, it now seemed apparent, the Gestapo, using the assembled information, would conduct a sweep through occupied Holland and arrest all known underground agents. Since arrest was tantamount to execution, the files in the Kleykamp building were, in effect, death warrants. In London, Dutch leaders begged the RAF to take action, to bomb The Hague. But, aware of the consequences, they asked for an air raid that would destroy only the art gallery and nothing else, not even the mansions close on either side of it, and certainly not the Peace Palace, only a few hundred yards away. They further asked that the raid be timed so that no one outside the gallery building would be hurt. But most difficult of all, the Dutch asked that the attack be planned so that if at the last minute the pilots could not put their bombs exactly on target, the Germans would somehow be fooled as to what the target would have been. Otherwise, the Dutch explained, the Gestapo files would merely be shifted somewhere else, and the valiant Dutch Resistance would be doomed.

It was a tall order, but the RAF accepted the challenge. Planning for the raid began under conditions of the strictest secrecy. Almost without hesitation, the Mosquito got the nod as the attack plane to be used; only weeks before, Mosquitoes of the 613th Squadron, 138th Wing, had successfully pulled off "Operation Jericho," the pin-point bombing of the Amiens Prison, which had en-

A Boeing B-17 Flying Fortress heavy bomber, whose exploits were perhaps best portrayed in the movie Twelve O'Clock High. *Now she flies in CAF air shows.*

A rare head-on view of the C.A.F.'s B-17, once seen only by the most daring of the Luftwaffe's fighter pilots.

Fifi, *the grand lady of the Confederate Air Force, one of the last surviving B-29 Superfortresses.*

Despite its lack of armament, the CAF's Heinkel He-111 was a potent weapon in Germany's Luftwaffe.

OPPOSITE PAGE
ABOVE: Produced too late for World War II action, the swift Sea Fury was the last and most modern of Britain's propeller-era aircraft. This one was a late addition to the Ghost Squadron.

OPPOSITE PAGE
BELOW: The Douglas C-47 "Skytrain" transport has seen service in various configurations for more than half a century! The CAF's model was a donation.

ABOVE: Mockup Japanese Zero fighters in a fly-by at Harlingen's Rebel Field. Re-enactment of the enemy attack against Pearl Harbor is a vivid reminder of the 1939—45 era of history that the CAF seeks to preserve for future generations.

BELOW: The North American AT-6 Texan advanced trainer, one of three standard American trainers in use by the Ghost Squadron.

Ryan Aircraft built the PT-22 in 1934 as a sports plane for those who could afford it. When the war began in late 1941, it was pressed into military service as a basic trainer. This is one of three trainer types operated by the CAF.

The CAF's venerable Hudson (or Lodestar) was first developed by Lockheed in 1938. In wartime use, it served widely in coastal reconaissance and light bombing. The first two German U-boat kills by the U. S. Navy in the Atlantic were credited to Hudsons.

In its rightful element, a Ghost Squadron P-38 Lightning is silhouetted against the setting Texas sun.

abled the prisoners, all members of the French Resistance who had been condemned to death, to escape. Because of the success of Jericho, the same "Mossie" pilots who had flown it got the assignment for the attack on The Hague. Preparation for the mission was thorough—maps of The Hague were blown up, their details studied, and a small scale but very accurate model of the section of the city to be hit was built, studied, and then restudied.

Early on the afternoon of April 11, 1944, their crews briefed, six Mosquitoes took off from their airfield in England, flying so low over the English Channel that salt spray condensed on their windshields. Just as planned, they kept their course so low even over the Dutch mainland that their presence was not detected by Nazi radar. Rushing in over The Hague at an altitude of fifty feet, Group Captain Bob Bateson, leading the attack, could make out a Gestapo sentry standing his post at the gallery door. The soldier made no move to run, apparently not believing that the blur he saw was an enemy bomber winging toward him below the level of adjoining buildings at a blistering 350 miles an hour. It was the last time in the sentry's life that he saw anything. Fighting the urge to pull back on the Mosquito's control stick, Bateson kept his plane pointed directly at the gallery's partially opened door until the last possible moment, then let his bombs go. The aim was perfect. First Bateson's bombs, then those of his following wingmen, skipped neatly across the pavement and through the open door. As if in slow motion, the building crumbled as the delayed-action fuses went off. Just as perfectly, the buildings nearby were untouched. As far as is known, no Dutch civilian was injured, but the Gestapo files and their damaging information vanished forever.

In terms of sheer suspense, the 6,000-mile flight of the CAF's Mosquito from England to Texas, in 1972, was nearly as dramatic. In fact, were it not for the sheer guts and determination of those who flew it, it may not ever have succeeded at all.

Consider first that by the time 1972 rolled around, the Mosquito was no longer a spring chicken, but a weathered old lady of thirty, well past the prime

The CAF's remarkable Mosquito after its 6,000-mile transatlantic flight from Luton, England, to Harlingen, Texas, in 1972.

of any airplane. Add to this the fact that unlike most of her contemporaries, the Mosquito was not of metal construction, but wood, and that in damp climates like that of England, wood rots in a surprisingly short time. Following acquisition of the Spitfire and Messerschmitts, however, the CAF longed for a Mosquito, rot or no rot, and in 1969, after a widespread search, it found one for sale in England. CAF Colonel Ed Jurist lost no time in jetting across the Atlantic and paying out the necessary cash. Two years were to pass, however, before Jurist and Duane Egli, another CAF member, were to return to London a second time to inspect the restoration work on the "Mossie" they had paid for.

Neither was satisfied with what had been done, especially when they realized that the aging bomber would have to be flown a third of the way around the world, and that in the previous fifteen years, its engines had been used less than fifty hours total. Egli embarked on an extensive rework program of his own, then put the virtually rebuilt bomber through a series of unusually rugged flight tests. In late fall 1971, he signaled Jurist that the Mosquito was as ready as it would ever be for the transatlantic flight, and in December 1971, the two pilots took off on a route longer and more hazardous than any the plane had flown, even in its prime, in combat. The first leg was scheduled to take them to Portugal, but an abrupt change in weather after takeoff in England forced a rerouting to Vigo, Spain. Following a maintenance check and radio repairs at Vigo, they proceeded to Santa Maria and Lajes Air Force Base in the Azores, then, in legs controlled largely by shifting weather and other factors, to St. Johns, Newfoundland, Halifax, Boston, New York, Lexington, Pine Bluff, and, finally, Harlingen, Texas, reporting for CAF duty on January 2, 1972. Altogether, the flight had taken twenty-two days. On a twenty-four-hour-a-day basis, that meant Mosquito Bomber Number RS-709 had covered an average of 11.36 miles per hour. That didn't exactly do justice to her World War II press clippings, but, then, she wasn't as young as she once was, either.

England to Texas: the transatlantic route of the Mosquito ferried by the CAF.

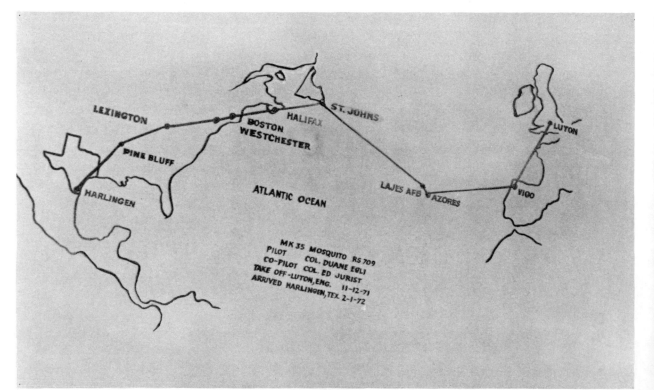

The single-engined Sea Fury (merely "Fury" in its land-based configuration) was Britain's last and most modern propeller fighter. Completed too late for service in World War II, it saw combat in Korea. Note the massive five-bladed propeller.

Powered with various engines, the Heinkel He-111 was designed by Germany before World War II and became one of the Luftwaffe's most widely used bombers. Being poorly armed, it was extremely vulnerable to attack.

Bubble nose of the Heinkel He-111.

Aircraft such as these, which portray Japanese World War II military craft, were built as replicas by the CAF, using mainly American trainers of the same era. The Ghost Squadron was instrumental in furnishing such mock-ups for the movie Tora! Tora! Tora! among others.

9 SAVING THE "HEAVIES"

One morning in June 1960, a four-engined Flying Fortress took off from a Southern California military airfield and groped for altitude over the desert below. Unlike thousands of bomb-laden "Forts" that droned in an endless stream over Europe and the Pacific in World War II, it was pilotless, a gutted, stripped-down drone guided by remote control from another aircraft several miles away. Suddenly, the giant bomber shuddered as it was struck by an IM-99 Bomarc missile, and plunged out of control to the impact area below. Though it is doubtful that anyone was aware of it at the time, there was a double-edged irony in the incident. The first was the fact that the manufacturer of the missile —the Boeing Company—was also the designer and builder of the airplane it destroyed. The drone, a QB-17, was one of 12,731 Flying Fortresses built, which became recognized as perhaps the most famous of all American World War II combat planes. The B-17 was the plane that dropped 640,000 tons of bombs in 291,508 sorties on European targets alone, a much-publicized bomber that inspired several books, movies, and television dramas. More ironic, though, was the fact that the 1960 flight was the last official military mission ever flown by a B-17. It ended a career that spanned more than twenty-three years, a military service reaching back to March 1, 1937, when the first of twelve YB-17s was delivered by Boeing to the Army Air Corps at Langley Field, Virginia. Yet the ignominious fate that befell the last of the "Forts" was only typical of the way that *all* seven light, medium, and heavy bombers of America's World War II air arm passed into oblivion, virtually forgotten, when V-J Day terminated their combat usefulness. As had been thousands of American fighters, bombers, too, were shipped to desert graveyards to await the bulldozer and the smelter, only a handful to be rescued for display in aviation museums or sold as surplus to private owners.

Restoring multiengined bombers to flying condition is vastly more expensive than single-engined fighters, and it was only fighters that the Confederate Air Force originally set about to locate and fly. Twin- and four-engined bombers represent double or quadruple the cost of fuel for fighters. They require heavier, longer runways, something the CAF in its infancy days at Mercedes, Texas, neither had nor could afford. Also, bigger planes demand larger hangars and higher insurance premiums, and they mean infinitely more problems of maintenance, simply because there is more airplane involved. Installing four new engines in a B-24 Liberator bomber, as an example, represents a cash outlay of at least $50,000; even a new paint job on the same aircraft today can run up a tab of $10,000 for the paint alone.

Yet, viewing the sad demise of the American World War II bomber, and the apathy toward its historical preservation as illustrated by the intentional destruction of the last active-duty B-17, and the scrapping of thousands of others, the CAF at a general staff meeting on May 15, 1963, threw budget restraints out the window and voted to seek a restorable example of each major Air Corps type to add to the CAF's fighter wing, which had been completed earlier in the same year.

"That was one of the most important meetings the CAF has ever held," recalls founder Lloyd Nolen, "for it set in motion the only collection of its kind in the world today: flying examples of all light, medium, and heavy American World War II bombers. The idea certainly didn't meet with unanimous approval at that meeting; some of our more conservative members argued that we couldn't afford bombers, and they were right. But all of us knew that if the collection wasn't started *then,* it might as well never have been. Wait much longer, and there wouldn't be any bombers left to start *with*."

Today, the Bomber Wing of the Ghost Squadron represents all of the seven "heavies" in the United States World War II flying arsenal. They are the twin-engined A-26 Invader and A-20 Havoc light bombers, the B-25 Mitchell and B-26 Marauder medium bombers, and the four-engined B-17 Flying Fortress, B-24 Liberator, and B-29 Superfortress heavy bombers. (Restoration of the B-29, without a doubt one of the most impressive undertakings of its kind anywhere, is described separately in the next chapter.)

In addition to these seven, the CAF has acquired and restored three Navy and one foreign bomber, the British Royal Air Force's Mosquito. The Bomb or Bomber Wing actually has eleven models, all in flying condition.

Because more surplus planes of its kind were around by the early sixties than its six Air Corps cousins, the twin-engined B-25 Mitchell was the Ghost Squadron's pioneer entry into the bomber field. Relatively fast (top speed: 275 miles per hour), rugged, dependable, and roomy, Mitchells were found to be ideal corporate errand-running and personnel-carrying aircraft after the war. For this reason several were scooped up by surplus buyers before the advent of swifter jets. The CAF acquired its first B-25 on May 10, 1961, from a private owner in Alice, Texas. A second was purchased in 1964, sponsored by Colonel Fred Rowse, as a permanent acquisition, and a third, which participates regularly in CAF air shows and other activities, was sponsored by CAF Colonel J. K. West. Three other Mitchells are privately owned by CAF members, but fly in CAF activities. That makes a total of six B-25s, ranking it with the P-51 Mustang and P-47 Thunderbolt as an airplane off the endangered list if for no other reason than its relative abundance. Named after the late Brigadier General Billy Mitchell, a pioneer advocate of air power, the B-25 was the best-known and the most widely used American medium bomber of the war. Less well known, however, is the fact that while more than 11,000 of them were built by North Ameri-

Fired up and rarin' to go, the North American B-25 Mitchell bomber was the CAF's first Bomber Wing acquisition. The "Mitch" was the most-used American medium bomber of World War II.

can Aviation Company, only 2,656 were flown by American pilots; the balance flew in the service of other nations, principally Britain, Russia, Free France, and Holland.

United States participation in World War II was barely four months old when the B-25 achieved its greatest fame, the sixteen-plane raid over Tokyo led by Lieutenant Colonel "Jimmy" Doolittle from the carrier *Hornet*. The attack was superbly timed. It occurred when the United States was still reeling from the blow at Pearl Harbor, and two months before the turning point defeat of the Japanese fleet in the Battle of Midway. All sixteen of the B-25s were lost when bad weather prevented their pilots from reaching assigned postraid bases in China. Seventy-one of the 80 crewmen on the raid survived, however, and Doolittle, the dashing prewar racing hero, afterward was promoted to brigadier general and awarded the Medal of Honor. More importantly, although the raid was viewed as a stunt by some, it was actually a brilliantly planned military attack with assigned targets that at the same time was a psychological shocker to the Japanese, who believed their home islands to be inviolate. After the raid, in fact, the Japanese were forced to retain many aircraft in their home islands, in anticipation of future raids, instead of deploying them to battlefronts of the Pacific.

Conceived in 1938 as an attack-bomber, the B-25's design for that role was unsuccessful, but redesigned as a medium bomber a year later, the Mitchell went on to achieve a reputation as perhaps the most adaptable bomber of them all. Design modifications throughout the war eventually equipped it with a tremendous bomb capacity, and it served as well as a "gunship," reconnaissance plane, and low-level attack-bomber; the Mitchell by 1943 became a terror of the Pacific

More than 11,000 B-25 Mitchells like this one were built for wartime service. Many made ideal corporate planes after the war.

sea-lanes after it was equipped with ten forward-firing guns and was perfected as a tactical skip-bomber.

The Mitchell was employed globally in World War II. The first attack on Bulgaria was carried out by ninety B-25s assigned to the Twelfth Air Force. On November 14, 1944, they dropped more than 155 tons of bombs on Sofia. The Twelfth also conducted the first American raid on Sarajevo, Yugoslavia, on November 29, 1944, attacking military installations and rail facilities. On February 15, 1944, Mitchells, accompanied by B-17s and B-26s, bombed the famous abbey at Monte Cassino, Italy, where enemy troops had blocked the advance of Allied forces.

In the Pacific and Asia, B-25s were as hard at work. With a crew of five, operating from Australia, they blasted Japanese forces in the Philippines, New Guinea, and Rabaul; in China, they were escorted by P-40s. In Burma, one bomb group gained fame as the "Bridge Busters," and from Alaska, yet another hit the Japanese home islands in July 1943, picking up where Doolittle's better-remembered raid had left off.

Pilot skill was one reason for the Mitchell's success in combat, but its excellence of design should not be forgotten, for the plane itself was highly praised by those who flew it, despite minor annoyances such as having brakes so touchy that many pilots checking out in it were almost thrown through the windshield until they got the hang of the plane's temperamental quirk. To obtain optimum tank and bomb stowage space, North American engineers raised the top of the Mitchell's fuselage and redesigned the crew's cockpit into its upper contour. The wing was set about mid-fuselage, giving the plane great stability. Its "greenhouse" nose arrangement gave B-25 crews the best forward visibility of any

Saving the "Heavies"   147

American light or medium bomber and for this reason it became a widely used camera plane, which could accommodate bulky equipment; after the war, B-25s were used widely for filming aerial sequences such as those in the early *Cinerama* series.

It was the firepower of the Mitchell, however, that earned it the most respect, particularly with the enemy. And no B-25s were respected more than that of Lieutenant Colonel Paul I. "Pappy" Gunn, whose constant rejiggering of the plane's armament became legend in the South Pacific. Demanding the ultimate in firepower, Gunn took a standard B-25G model, on which a single 75-millimeter cannon had been nose-mounted, and added four forward-firing .50-caliber machine guns alongside the nose of the fuselage. The 900-pound single cannon was temperamental enough; its recoil, pilots swore, "stopped the plane in midair and then shoved it *backwards*," but the additional machine guns almost proved the undoing of Gunn's flying gun platform. Test-firing the lethal package of cannon and machine gun ripped a section loose from the bomb bay and caused cracks to appear along the wing, fuselage, and engine nacelles.

Undismayed, Gunn put his technicians to work strengthening the weak spots, and when the beefed-up result finally flew into battle, it could deliver more concentrated firepower than any airplane of its day. As a bomber, B-25s in later series could tote a 5,000-pound bombing payload; no plane better deserved the "flying arsenal" nickname it soon earned.

Produced barely in time to see action in World War II, the Douglas B-26 was the next bomber the CAF wanted. Originally designated the A-26 for wartime service, it should not be confused with the Martin B-26 Marauder of the same period. Designed as a follow-up airplane to the A-20 Havoc, the Invader made its combat debut over Europe on November 19, 1944, only six months before Germany's surrender. When production ceased after V-J Day in August 1945, 2,502 Invaders had been produced. That left quite a surplus of late-model attack-bombers, so the Air Force put them to work both in the Korean War, in

The CAF's A-26 Invader was acquired in good condition in 1969. It was the standard bomber of the post-World War II Air Force.

A Douglas A-26 Invader of the Bomber Wing. Designed in 1941, the Invader saw military action for twenty-five years. Here it is shown wearing its Ninth Air Force colors.

which they were used mainly to harass North Korean supply lines at night, and, to a limited extent, in Vietnam, where they also served in night interdiction along the Ho Chi Minh Trail.

Over a period of almost twenty-nine years, its bomb capacity, variable armament, and maneuverability made the Invader a powerful offensive weapon in three wars. It is interesting to note that it carried nearly twice the bombload required by the original specifications laid down by the Air Force, and exceeded every performance guarantee. The A-26/B-26 was equally adept as an attack-bomber, light bomber, or fighter-bomber. With a top speed of 359 miles per hour, the Invader was powered with two Pratt and Whitney radial R-2800 engines, each turning up 2,000 horsepower, and had a maximum gross weight of 30,000 pounds.

Fortunately, the CAF was able to locate an A-26 in top condition in 1964. It was sponsored by W. C. Edwards as a permanent acquisition by the organization.

The Ghost Squadron's third "heavy" was a twin-engined A-20 Havoc attack-bomber. Developed by Douglas Aircraft in 1938, the Havoc was the most widely used light bomber of World War II, though it gathered little of the public acclaim of the more glamorous B-25 Mitchell or B-17 Flying Fortress; except for its rescue by the CAF, it might well have faded into obscurity. The A-20 participated in no daring daylight raid over Tokyo, nor did it fly any missions as swashbuckling in their nature as those of the famed Flying Tigers. Almost forgotten by aviation historians, it simply served as faithfully in as many theaters,

A study in contrasts: a single-engined private plane takes off from Rebel Field over the silhouette of a twin-engined Mitchell.

and took as much punishment to bring its crews home safely as any of its better-remembered peers. The Havoc, in fact, saw battle from the Battle of France in 1940 until the last shot of World War II was fired in August 1945. Its career between those dates reads like a gazetteer of World War II combat aviation history.

The Havoc was a new concept in aerial weaponry. The brainchild of Donald Douglas, Jack Northrop, and Ed Heinemann, it was designed for a speed of 250 miles an hour, a bombload of 2,000 pounds, a crew of two, and three small-caliber machine guns. The Army Air Corps had never previously accepted a twin-engined attack-bomber, and although those specifications were considered reasonable at the time, world events, such as the Spanish Civil War, rendered them obsolete even before Douglas could produce a prototype. Meanwhile, the French Air Force had watched flight tests of the A-20's two experimental predecessors, the Douglas Model 7A and 7B, and were impressed; if Douglas could beef up its new product, they would agree to order at least 400 of them for defending France against the coming Nazi onslaught. The product of the changes —the Douglas DB-7—became the prototype of the A-20 Havoc.

With World War II in Europe imminent, Douglas rushed ahead with A-20 production, but only 100 planes were delivered to France before the German *Blitzkrieg* got rolling full steam. A few of these managed to get airborne when the attack against France began, although those that did get aloft inflicted heavy

The Douglas A-20 Havoc was the most widely used light bomber of World War II. Douglas built 7,000 copies of this model, more than half of which went to Russia under the Lend-Lease program. Here's the CAF's prize in USAF colors.

damage against invading tanks near St. Quentin in late May of that year. Subsequent orders for the A-20 by France were diverted to Britain, and by this time the little bomber had grown considerably faster, heavier, better-performing, and capable of delivering a far more lethal punch to the enemy.

Nicknamed "Bostons" by the British, Havocs were pressed into service against Rommel's Afrika Korps in the Great Western Desert, where their contribution to the defeat of the "Desert Fox" is perhaps best-remembered of all their service worldwide. They were the major weapon of the Royal Air Force when, flying through fog and low clouds almost on the ground, they swept against Nazi tank units attempting to surprise less-seasoned American armor units at Kasserine Pass in mid-February 1943.

Even earlier, on July 4, 1942, twelve Havocs flew the first American raid over Europe, attacking German military installations in Holland. This raid marked the beginning of America's daylight bombing experience in Europe. They flew night raids in Europe, too, and converted Havocs performed collateral duties as aerial mine layers, and as searchlight ships, carrying lights in their noses to illuminate German formations.

In the Pacific, the Havoc achieved distinction particularly in attacking Japanese shipping in the Bismarck Sea in March 1943. Again, it was the A-20's low-level flying agility that did the trick; by the end of the engagement, Havocs had assisted in sinking or damaging three cruisers, seven destroyers, and twelve merchant ships—all in formations in which they flew no higher than the masts of the enemy vessels. Its low-level flying ability later made it an ideal vehicle for spraying insecticides on fields in Italy; the flying finesse required for that job is illustrated by the fact that to succeed, "spray missions" mean flying at just above stall speed and at only fifty feet off the ground.

After World War II, the Havoc was a particularly scarce airplane, especially since out of only 7,000 of them built, more than half had gone to Russia. The CAF found its Havoc in Boise, Idaho, and because of its run-down condition, was able to buy it for only $1,000. Repairs cost quadruple that figure—$4,000. After this work was completed, it was ferried to Harlingen, Texas, to join the Ghost Squadron's fledgling bomber arm.

The "other" B-26—the Martin Marauder—rounded out the CAF's collection in the twin-engined field. Its chief claim to aviation fame was that it had the lowest combat loss rate of any Allied bomber—less than one half of 1 per cent. First flown in November 1940, the design of the Marauder showed such promise that 1,131 of them were ordered by the Air Corps. The plane began flying combat missions in the Southwest Pacific in spring 1942, but most B-26s subsequently assigned to operational theaters were sent to England and the Mediterranean area. Bombing from medium altitudes of 10,000 to 15,000 feet, Marauders flew more than 110,000 sorties and dropped 150,000 tons of bombs by the end of World War II. It had been used by British, Free French, Australian, South African, Canadian, and Greek forces in addition to U.S. units. In 1945, when B-26 production was halted by Martin, 5,266 had been built. More than 250 Marauders completed 100 missions each. One, named *Flak Bait,* was the first Allied bomber to complete 200 missions.

In view of early development problems that almost ended the Marauder's career before it began, its combat record seems especially impressive. The B-26 was the result of a response to the Air Corps's request for a fast, heavily armed medium bomber. The accent was on the word *fast,* for what the Air Corps wanted was a plane that could perform a variety of medium-altitude missions of the "hit-and-run" variety: fly in fast, drop the bombload, and get out just as

The CAF's A-20 warms up on a runway in Boise, Idaho, prior to a ferry flight to Harlingen.

A side view of the CAF's A-20 during restoration. Note the rear windows installed during her postwar civilian years.

The final twin-engined member of the CAF Bomber Wing, the Martin B-26 Marauder was the busiest medium bomber in the war, seeing service from Europe to the Pacific.

quickly. Martin's answer was a twin-engined plane that had a range of well over 2,000 miles, a service ceiling of 20,000 feet, and maximum speed of 285 miles per hour delivered by two Pratt and Whitney R-2800 radials with 1,900 horsepower each. Originally, the B-26 was designed to carry a crew of five, and was to be armed with four machine guns in addition to its bomb payload.

So badly was the Air Corps in need of such a plane that the Marauder was rushed into production without a prototype, in other words, "straight off the drawing board," a decision which both the Air Corps and Martin—and doubtless many pilots who flew it—may have later regretted. The Marauder's major problem was its high rate of landing accidents, an annoyance attributed both to its weight—32,000 pounds—and the fast landing speed (130 miles an hour) made necessary by the relatively small surface area of its stubby wings. A skilled pilot could overcome this problem, but a green one often found himself cursing the plane from the vantage point of the cow pasture nearest the runway. Despite the abnormally high incidence of landing accidents, production continued at Martin while engineers redesigned and repositioned the wings. That helped some, but constant shuffling of its armament and crew configuration continued to add more weight, which in turn offset the advantage of greater wing area. In late 1941, three B-26s were ferried to England for evaluation by the Royal Air Force, which was not exactly overwhelmed with awe but which agreed to withhold a final judgment until modifications promised by Martin could be made. By the following spring, so many training accidents had occurred that the Air Corps convened a special board of investigation, and production at the Martin plant was temporarily halted. In combat, though, particularly in the Pacific, the B-26 continued to fly and amass its creditable low-loss record.

During its career, the Marauder filled many combat roles other than that for which it was designed. Although it proved unsuccessful as a torpedo-bomber (against the Japanese in the Aleutians and in the Battle of Midway) it excelled as a multiplace fighter. It proved unsuited as a "treetop bomber" (its high stall speed made it too fast for accuracy) but at medium altitudes it became a potent weapon particularly in night operations, flying from airfields in England, against enemy bridges and transportation targets on the Continent. Pilots lauded the fact that the B-26 could take considerable punishment and still return to home base safely; it easily could be flown with one of its two engines knocked out.

The B-26, then, shared with the P-40 fighter and a few other World War II vintage combat birds the reputation of having a number of shortcomings but overcoming them with first-rate performance. The CAF obviously wanted a flyable B-26 to make its combat collection complete, shortcomings or no shortcomings, but once again, Marauders were in considerably short supply by the early sixties. In 1967, however, a Marauder in need of minor repair but still flyable was located in private ownership in Denver, Colorado, and flown to Texas by CAF members Vernon Thorp, Gary Levitz, and Lefty Gardner. Several months later, the right landing gear collapsed during an engine run-up, and the plane sustained heavy damage to the wing and propeller. Budget-bare, the CAF passed the hat among its members and scraped up the necessary funds to repair the B-26. Today, the CAF's B-26 is considered one of the rarest planes in the world.

Its twin-engined bomber goal fulfilled, the CAF next began the most ambitious search in its history: locating and restoring to flying status one each of the three four-engined heavy bomber stalwarts of World War II: the Consolidated B-24 Liberator, the B-17 Flying Fortress, and B-29 Superfortress. The epic B-29 restoration saga, as related in the next chapter, was not to end for several years, although those involving the B-17 and B-24 were no less arduous nor less demanding on the CAF's pocketbook and patience.

The friendly rivalry between B-17 and B-24 crews became legend in World War II. The "Fort" emerged at war's end cloaked in far more glamour than the Liberator that succeeded her, yet the credit for firmly establishing the role of the strategic bomber in modern warfare must be shared equally by both, as well as by the mighty B-29, which saw service in the Pacific only. Though they were rivals in a sense, the Flying Fortress and the Liberator also complemented each other, the "Fort" seeing action over a longer period, yet achieving nothing over its later cousin as far as rugged durability, faithful service, and combat effectiveness were concerned. It might be said that the B-17 fought the early battle for acceptance of the strategic bomber in modern warfare, and the B-24 came along later to help prove the value of such strategy.

Described by General H. H. "Hap" Arnold as "the backbone of our world-wide aerial offensive," the B-17 and its development were unique in aviation history. The Boeing Company, steadfastly devoted to its belief in the Fortress as *the* heavy bomber of the future, assumed full expense for the design and production of the first Fortress and risked its corporate future on this belief. The B-17's origin dates back to August 1934, when the Army Air Corps invited manufacturers to submit a new design for "a multiengined bomber capable of a maximum speed of 200 to 250 miles per hour at 10,000 feet, a service ceiling of 20,000 to 25,000 feet, and an endurance of between six and ten hours." The requirement did not specify how many engines "multiengined" meant, although in general

One of the grandest airplanes of all time, the Boeing B-17 Flying Fortress, a durable, tough, fighting lady whose wartime service spanned the globe, is now a star of the CAF Bomber Squadron.

usage, *multi* is accepted as "more than two." At any rate, Boeing accepted the challenge on September 26, 1934, when its board of directors earmarked $275,000—a huge investment in those days—toward the design and construction of a single four-engined prototype, dubbed the Model 299. Shortly after sunrise eight months later, on July 28, 1935, test pilot Les Tower lifted the 299 off the Boeing runway at Renton, Washington, for her maiden flight. Though brief in duration, the flight proved a huge success. It led to increasingly longer tests, the final one covering more than 2,000 miles from Seattle to the Air Corps's Wright Field in Ohio, at an average speed of 233 miles an hour. Impressed Air Corps officials designated the prototype as the XB-17. Despite a tragic crash on October 30, 1935, which killed an Air Corps evaluator and as a result of which Les Tower himself later died from injuries, and although Boeing lost the design contract, the company was nevertheless encouraged to push ahead, and the Air Corps later placed an order for thirteen YB-17s and a fourteenth airframe for static testing. The planes thus produced were then subjected to the most rigorous shakedown of any military aircraft built up to that time, the accent being on well-publicized long-haul flights to prove the Fortress' inherent capability as a long-range "continental bomber." Boeing's unswerving faith had paid off, and a long evolution of B-17s in various configurations—each one tougher and more effective than the one before—began. A total of 12,731 Fortresses was built in all series, including 6,981 by Boeing, 3,000 by Douglas, and 2,750 by Lockheed under subcontract.

In July 1941, the B-17 in Royal Air Force service first performed the job for which it was built—precision bombing of German installations from heights which enemy cannon could not reach. The following December, seventeen "Forts" flew the first U.S. missions in the Pacific. The Japanese Navy learned of the B-17's power in May 1942, in the Battle of the Coral Sea; earlier, immediately following Pearl Harbor, B-17s of the 19th Bombardment Group based at Clark Field in the Philippines had struck back at the Japanese, and in twelve months more than 600 Japanese aircraft had been shot down and a number of ships sunk.

The Battle of the Coral Sea was the world's first great engagement between ships and land-based planes, and it convinced the last of the military diehards that airplanes were not merely an adjunct to ground operations, but a major weapon in their own right. Many persons, too, including the Nazis, did not believe that any bombing program could do major damage to Germany. They pointed to the fact that the Luftwaffe had tried to bomb Britain into submission and had failed, and that strategic bombing over land was a matter of night raids. Damage was done, but not enough to be decisive in the long run. The summer of 1942 proved this theory wrong, too, when the first B-17Es manned by American crews landed in England. These were bombers of a new breed, bristling with gun turrets and very different from the earlier Flying "Forts," which proved to have had some blind spots. They struck first on August 17 at Rouen, a German rail center eighty-seven miles northwest of Paris. Twelve "Forts" rained destruction on freight yards, trains, and roundhouses, while others carried out diversionary raids on Cherbourg and Dunkirk. It was broad daylight, a time that then-accepted military policy dictated that heavy bombers should be at home, but the B-17Es came in at 25,000 feet and effectively hit their targets. As importantly, all returned safely to England. That was the beginning of the "Fort"'s historic day-to-day role in pummeling German targets, especially factories and producers of raw material, the loss of which spelled the beginning of the end of Hitler's Third Reich.

The tremendous toughness of the Fortress became a legend. Many B-17s

A Confederate Air Force B-17 "Fort" participates in an air show as parachutists drift down off its wing.

came home after a raid riddled with hundreds of bullet and flak holes, with one or two engines shot out, with wings and tail surfaces shredded. Perhaps the oddest testimonial to this toughness—but in reverse—involved a B-17 mission over Germany in which Sergeant James Raley of Henderson, Kentucky, was a tail gunner on one of the planes. A member of the Fifteenth Air Force, Raley heard over the intercom that the plane was at 19,000 feet; suddenly, he heard a loud noise and was thrown violently around his gun position. Trapped inside the tail turret, Raley could feel the plane spinning earthward. He knew he was falling, and from 19,000 feet, there was no escape. Peering through a window, he saw another Fortress burning and plummeting toward the ground. Raley's confidence in his pilot shot up several notches when he felt his plane slide along the ground in a belly landing and come to a rest against a stand of pine trees. Fearful of fire, he worked his way toward the forward part of the plane . . . only to discover there *was* no forward part of the plane. Astonishingly, Raley had glided 19,000 feet to earth in the tail section only; apparently, the huge section had sheared off in such a way that the wide horizontal stabilizer had become a perfect airfoil. It provided lift just as a wing would. Shaken but only bruised, Raley walked for weeks through the Italian mountains and eventually rejoined his outfit. The other nine members of the crew were never heard from again.

However, despite their ruggedness, many Flying Fortresses never made it home. A total of 4,750 were lost on combat missions, more than any other type of aircraft. That so many were lost was perhaps due as much to the enemy's great concentration of flak and fighter attacks against them—a signal of the bomber's effectiveness—as to the fact that they went into combat in such great numbers; thousand-plane B-17 raids were common toward the middle and end of the war in the European Theater.

Enemy fighter planes were hard-pressed to stop the huge B-17 armadas, however. With their tremendous, deadly crisscross patterns of firepower, Fortress gunners shot down an average of twenty-three fighters on a thousand-plane raid, almost double the number of enemy planes shot down by an equal number of U.S. fighters.

The B-17 added many other duties to its basic role as a bomber during and following World War II. Some were converted to cargo ships, photo planes, and personnel carriers. They became launching ramps for experimental weapons such as the GB-1 glide bombs and JB-2 "buzz bombs," and, as this chapter's opening related, they were used as targets themselves. It was a B-17 that flew through the mushroom cloud of the postwar Bikini nuclear test, gathering radioactive samples, and still others were recruited for air-sea rescue work. But thousands of other B-17s were sent to desert storage areas, like that at Kingman, Arizona, to wait out their retirement years, or to be scrapped.

Fortunately, a handful were picked up by historical societies, aviation museums, and other civic-minded groups for historical preservation. The most famous example, perhaps, is the *Memphis Belle,* the first Fortress to complete twenty-five missions. Purchased after the war and restored to fighting trim by citizens of the Southern city whose name she carried into battle, the *Memphis Belle* was later enshrined as a war memorial in front of a National Guard armory in that city. But even this aging veteran of the 1941–45 air war fell on hard times, a victim of public apathy; within a year after Memphis citizens gathered in nostalgic dedication, she bore wounds of rock-throwing vandals nearly as serious as the flak holes that had become her badge of honor over Europe.

Before roomy, swift personal jets came on the scene, a few Fortresses were bought by American corporations to transport large groups of employees. They

With her four engines roaring, the CAF's Fortress, in her first color scheme, prepares for takeoff.

were expensive planes to maintain, but a lot cheaper than sending the same number of executives around the country via scheduled airlines. With some firms, surplus B-17s served dual roles, such as being flown as personnel carriers part of the time and hauling supplies the rest. Such a plane was the B-17 acquired in 1967 by the Confederate Air Force.

A B-17G-95-DL built for Boeing by Douglas near the end of World War II, it never saw combat, but for a brief period, with its bomb bay doors sealed shut and long-range fuel tanks added, served as an antisubmarine patrol-bomber for the Navy. It was, in fact, one of only thirty-one B-17s, redesignated PB-1Ws, flown by the Navy before a more sophisticated propeller-driven antisubmarine plane, built by Lockheed, came into use. Its Navy career ended, the B-17 spent three years gathering desert dust at Litchfield Park, Arizona; before the smelter could consume it, however, it was sold as surplus to the Aero Service Corporation, a division of Litton Industries, home-based in Philadelphia. Litton modified the bomber slightly, adding a magnetometer for use in industrial research.

The CAF, meanwhile, had launched a nationwide search for a privately owned B-17 after receiving a list from the Federal Aviation Administration of all known B-17 owners. The name of Litton Industries appeared prominently on the list. Litton executives had heard of the CAF, supported its historical mission and were thus already aware of the purpose to which the old bomber would be put when they were approached by Ghost Squadron officials in Philadelphia in 1967. Cost was a major consideration, especially after Litton, sympathetic but adhering to company policy, reported that for legal reasons it could not consider donating the plane. Litton would agree to sell the B-17, however, if certain conditions could be agreed upon. What Litton wanted was the right to lease the plane back for two months out of each of four years following the CAF's acquisition, for which it would pay all maintenance costs, plus $120 per hour for flight time, and $1,500 per month for standby time. To CAF Colonels Lefty Gardner and Thomas Short that day in Philadelphia, that seemed reasonable enough, since the

A B-17 in its early Ghost Squadron days. No longer assigned to hauling bombs, this Flying Fortress became a handy cargo carrier for the CAF.

CAF would use the plane only a part of the year anyway. And when they inspected the B-17, they were doubly certain it was the ideal B-17 for the Ghost Squadron's growing collection. It had never been in combat, and it had been flown an average of only 225 hours per year in the previous nine years, and was in excellent condition.

With fingers crossed, Gardner gingerly approached the subject of price. From previous research, he knew that the fair market value of a B-17 in such good condition would run around $85,000. To his happy surprise, Litton wanted only $50,000.

Though the price was right, the CAF didn't have enough cash on hand at the time to cover even the $30,000 Litton asked as a down payment. The money was raised—in less than three months—by forming a "B-17 Flying Fortress Squadron" of 100 members, admission to which was a donation of $350. On July 3, 1967, formal title to the Flying "Fort" was turned over to the CAF by Litton. The only remaining concern of the Ghost Squadron was how to paint the plane. At the suggestion of General Curtis E. LeMay, a top World War II Air Corps commander, it was finally daubed in the combat colors of the 305th Bomb Group of the Eighth Air Force. Today, still in top condition, the Fortress flies frequently in CAF air shows. One of its highly popular acts is touching down on one wheel with smoke billowing out of one engine and Japanese Zero fighters in hot pursuit in a re-creation of the *Tora! Tora! Tora!* attack on Pearl Harbor. Landing a Fortress on a single wheel is not for the neophyte. In this description, which lacks none of the dry humor that has become a hallmark of the organization, the late Van Skiles, one of several CAF members checked out to fly the bomber, sums up how the unusual act is done and how it originated:

"Check-out in the B-17 was routine. Study the manual, blindfold cockpit check, then off into the blue. The Fortress is honest, and though a little heavy on the controls, simple to fly. I had spent twelve years in the cockpit of a DC-3 for Pan American and Trans-Texas Airways, and there was a lot of similarity in

Controls of the CAF B-17 Flying "Fort."

handling characteristics. I just had to remember to do everything four times instead of twice. The big thing was to get used to the unusual Boeing arrangement of four throttles. To get proper control, particularly for taxi and takeoff, they had to be operated palm-up. This was awkward at first, but it worked.

"One of my first CAF assignments was to fly the B-17 with the New Mexico Wing in their air show. Upon arrival in New Mexico, I was notified by the FAA that they were grounding the Fort because the right main tire had worn through three plys of the tread. I managed to convince them that it was still safe (there were 17 good plys remaining). For the rest of the show it was the co-pilot's job to see that we stopped with the bare spot hidden. After takeoff, it was also his job to stop the wheel with the worn spot on top. Upon landing, I would bounce the wheel smartly to get it spinning, then let it gently down to prevent skinning any more plys off. B-17 tires aren't available at just any airport, and, besides, they cost a whole lot of money.

"While briefing for one of my first air shows, we conceived the idea of extending only one main gear and shooting an approach with the announcer getting all excited, the safety man on the runway firing flares, and the crash wagons cranking up. We didn't broadcast it much to the rest of the colonels but we should have; the act must have been convincing as several colonels told me to let them know ahead of time before I pulled that again. They nearly had a cardiac arrest because their beautiful B-17 was about to be written off. Talking about it and doing it are two different things sometimes, and combine that with the stress of show flying and incidents will happen. Once, while sailing down the runway on one wheel with the other retracted, I decided it was time to get airborne, and called for 'props, *full low.*' I was thinking *pitch,* and the co-pilot was thinking *rpm!* When you are in that position with the mills heading for 1200 rpm, things get real busy. Nowadays, we get the props in full pitch before coming across the field."

Acquiring a flyable B-24 Liberator proved more complicated than finding a B-17. Despite the fact that more than 18,000 of them were built—one of the longest production runs of any American aircraft—none in flying condition were known to exist when the CAF voted to form its Bomb Wing in 1963. The B-24 flown today by the CAF reeks with history, for during its career, stretching more than three decades, it was owned by three companies, once suffered a serious accident, was scheduled for British service but never reached Britain, and managed to serve the United States military along the way. Unlike the CAF's B-17, which was a model near the end of the Boeing production, the Liberator was only the eighteenth B-24 built. It was produced by the Fort Worth, Texas, division of Consolidated Aircraft (later to become Convair, a division of General Dynamics). Thus it was that a thirty-year-old airplane that first flew over the great expanse of Texas finally returned to the Lone Star State as a fitting flying memorial to her 18,000 sisters turned out by Consolidated, as well as Ford, Douglas, and North American under subcontract.

First flown in 1939, four years after the B-17 in whose shadow it would always seem to play second fiddle, the Liberator was a powerful and versatile strategic World War II heavy bomber. More than a bomber, though, it was an airplane whose adaptability seemed to be limitless. It became a long-range transport and a top-rate reconnaissance aircraft, and served not only the Americans but the British, Australians, Canadians, and South Africans as well. In its many different configurations the B-24 saw action and duty in all parts of the world.

Its finest combat hour, perhaps, was the famed Ploesti raid in Rumania,

A powerful World War II bomber, the four-engined Consolidated B-24 Liberator first flew in 1939, was perhaps overshadowed by the more famous B-17, but nonetheless made its own headlines. The famous low-level raid against the Ploesti oil refineries in Rumania was but one example. Here the CAF's B-24 is shown in its pre-98th Bomb Group color scheme.

which, though described as a disaster by some aviation historians, nevertheless won Medals of Honor for five of its participants, and proved the B-24's worth as a thoroughly rugged, durable plane that could take astonishing punishment and still come home safely.

The Ploesti raid on August 1, 1943, involved 177 Liberators whose crews had been detached from the Sicilian campaign for an intense ten-day briefing and familiarization flights over the North African desert against a mock-up of the Ploesti oil refinery target. On the day of the raid several of the B-24s never made it off the ground, due to mechanical problems, and despite the fact that the raiders lost the element of surprise when one of the advance units wandered off course and alerted enemy defenses, enough got through to turn Ploesti into a smoking ruin and reduce refining capacity by almost half. As an indication of the effectiveness of enemy defense, fifty-four of the raiding B-24s never made it home, but many of those that did were so badly shredded by flak they resembled camouflaged Swiss cheese.

Not long after Ploesti, in mid-August, Liberators made their first attack on Germany, flying from the Mediterranean; their extremely long range made them an ideal strategic bomber in the Pacific, too, where they flew over vast stretches of ocean to bomb targets such as Truk and Rabaul. They were used widely in the Aleutians and, later in the war, made many daylight raids on Japanese cities. In various configurations, B-24s were also used as VIP transports, for weather research, and in antisubmarine patrol.

No one could call the Liberator "pretty," unless it is agreed that beauty lies in the eye of the beholder. Its crews often referred to it as the "flying boxcar," or "the tub," and pilots sometimes found it difficult to fly. It was a plane requiring plenty of muscle, especially if it was poorly loaded. Because of its unique high-

A pilot's-eye view from the CAF's Liberator.

wing design, center of gravity was critical but, properly loaded, the B-24 had a greater cargo or bomb capacity than the B-17.

Despite the huge number of them produced, B-24s did a disappearing act after the war. By 1951, only a single B-24 was in active service with the Air Force and another 5,500 were turned over to the Reconstruction Finance Corporation. Many were scrapped. After V-J Day, the Royal Air Force put several others to work as troop carriers, in aerial surveying and patrol, and a handful of highly modified B-24s were used for a while by the U. S. Coast Guard. For historical purposes, however, the Liberator was practically nonexistent. Until the CAF's acquisition, the most notable exception was the *Strawberry Bitch,* saved from the scrap heap by the Air Force, restored, and placed on display at the Air Force Museum at Dayton, Ohio. The *Strawberry Bitch* had flown fifty-nine missions with the 512th Bomb Squadron of the 376th Bomb Group, mostly out of Italy, and had been shot up and patched so many times it was a wonder she survived the war.

The B-24 eventually acquired by the Ghost Squadron began life as AM-927, the designation given her under the Lend-Lease program. Though she never reached England, part of the numerical designation stuck, and for years she was referred to simply as "Old 927." After several test flights in Texas, the Liberator was involved in a serious accident in Canada, where she had been ferried for transfer to the RAF. The plane was returned to Texas for repairs, but instead of making the trip north again, she was reclaimed by Consolidated as a VIP transport, and for hauling cargo and supplies connected with the company's contract with the Defense Department.

In 1948, three years after the war ended, the B-24 was purchased as a transport by the Continental Can Company. Fitted with sleeping berths and reclining chairs, it shuttled between Continental Can's Morristown, New Jersey, home plant and other company bases for the next eleven years. Purchase by Continental of a new turboprop in 1959 signaled retirement for "Old 927" and for a while, scrapping loomed as her fate.

However, about the same time, *Petroleos Mexicanos* (usually shortened to the acronym Pemex), the government-controlled oil industry of Mexico, was looking around for a large, long-range four-engined transport to connect the extensive Central and South American territory it covered. The title to "Old 927" passed from Continental Can to Pemex in 1959, and a new career lasting nearly nine years began.

In mid-1967, four years after deciding to form a bomber wing, the CAF assigned a high priority to the B-24. CAF executives had known of the existence of "Old 927," but learned too late that it was no longer the property of Continental Can. Victor Agather, a CAF colonel living in Mexico City, who was to spearhead a later campaign to restore a B-29, opened the sensitive negotiations with Pemex to acquire the B-24. For once, the timing was perfect; Pemex, Agather reported to CAF headquarters, had planned to scrap the Liberator as soon as it located a suitable replacement. Pemex wanted a used DC-6, but had been unsuccessful in finding the right model at the right price, for its purposes.

A group of Pemex executives were invited to San Antonio, Texas, where the CAF had managed to scout up a surplus commercial DC-6 airliner that was available for $240,000. Pemex was obviously pleased that the CAF would go to such great lengths to smooth the way for transfer of the B-24 to CAF hands, and agreed to part with the four-engined bomber that had served the company so

Wing and wing, the CAF's B-17 Flying Fortress and Consolidated B-24 Liberator in before and after color schemes.

well. But there was one hitch: while Pemex would sell the plane, it insisted on retaining its four engines because they were hard-to-find replacements for the engines on the company's fleet of DC-3s.

The CAF reluctantly agreed, but that left the obvious follow-up problem of where to find new or slightly used engines for the B-24. After all, buying the B-24 as an engineless static hardly fulfilled the Ghost Squadron's basic mission, and by the late-sixties, engines of this type, even used ones, judging by their price, seemed to be platinum-plated. Finally, in an Oklahoma city warehouse, CAF Colonel Lefty Gardner located four such engines in good condition that carried a price tag of $24,000. The necessary money was borrowed from a sympathetic Texas banker and a swap was arranged with Pemex; to save the time and cost of removing the B-24's engines, Pemex was offered the newer ones instead, and everybody was happy. Late in 1970, sporting a new $10,000 paint job in the markings of the 98th Bomb Group of the Ninth Air Force, gallant "Old 927" flew for the first time in CAF service. As of this writing, it is believed to be the only B-24 flying in the world today.

With a single exception, that completed the Ghost Squadron's Air Corps Bomb Wing. The missing plane, of course, was the B-29 Superfortress, the historic four-engined behemoth that dropped the atomic bomb on Hiroshima to end World War II. And *that* acquisition, as it turned out, would prove more costly, at times more exasperating, and more time-consuming than all the other "heavies" put together.

Low-level fury: a B-25 Mitchell bomber and an A-26 Invader perform for the crowd. One can see why both planes could double as fighter-bombers in wartime service.

10

THE SAGA OF FIFI

Few would debate the statement that the most significant air combat mission ever flown was that of the B-29 Superfortress that dropped the atomic bomb on Hiroshima, Japan, on August 6, 1945. In one blinding, searing split-second that resulted in the loss of 70,000 human lives, and in which the city was reduced to smoking, radioactive-contaminated rubble, World War II was effectively ended. And it was ended at a huge savings in Allied lives that, intelligence had indicated, would have been the price paid for an invasion of the Japanese home islands.

Of necessity, planning for the Hiroshima raid was conducted under conditions of extraordinary secrecy. Only a small number of military strategists even knew that the bomb existed. Although the Air Corps ground crewmen who were detailed to load the bomb were obviously aware that it was no ordinary weapon (nicknamed "Little Boy," it wasn't; it measured 10 feet long and 28 inches in diameter and weighed a hefty 4½ tons), they could hardly begin to imagine the awesome impact it would have on Hiroshima—and world history—a few hours later.

Members of the flight crew of the Superfort, the *Enola Gay,* were not told of the unusual nature of the mission until after the aircraft ponderously lifted off the runway on Tinian Island, in the Marianas archipelago of Micronesia. But surely they suspected something big was in the offing. Skilled, experienced combat veterans all, they had been handpicked for the mission, not by Captain Robert A. Lewis, who normally piloted the *Enola Gay,* but by an aviator three notches Lewis' senior, Colonel Paul W. Tibbets, Jr., commander of the 509th Composite Group.

Five other B-29s accompanied the *Enola Gay* on her mission. Three were assigned to fly ahead as weather observers. Two more carried scientific equipment to measure and record the effect of the bomb. A sixth was held in reserve in case the *Enola Gay* developed engine trouble or was otherwise unready for the mission.

Although the power of the bomb had been demonstrated in a ground test at

The Boeing B-29 Superfortress, largest, most advanced heavy bomber produced by any nation in World War II. The B-29 saw action in the Pacific only, for which it was specifically designed and built.

Alamogordo, not even the most knowledgeable military planner had any experience to judge what the blast might do to the airplane that dropped it in combat. The final two Superforts carried special observation crews and cameramen to record the history-shattering event.

The mission of the *Enola Gay* and her escort B-29s took 12 hours, 13 minutes.

Three days later, on August 9, a second atomic bomb—more appropriately nicknamed "Fat Man" and of the plutonium type rather than uranium—was dropped on Nagasaki.

The last-ditch stand, iron will, and morale of the Japanese were shattered; five days later, on August 14, 1945, the war ended with Japan's surrender.

Although secrecy was a byword of the mighty Superfort in her most impor-

One who will never forget: Paul W. Tibbets, Jr., commander of the Enola Gay, *which changed history at Hiroshima, Japan, August 6, 1945.*

tant task, the atomic bomb missions were not the first time the airplane was veiled in tight security. From the beginning, in fact, unparalleled secrecy prevailed.

The B-29's development, like that of the B-26 Marauder, was ordered into production "off the drawing boards." Because the nation was then at war, not a word was said about it when it made its maiden flight on September 21, 1942. Nor was any mention made that production contracts for the airplane—to that time not yet even tested in the air—had been signed, new plants were being built to produce it, and a nationwide subcontracting program was under way to turn out combat-ready copies by the hundreds.

The secrecy still held as the bombers, biggest ever built, started rolling from plants of the Boeing Company in Wichita, Kansas, and Renton, Washington, and from the Martin factory in Omaha, Nebraska, and the Bell plant in Marietta, Georgia.

Even after the Superforts tasted combat for the first time—when 100 of them made a daring daylight raid on Bangkok from a base in India on June 5, 1944—only faint and inaccurate details appeared in the American press. It was not until ten days later—June 15—that the world began to learn about the fantastic new American bomber that had been designed, built, tested, and sent to combat virtually behind closed doors.

The June 15 mission was a psychological shocker for Japan, especially since it involved a flight of fifty "Supers" that hit vital steel mills at Yawata in Japan's homeland. One of the planes was the *General H. H. Arnold Special* and it was to make history in a different way later on. Named for the Air Corps's top commander, this Superfort, built in Boeing's Wichita plant, went on to participate in ten other successful missions over Japan before making a forced landing near Vladivostok, Siberia. Though the crew was released by Russia, the B-29 was permanently interned; in 1947, American aviation engineers, viewing photographs released by Russia of the Soviets' new seventy-two-passenger Tupolev Tu-4 transport, were moved to comment that it looked remarkably like the B-29.

The Superfortress was not a single-design aircraft. It was the end result of bomber evolution that could trace its genesis at Boeing back to 1937. By the mid-thirties, Hitler was already on the rise in Europe and Japan's designs on the Pacific scarcely went unnoticed by a handful of dedicated American strategists who even then could see war clouds looming. Aware of the inevitable move toward war and aware that, unlike World War I, the new conflict would possibly pose a direct threat to industrialization of America itself, they called for and received funding for a series of several types of aircraft with a range up to 4,000 miles. Boeing had already built the XB-15, a four-engined high-altitude airplane. Although the XB-15 proved too much airplane for the engines originally installed, the single model delivered to the Air Corps proved worthy as a workhorse transport for long-distance cargo-carrying missions. Since Boeing by 1935 had successfully flown its Model 299—forerunner of the famous B-17 Flying Fortress—the company was considered far ahead of its competitors in the development of a long-range, high-altitude "hemisphere defense" bomber.

At the Air Corps's urging, Boeing shuffled its priorities and soon came up with two designs for the "hemisphere defense" plane. The first, the Model 322, in many ways was a marriage of prototype designs of Boeing's 307 Stratoliner, because of its large, circular section fuselage, and the Flying Fortress, because of the Fortress-like wing and tail assembly. Boeing designers estimated that the 322 would have a maximum speed of more than 300 miles an hour and could carry a maximum bombload approaching five tons.

Even as war approached, Congress continued to keep a tight rein on military purse strings. With only so much money to go around, the Air Corps reluctantly shelved the 322 in favor of pushing development of the Flying Fortress.

But for the persistence of Boeing, the B-29 might never have got off the ground until it was too late to serve in World War II. Denied government funding, Boeing pushed on its own as a private venture, experimenting with different designs, airframes, engines, and one special feature that was retained not only through the development of Superfortresses but of postwar civilian transports as well: the pressurized fuselage.

Boeing's second direct predecessor of the B-29, the Model 333, proved to be a challenge of compromise. Allison engines were installed first, but although compact, they were not powerful enough to sustain the plane at high altitudes and over long distances. Pratt and Whitney radials adequately overcame the power problem, but presented another; because they occupied so much space in the wings, fuel storage capacity was reduced and, in turn, so was the range of action. Although the Model 333 so fitted could carry one ton of bombs 2,500 miles —an amazing distance in those days—it was only a fraction of the range needed for a true hemisphere defense bomber. Back to their drawing boards went the Boeing designers. Again, the solution was a matter of constant experimentation, trial and error, compromise, and a healthy measure of just plain luck. To beef up fuel capacity, the prototype's wingspan was expanded to 140 feet, 3 inches. That almost doubled its range—from 2,500 to 4,500 miles—but it also had increased its gross weight to more than 65,000 pounds. Still, by July 1939—only two months before Hitler's attack on Poland formally ignited World War II—the wrinkles of experimentation were at last being ironed out and the Superfort began to assume a definite form.

With the war fully under way, the Air Corps in November 1939 defined the specifications for a superbomber needed later to replace the B-17 and the Consolidated B-24. The requirements: it must have a speed of 400 miles, a range of 5,333 miles, and be capable of carrying a 2,000-pound bombload.

A race against time began. It was a race against rapidly moving world developments and that time was rapidly running out. What Boeing engineers faced— as did their counterparts at Lockheed, Douglas, and Consolidated, to whom General Arnold issued similar design demands—seemed virtually impossible.

Their fundamental challenge was an aerodynamic puzzle of propelling a mass more than twice the weight of the B-17 at a speed much faster than the Fortress. New engines were available, giving the B-29 almost twice the power of the Flying Fortress, but there was still an exasperating basic rule to be considered.

Roughly speaking, the horsepower goes up as the cube of the velocity, which means that eight times the power was needed to double the speed, instead of twice the power. Too, when weight is doubled, induced drag is increased. That, of course, also means more horsepower is needed. So what Boeing needed was an airplane with no more drag than the B-17, but twice as big, and with flight and landing characteristics never before achieved.

Boeing's answer: an unusual combination of flight and landing characteristics which compromised neither. Enormous wing flaps were originated. They were larger, in fact, than wings of many fighter planes, the largest ever put on an airplane up to that time. They performed well, providing the necessary lift at the crucial moments of landing and takeoff.

The pressurized fuselage was innovative, and allowed bombing crews to work at high altitude without cumbersome, duty-impairing oxygen systems, but it also presented problems. The shape of the fuselage, the armament, the ammunition feed lines, the bomb bays—all had to be designed to work in harmony with the pressure system. But work out the problems Boeing did, and to their later profit, too, in the years following the war; the pressurization system was carried forward into the company's 707 jet—first major American jet passenger carrier —and, with only little modification, into later airplanes such as the Boeing 727, 737, and 747 and the Douglas DC-10.

The pressurization system also required a new method of controlling the B-29's gun turrets. Late models of the B-17 Flying Fortress were equipped with power-operated turrets, but even these later designs wouldn't serve the B-29 because of its pressurized fuselage, and also because their exterior bulk increased drag and reduced maximum speed. Given the problem by Boeing, the General Electric Company came up with a workable answer. By a remote control system, B-29 turrets could be operated from *inside* the plane, the guns themselves firing on the outside. Another advantage of the new system was that a gunner could control more than one turret at a time.

Another innovation of the B-29 was its inertial navigation system. Admittedly crude by modern standards, it nevertheless revolutionized and vastly improved navigation systems for long overwater flights. Until the advent of the Air Position Indicator* (API) aircraft crews had to rely on radio systems, visual fixes, or celestial navigation. The API, however, facilitated precise course-plotting even during radio blackouts and when overcast skies made celestial navigation impossible.

Today, all long-range commercial jets use inertial guidance systems whether crossing the Atlantic or Pacific, following the Great Circle routes. Because of its precision, inertial guidance system equipment pays for itself in fuel costs within a few international flights. It was a highly sophisticated version of this system— pioneered in the B-29—that guided Apollo astronauts to the moon.

With design in hand and engineers furiously at work to develop new equipment the revolutionary bomber would require, Boeing launched a fantastically rigid program of testing various parts of the Superfort's structure. Full-sized major sections of the fuselage, wing, and tail assembly were hammered, stretched, crushed, even shot through with cannon shells and deliberately pulled to pieces to determine just how much punishment the B-29 could absorb. The results of each such "torture test" brought about minor modifications, but Boeing had completed the basic design well; an exceptionally "clean" airplane, it was noteworthy that no changes were required in the basic structure.

The first XB-29 made its maiden test flight on September 21, 1942, more than five months *after* the first production model rolled off the assembly line at the Boeing's Wichita plant. It was a daring gamble and one that could have been financially disastrous had the flying prototype proved to be a failure. But daring gambles are common in war and as has been said many times before, the pressures of war seem uniquely calculated to stimulate genius and talent that may have lain dormant under less stressful situations. The Boeing engineers had done their work well; the first XB-29 passed Air Corps inspection with flying colors.

Minor problems and a major tragedy followed. The minor problems involved "bugs" that further modification could eliminate. The tragedy—the crash of the second XB-29 due to an engine fire, which killed eighteen Boeing workers including ten of Boeing's top Superfort specialists—could not be undone, but the pressures of war perhaps justify even that sort of calculated risk.

By July 1943, with additional Boeing plants and two other companies busily

* The API is alternately called the Approximate Position Indicator.

assembling production models at four sites, seven XB-29s had been delivered to the Air Force. They were quickly pressed into service as training vehicles for combat B-29 crews. In Washington, meanwhile, military strategists reached a critical decision: because it was especially adapted to long-range missions, the Superfortress would be sent only to the Pacific. The B-25 Mitchell, the B-24 Liberator, and the now-venerable B-17 Flying Fortress were holding their own in Europe. In the Pacific, island-hopping American forces faced staggering geographic odds; after all, those forces were strung taut across an ocean that covered fully one third of the earth's surface. In territory known vastly better by the enemy, Allied ground forces were sorely in need of constant, daily heavy bomber support both to soften potential invasion targets and deliver punishing blows to the Japanese industrial capacity.

As the mainland B-29 plants assembled the huge bombers on a twenty-four-hour-per-day wartime footing, bases were being readied in India and China to serve them. Japan still held the islands closer to her homeland from which the bulk of B-29 attacks would be mounted later in the war. Although the Allies had swept steadily westward, eastward, and northward after the turning-point naval Battle of Midway in 1942, the hard-won islands were too far distant from their targets for even the long-range B-29 with a minimum bombload. Because the Himalayas were such a barrier to moving supplies from India to China, it was decided to build the main bases in India itself, where major supplies would be maintained, using China bases as advanced staging sites. Accordingly, sites for several airfields were designated near Chengtu in central China, and work quickly got underway to complete them. There was considerable irony, and a graphic demonstration of the differences in Eastern and Western cultures, in this situation. In America, production plants were turning out the most advanced revolutionary, large airplane ever built to that time. But in ageless China, from which they would fly to perform their wartime task, it was hoes, hammers, and ancient hand-pulled stone rollers that were used to level the airfield sites, and hand-crushed stone that formed the runways themselves.

The B-29's baptism of fire was the raid on June 5, 1944, against Japanese-held Bangkok. It proved how effective the B-29's secrecy had been; totally unaware of the new bomber's existence, the Japanese routinely reported that it had been carried out by B-24 Liberators. Once the secret was out, however, the defending Japanese became suddenly—and frighteningly—aware that here was no ordinary adversary. When the first operational Superforts went into action in Asia, the Japanese lacked an effective technique for stopping them. Capable of flying above the limits of standard antiaircraft batteries, the 29s seemed invulnerable to damage by fighter planes. For months, Japanese pilots misjudged both the B-29's speed and maneuverability, and the evasive tactics perfected by its crew. The report of a single raid underscores the outstanding defense ability of the Superfort. Assigned to bomb Japanese-held An-shan, Manchuria, on September 26, 1944, swarms of Tojo fighters rose up to the challenge of the eighty-nine attacking American bombers. Yet after nearly an hour of furious combat, all eighty-nine B-29s returned safely to their home base.

The final push toward Tokyo began in late 1944 after the crucial Mariana Islands were taken by amphibious forces starting in June of that year. Saipan fell in July, Guam and Tinian in August, but only after some of the costliest fighting of the Pacific war. Navy SeaBees and Army construction crews moved in at once and began enlarging the airstrips the Japanese had built there, as well as laying some new ones. Tinian was the major base of five B-29 sites; the first B-29 to use it as a fly-off point for bombing Japan arrived there on October 12, 1944.

Although the frequently debated decision to drop the atomic bomb on Japan thrust the Boeing Superfortress dramatically and instantly into aviation history books, its most important contribution to the Pacific war effort doubtless was not a single raid, or two. It was the incessant, day-by-day strategic, saturation bombing of Japanese targets that effectively softened Japan's war production capability, and thus her waning ability to defend herself. The first attack by B-29s based in the Marianas was a daylight raid made by eighty Superforts, which bombed Tokyo on November 24, 1944. Disturbed by reports of poor results, military commanders decided that the high altitude precluded effective precision bombing. The decision to use the B-29 to attack at night instead launched their famous low-level incendiary missions over Japanese cities. Because the Japanese lacked a night-fighter defense, the fact that the Superforts did not have to attain the previous high altitudes and use up valuable fuel allowed them to carry far greater bombloads than before.

In the first of the low-level night incendiary raids, on March 9, 1945, Superforts carried out the most destructive bombing raid in history. The attack, involving 299 B-29s, leveled seventeen square miles of Tokyo and more than 80,000 people were killed. Although that raid involved hundreds of times more bomb tonnage, and considerably more bombers, in terms of destruction it exceeded even the Hiroshima and Nagasaki atomic bombings of five months later.

In the week that followed, thirty-two square miles of four other cities virtually disappeared in the fire storm of Superfort incendiaries. As the raids increased in intensity, a domino-effect ensued. As factory after factory that built defense fighter planes and vital parts succumbed to the B-29s' daily punishment,† and with much of its remaining aircraft desperately committed elsewhere, the fighter resistance itself over Japan virtually ceased. With practically no air opposition, Air Corps commanders could strip out all armament from the Superforts, except two tail machine guns for safety's sake, and use the weight savings for bombs and fuel. The first B-29s to enter Pacific combat, with a gross weight of 137,500 pounds each, were equipped to carry up to 20,000 pounds of bombs. By eliminating much of the armament, and with reduced fuel required because of the low-altitude attack strategy, B-29s could add 4,000 more pounds of payload, raising their bomb capacity to 20,000 pounds. Within the next few months, the Air Force had committed twenty-one combat groups of Superforts, and the addition of two tons of bombs each had a dramatic effect on Japanese cities and industrial plants.

By spring of the war's final year, Japan's three major cities of Tokyo, Nagoya, and Yokohama—all critical to war production—had been practically wiped off the map. Meanwhile, 600 Superforts were diverted to other tasks: bombing Japanese shipping, mining Japanese harbors, and gathering photo-reconnaissance information over Japanese cities.

Hiroshima was the stunning peak of the Superfort's combat career. By the end of World War II, a total of 3,970 of the big four-engined bombers had been built, 2,766 of them by Boeing, 668 by Bell, and 536 by Martin. In its final version, constantly improved upon by battle experience, the B-29 could boast a maximum speed of 375 miles an hour at 30,000 feet, a ceiling of more than 35,000 feet, and a range of more than 4,500 miles.

Following the war, Superforts performed several other firsts. In November

---

† The Japanese were caught flat-footed by low-level attacks; their antiaircraft fuses were not set for low altitudes.

1945, a B-29 named *Pacusan Dreamboat* lifted off a runway on Guam and landed at Washington, D.C., thirty-five hours later. The distance—8,198 miles—was a world record. A few days later, the same airplane flew from Burbank, California, to New York in 5 hours, 27 minutes to set a speed mark, and in October 1946, another nonstop record was established, this time from Honolulu to Cairo, 9,500 miles, in 39 hours, 36 minutes.

While these facts kept the Superfort's identity alive, it appeared to be permanently retired from combat. Jets had made their appearance even before the end of World War II, and aircraft designers were at work designing a new generation of aircraft powered not by propellers, but by the more powerful, efficient turbine engine.

But the record-setting, war-ending Superfort was not to be retired without one more taste of combat. In June 1950, when the Korean War began, Superforts again were rushed into action, repeating the heavy-load, long-distance strategic bombing techniques that had proved so effective against Japan five years earlier.

Following Korea, more and more uses were found for them, including the vital job of typhoon hunting and weather watching. In the WB-29 configuration, operated by what later became the Military Airlift Command, they ranged the globe, relaying important weather information that enabled forecasters in the United States to become more accurate in their predictions.

The B-29 also pioneered aerial refueling. First as the KB-29, which used a hose-and-grapnel system, then as the KB-29P, using the Boeing-developed Flying Boom, it opened the way for even greater use of heavy bombers. In 1949, four KB-29Ms provided the aerial refueling for the B-50 *Lucky Lady II,* which made the first around-the-world nonstop flight. Other postwar configurations sounded, because of their letter designations, like an alphabet soup. The B-29B, which, except for the tail gunner's position, had its turrets and sighting blisters removed and contained extra radio and radar equipment; the EB-29B, used as a television relay station; the XB-29E, a fire control test model; the B-29F, which was winterized for duty in Alaska. The XB-29G served as a flying test bed for turbojet engines and the XB-29H was used for special armament tests. The YB-29J served as a surface test model for improved engines and the SB-29 was employed in search and rescue missions. Finally, there was the TB-29 trainer and the B-29MR, which became a receiver airplane for British hose-type refueling tests.

Then, oblivion.

No one knows for sure when the last active duty B-29 flew. Doubtless it was no later than the mid-fifties after it had been reconfigured to participate in its various postwar missions. It seems strange and ironic that not even the Air Force could provide accurate information on the location or disposition of its most famous bomber when, in the summer of 1966, the Confederate Air Force approached the Pentagon in a search for a single surplus model that could be restored to flying condition.

For the CAF, adding a Superfort was a high-priority item, an absolute must. "Of all the airplanes we'd managed to locate and restore," remembers Lloyd Nolen, the CAF's founder, "we developed a special desire for the Superfort. It was not only the last word in World War II aircraft design and performance; it was the one ship that would complete our collection." The B-29 project started a mere search; it ended as a full-blown crusade.

Obviously, restoring a B-29 would be the CAF's most expensive undertaking to date. But Nolen and his fellow colonels were not concerned about raising the necessary money, for in their own ranks they had discovered a man who not only had been closely associated with the development of the plane during the war, and who still held a nostalgic regard for it, but one who also had pledged full logistics and financial support in sponsoring a restoration.

Little could anyone in the CAF have dreamed, however, that the project would drag on for fully eight frustrating years, involve thousands of miles of travel, cost $85,000, and that only the intervention of a United States senator would finally pry permission to fly the result from an unbelievably adamant Pentagon.

By all odds, Victor N. Agather was the ideal choice to spearhead the B-29 project. A slightly built, warm, generous, but thoroughly determined man, he had been intimately tied to the B-29 for more than five years of his life before, during, and following World War II. The great airplane had, in his words, "become a part of my blood and my genes." Agather, presently a successful American businessman living in Mexico City, joined the Army Air Corps in 1934, served one hitch, was discharged, and then was recalled to active duty when war appeared imminent. While stationed at Wright Field in Dayton, Ohio, he was selected by General Erik Melson (round-the-world pilot) and personal adviser to Hap Arnold to serve on the development staff of the B-29, which was just then coming off the drawing boards. He spent the following few months with Boeing engineers and Air Corps flight test units at the various Superfort factories that had begun to proliferate around the country.

In 1944, about the time the plane was beginning to make itself known in the Pacific, he was assigned to India, China, and then the Pacific, where, in the Marianas, his growing expertise could be brought into play as strategists prepared the B-29 for its assault on the Japanese mainland. Even when the war ended, Agather asked for and was given duty connected with the plane; transferred home to the United States, he spent the balance of his military career training ground and flight crews in B-29 postwar operations.

By the mid-sixties, Agather had remembered the B-29 well, but in an initial attempt to locate a surplus model the CAF could restore, he learned to his dismay that apparently not everyone shared his nostalgia and affection. The Air Force, which had controlled the bomber from the beginning, was the obvious starting point. Agather routinely wrote the Pentagon, outlining the CAF's plans. Back came a reply. With the exception of three or four Superforts on static displays in aviation museums, the Air Force said, there were none left intact anywhere in the world. Except for the museum models (including the *Bockscar,* the B-29 that bombed Nagasaki, which the Air Force had preserved at its own museum in Dayton, Ohio), all had been chopped up and consigned to the smelter as scrap. It seemed incredible that only a handful of Superforts remained, yet, the Air Force insisted, it was true.

"We refused to accept that," Agather recalls. "It wasn't that we were accusing the Air Force of lying, only that we felt certain there was a colossal snafu in their records somewhere. So, we decided to go out and look for ourselves."

Through its growing network of members, the CAF spread the word: *find a B-29.* CAF colonels living near military bases were asked to make local inquiries; perhaps they'd luck out and accidentally find a model that had been stashed away in a back lot and forgotten. At Agather's office in Mexico City, the telephone circuits buzzed with calls to wartime friends who had worked with him on the Superfort project. Other calls went to the museums that had a B-29 on

Restoring a B-29 seemed an almost insurmountable task; witness the beginning, in the California desert, where row upon row of Superforts awaited oblivion.

Victor N. Agather, whose determination and generous pocketbook helped bring a B-29 to the ranks of the Confederate Air Force.

display; in acquiring their own model, the callers asked, had any other B-29s been spotted?

One summer day in 1966, Agather's persistence at last seemed rewarded. The grapevine had unearthed not one but *thirty-seven* B-29s; his hopes sank, however, when he was told where they were and what they had been intended to be used for. Spread across a field at the Army's Aberdeen Proving Ground in Maryland, they had been designated as target planes; specifically, they were to be pressurized and then shot through with cannon to determine the effect of high-impact ballistics on pressurized fuselages, something that had never really been fully proven even in combat. If the tests had not yet taken place and the planes were intact, there was still hope; muttering a silent prayer, Agather climbed on the first plane for Aberdeen. As luck would have it, the B-29s were still very much intact, but close inspection determined that what cannon had not yet accomplished, the elements had: all critical parts of the planes such as main and rear spars had been badly corroded by wind and rain. "We decided that the cost of restoration would have been prohibitive," Agather remembers. "So we just went quietly home."

Aberdeen was a disappointment, but the fact that thirty-seven Superforts had been located despite the Air Force's insistence that none existed anywhere only buoyed Agather's hopes. Patiently, he pushed on, and a few months later, once again his patience paid off. The National Aeronautics and Space Administration (NASA) had used the B-29 as a "mother ship" in a series of test drops of the rocket-powered X-1, he learned, and one such model had been declared surplus and donated for static display to the Allied Aircraft Museum in Tucson, Arizona. Agather lost no time in contacting the operators of the museum. Would they consider selling the Superfort? After hearing more about the CAF and its historical mission, the museum agreed, and a few days later received the cash down payment to secure the purchase option that had been agreed upon. About the same time, entirely by coincidence, Agather had been approached by the Junior Chamber of Commerce of a major American city, which had been looking for a suitable combat airplane to sponsor as a restoration. Agather suggested the Tucson B-29. Weeks of indecision by the Jaycees followed. Due to that delay, plus a snarl in the mail between Mexico City and Tucson upon which Agather's second option check depended, the option expired. Although Agather managed to convince the Tucson museum operators about what had happened, it was too late. In the interim, the Superfort had been sold by the Tucson museum instead to a West Coast group which at that time operated a cosmetic firm that had planned to use the famous ship for commercial purposes. "I don't mind saying that the loss of that B-29 almost broke my heart," Agather says, recalling how he flew immediately to California in an unsuccessful attempt to renegotiate purchase of the plane. (Later, another of the West Coast group's aircraft, a surplus military ship, was involved in a tragic crash into a Sacramento, California, ice cream parlor that took twenty lives; in the angry furor over responsibility that ensued, the Federal Aviation Administration became even more reluctant to license any former military planes; Victor Agather believes, with good reason, that accident was also largely responsible for the Pentagon's adamant refusal to let the CAF fly a B-29 even if it eventually found one. Ironically, the B-29 he almost obtained was left in the salt air of Oakland International Airport so long it eventually corroded beyond repair.)

Failure, especially repeated failure, daunts and discourages some men. But as the saga of Project Superfort continued to unfold, it became obvious that Vic Agather was not numbered among them. If anything, the disappointments at Aberdeen, Tucson, and Oakland only whetted his enthusiasm and determination, and that of Lloyd Nolen, Lefty Gardner, and other CAF colonels who by now were also deeply involved in the search. In Mexico City, Agather reached nearly twenty years back into his memory, recalling the days when squadron after squadron of bomb-heavy Superforts lumbered off the jury-built runways of Guam, Tinian, Saipan, and Iwo Jima, destined for Japan. Many, badly shot up in their missions, had not made it back at all, belly landing instead on small volcanic islands north of the Marianas. Some, he recalled, plunged into the ocean just after takeoff, due to mechanical failure or foul weather. Still others had bellied in on their return from Japan to air bases in the Changtu area of China. Bringing a B-29 out of Communist China was of course out of the question, especially in the days before diplomatic relations between the two countries, deep-frozen since 1948, began thawing once again.

A phone call from a CAF colonel interrupted Agather's daydreaming plans to take the biggest gamble yet in the search for a B-29, to begin personally scouring the battlefields where it had achieved fame in battle. Another stateside B-29 had been spotted, this one abandoned in a closed military airport near Provo, Utah. Once again, Lefty Gardner and Darrel Skorich converged on the spot, only to discover that although the plane was generally in good shape, most of its vital systems had been so badly cannibalized by souvenir hunters that finding workable replacements appeared extremely doubtful. Reluctantly, they returned home.

Almost at the same time, the CAF's headquarters office in Harlingen, Texas, received an excited telephone call from Roger Baker, a CAF colonel whose regular job was piloting a commercial airliner on a nonstop run between Los Angeles and New York. Nearly breathless, Baker explained that he had just landed his Boeing 707 at Los Angeles International Airport half an hour earlier, and during his descent over the Mojave Desert of Southern California, he had seen what appeared to be a ghost or, more properly, several ghosts.

"There were B-29s down there, a *lot* of them!" Baker almost shouted into the telephone. "Fifteen, maybe twenty, parked neatly in a row."

The voice on the other end, in Harlingen, sounded skeptical. "Twenty-nines? Hell, the Air Force says there *aren't* any more 29s. Sure you haven't been working too hard, Rog?"

"Neither working too hard nor smoking marijuana," Baker shot back. "Those were B-29s, and to prove it, I'm going to drive up there right now!"

China Lake, on the Mojave Desert, is a Navy installation, not Air Force, so it may be understandable why the Air Force reiterated its claim that no B-29s existed when the CAF made a hurried call to Washington to verify or substantiate Baker's report. A follow-up call to the Navy, however, struck pay dirt. Yes, there were B-29s at China Lake—about thirty of them. No, they didn't belong to the Navy, the Air Force technically still had jurisdiction over them, and, no, it wasn't the Navy's business that the Air Force couldn't keep better track of the airplanes it owned. Yes, if the CAF wanted one of the Superforts it would have to contact the Air Force, and yes, the Navy would be happy to bring the inventory records of its traditional service rival up to date.

Its embarrassment quickly forgotten, the Air Force was easily persuaded to donate one of the China Lake B-29s to the CAF collection. The CAF was invited to take its own pick of the thirty. Even more generously, the Air Force agreed that since the Superforts were designated as ballistics targets anyway, it wouldn't mind if Agather's group cannibalized good-condition spare parts from these planes.

Unlike those on the planes at Aberdeen, a part-by-part inspection of the Superforts at China Lake showed them to be structurally sound; nearly seventeen years in the dry, virtually rainless California desert climate had not affected them as had Aberdeen's muggy, humid weather. The job of restoration hardly loomed as an easy one, however; even in the plane chosen, the instruments that were missing had not been carefully taken out, but ripped loose forcefully, meaning that not only the instruments but the wiring connecting them would have to be replaced as well. Starters had been stolen to be used as truck winches. Landing gear motors were missing. But these were details that Agather could live with. What counted was whether or not the aging Superfort—Boeing B-29 Serial number 44-62070, to be precise—was sound enough to be restored to first-class flying condition.

Deciding that it was, one of the most extensive and astonishing restoration programs in the history of the CAF got underway. After formally turning over the plane to the CAF, the Air Force and the FAA agreed that if restoration met their stringent demands, the B-29 could be flown on a one-time-only basis from China Lake to its new home in Harlingen.

CAF volunteers leaped at the prospect, with Colonel Lefty Gardner being appointed B-29 Project Officer, a responsibility he had assumed many times on other CAF missions. Under supervision of Colonel Duane Egli, who had restored and flown the DeHavilland Mosquito bomber from England, CAF members rescheduled vacations and took time off without pay to help out. The B-29's vital electrical systems were rewired, and the old systems removed. Con-

The flight engineer's panel, or what was left of it, on a China Lake B-29.

The B-29's enormous bomb capacity can be imagined by this view from its bomb bay, as Victor Agather checks the progress of the restoration with a fellow CAF member.

trol surfaces were stripped of their old coverings and re-covered with new ones. Control cables were carefully tested, replaced where necessary. Many new parts were needed but a nationwide telephone canvass of surplus military sales houses fortunately turned up every one required.

It was now early May 1971—nearly five years since the CAF launched its search. The critical day finally arrived. It was time to test the engines. As an engineer held down the starter and primer on Number-3 engine, there was a resounding roar of eighteen cylinders, smoke pouring forth and flame spurting from huge exhaust stacks and the great plane began to breathe life once again. To those standing nearby, it was a nostalgic moment, and for those in their mid-forties and early fifties, perhaps, a poignant reminder of the momentous era of their youths.

Restoration of the B-29 to flight condition was completed by summer. Content that the plane was competently restored and safe to fly, the FAA issued a one-time ferry permit. Pilots selected were Randy Sohn and Lefty Gardner, two men ideally qualified for the job. Gardner had flown B-17s and B-24s during the war. As CAF staff procurement officer, he had returned more ancient aircraft to CAF headquarters than any other pilot.

Sohn, an airline captain with then North Central Airlines, had flown KC-97s with the Minnesota Air Guard in recent years, an aircraft very similar to the B-29.

The B-29 rumbled down the China Lake runway on the morning of August 2, 1971, with Sohn, Gardner, Jim McCafferty, Roger Baker, and Darrel Skorich aboard, and set a course for Harlingen, Texas, 1,500 miles away. Six hours and

Pilot's view from the restored B-29 cockpit. The Superfortress' immediate predecessor, a B-17 Flying Fortress, is parked to the right at Harlingen; to the left, a glimpse of the CAF's B-24.

thirty-eight minutes later, a battery of newspaper and television photographers recorded the jubilant pandemonium that broke loose at the sight of the first Superfortress to land anywhere in the world in nearly two decades. Unbelievably, this first flight after seventeen years of neglect was made without a single mechanical problem, a tribute not only to the CAF maintenance crews, but to the American aviation industry of 1944–45 and more particularly the Boeing Company and Wright Aeronautical Company.

It was three years later, however, before the Air Force allowed the B-29—now named *Fifi,* after sponsor Vic Agather's wife—to be flown again. The CAF admittedly had been given only a one-time ferry permit to fly the plane from California to Texas. But Agather and others involved had assumed, wrongly, that after the FAA certification tests that followed, tests that indeed led to an Air Worthiness Certificate, the historic ship could be flown in CAF air shows as had all of its restored predecessors. Just the opposite was the case, however; despite dozens of letters and telephone calls back and forth between Harlingen and Washington and several in-person appointments with recalcitrant Pentagon officials, the Air Force remained steadfast; the B-29 could not be flown again, ever.

Clearly, the CAF was getting nowhere, and probably it never would have had it not been for the personal help of one of its most staunch supporters, a CAF colonel himself: Barry M. Goldwater.

To say that Senator Goldwater merely intervened in the CAF's behalf would be the understatement of the year. A veteran flier himself and an outspoken supporter of military airpower, Goldwater jumped into the controversy with both feet. To Goldwater, the Air Force's position was not only arbitrary, it smacked of outright contradiction. "I have run into some crazy things in my life but I don't think I have ever come into contact with a crazier one than this with the Air Force and the B-29," he fumed in one letter to a top Air Force executive, typical of dozens over a two-year period. "I cannot understand why the CAF, which has a model of nearly every aircraft that flew in World War II, including

British and German, is not allowed to fly the B-29 in air shows around the country as they do with others. I hope we can put an end to this badminton game that is going on with the poor old '29' being the bird that is being kicked back and forth; this is *not* the Air Force!"

Finally, the Air Force relented and agreed to remove the "no-flight" clause from its deed of the aircraft, but only on condition that the CAF buy a $10 million public liability insurance policy. The condition was as financially impossible to the CAF as was retaining the no-flight clause, but with more help from Goldwater, the liability was lowered to a level the organization could afford.

The FAA issued its Air Worthiness Certificate on September 25, 1974. After an extensive flight testing program, all flight restrictions were removed. Eight years after the CAF began looking for the last plane to complete its flying inventory, the B-29 Superfortress formally arrived.

Today, sometimes with Vic Agather at the controls and sometimes under the command of other, qualified CAF members, *Fifi* is a regular and visually thrilling part of the Ghost Squadron's air shows, particularly that held in Harlingen each year. Not every admirer of the B-29 can get to Harlingen, of course, and it is this problem that the CAF is attempting to solve by taking its growing fleet of planes around the country on tour. "It has always been my feeling," Agather puts it, "that a flying museum should be taken to the public, and not require the public to go to the museum. Our hope is that the B-29 along with

CAF maintenance crew primes one of the engines on the Ghost Squadron's Fifi.

Wheels down, Fifi *prepares to land at Harlingen.*

other CAF aircraft can tour as many cities as possible. One only has to be present at a demonstration to realize the public demand to see and hear these aircraft in flight. I believe we have this as an obligation to the heritage of the United States."

A sampling of *Fifi*'s admirers at Harlingen one recent year provides ample proof of the "public demand" to which Agather refers. Four of the visitors, all men in their mid-fifties, explained to Agather that one of them had read about the restored B-29 and the upcoming air show in Harlingen, and contacted the other three by telephone. "We are the last surviving members of an eleven-man crew who flew thirty-one missions over Japan in a '29,' " one of them explained. "Today is the first time we've seen each other since 1945."

A graying lady was next. She held a sheaf of papers in her hand. Quietly waiting until Agather had a free moment, she asked if he could tell her the serial number of the plane.

"It's Number 44-62070," he replied from memory.

A smile flashed across the visitor's face as she quickly shuffled through the papers. Leading Agather through the bomb bay, she went immediately to a cross frame bracket where the serial number appeared. "I put that number there," she beamed with delight. "I helped *build* this Superfort!"

Finally, there was an eight-year-old boy whose name escapes Agather's memory. While the others were talking, he walked slowly about the plane several times, his eyes critically absorbing every detail. Here and there he stopped, letting his fingers run over rivets, brackets, wires, braces, the aluminum skin itself. Here was a lad, Agather mused to himself, who seemed to have more than a passing interest in the historic aircraft. Finally, he approached the youngster and asked, "Son, is there some way I can help you?"

"Yes, sir," the boy replied firmly and without a trace of a smile. "I'd like to know why the APQ-13 antenna is not installed!"

HOW TO KEEP 'EM FLYING

If you think you're performing miracles keeping that venerable second family car ticking, consider the masochistic life of Vince Carruth, the "patch 'em up, keep 'em flying" miracle man whose title is maintenance chief of the Confederate Air Force. At about the same time one recent year, Carruth was scurrying around half of south Texas with three job orders in hand, each of which would seem utterly calculated to gray the hair of a less-determined man and propel him toward the aspirin bottle. First, he had to find replacement spark plugs for the engine of the CAF's latest acquisition, a single-engined German Storch observation plane. A simple assignment? At first glance, yes. In Carruth's case, however, the predicament was woefully familiar: the 12-millimeter plugs were of European, not American manufacture, and though a limited number of that particular kind of plug were known to be manufactured in the United States, finding them was about as easy as locating the proverbial needle in the haystack.

At the same time, Carruth was trying to locate a number of engine parts for an ailing P-51 Mustang fighter. And last, he needed a replacement master brake cylinder for a P-40 Warhawk whose original one had surrendered a few days earlier after three decades of valiant service.

How Vince Carruth managed to solve the three problems typifies the herculean task of keeping more than threescore combat planes airborne a generation after thousands of their contemporaries have been relegated to the boneyard.

Let Carruth remember it:

"The spark plug problem was one we'd been through before. Usually when we run into a situation like that, we first try to locate the previous owner of the plane, figuring he'd been up the same creek himself. In the Storch's case, we traced the last owner to a town in New England; yes, he *had* found replacement plugs, but only by contacting an obscure source in France. We doubled back over the same trail, bought the last eight plugs the French outfit had, and got the bird running again. Then, realizing that was the end of the lot, we looked ahead to how we'd solve the same problem the next time it occurred."

Some men climb Everest, others try to balance the federal budget. Vince Carruth's job is just as easy; all he has to do is keep a bunch of aging relics alive and well and flying.

In a phrase, Carruth decided to jury-rig.

"We knew that an American plug manufacturer, Champion, made a 12-millimeter plug. But where the ignition lead hooks on, the size is American Standard, not metric. So what we had to do was to change the lead to the head of the plug. We manufactured an elbow with two different threads, metric at one end, American Standard at the other. It's a lot of work for a part as minor as a spark plug, but if you're trying to keep a bird in the air, what other choice is there?"

Finding parts for the Mustang's liquid-cooled, in-line engine proved almost as frustrating. "Fortunately, P-51s were among the most popular fighters after the war," Carruth remembers, "so there were a lot of parts for them around. And until cheaper, more efficient engines came along, a lot of surplus Allison and Merlin liquid-cooled power plants were bought to drive water pumps, oil well pumps, that sort of thing. So, when we couldn't find the parts we needed from the aviation sources, we started badgering farmers and ranchers. We crossed our fingers, hoping one would remember an old Merlin or Allison stuck away in a barn somewhere. We were lucky, we found what we needed, but it ate up a lot of valuable time."

As far as the P-40's problem was concerned, remanufacturing proved to be the answer. "Over the years, we've developed a card-index information system which lists just about every part we'll anticipate we'll ever need, right down to the last nut and bolt. The cards also list, from past experience, where we might find those parts. In the case of the P-40, our cards told us that a small company up in Dallas could make the parts we needed, and what we specifically needed were seals for the hydraulic actuating cylinders. The Dallas outfit took the measurements off the old seals, and made us new ones. They aren't as good as the originals, because they'll accept only automotive brake fluid, not heavy-duty aircraft fluid, but until we figure out a way to convert them over, they'll have to do."

Carruth, a former Navy fighter pilot who served most of World War II as an aircraft carrier "paddle man" (a landing signal officer) runs his maintenance operation in Harlingen with a minimum of manpower and a maximum of know-how. Besides himself, the CAF has allotted two assistant mechanics for engine-work, two sheet-metal mechanics to keep the Ghost Squadron's skins knitted together, and a couple of "line boys," aviation-minded young men who learn their trade by wiping down the airplanes, sweeping hangar floors, and changing oil drip pans. The mechanics, of course, must be licensed, and are answerable to the Federal Aviation Administration, which oversees the CAF's aging war birds with increasing concern each passing year. There will come a time, doubtless, when the Ghost Squadron may be down to a handful of aircraft, for it is obvious that a fleet of planes rushed through production and into combat almost forty years ago cannot be kept flying indefinitely. Meanwhile, Vince Carruth and his staff seem to be performing small daily miracles to ensure that the CAF's four related goals are met as long as possible. Those goals:

(1) To acquire a complete collection of prominent World War II combat aircraft; (2) to develop facilities for the display of these aircraft; (3) to provide the necessary maintenance program to keep them in flying condition for as many years as possible; and (4) to establish an organization having the dedication, enthusiasm, and *esprit de corps* necessary to operate, maintain, and preserve the airplanes.

With acquisition of the final plane needed to complete the World War II collection, and development of ground facilities at Harlingen, Objectives 1 and 2

The challenge: turn this mess into . . .

. . . a workable engine once again. But even after the job is done, constant maintenance is a must.

were met several years ago. That the CAF remains in operation despite mounting obstacles of cost and time would seem to indicate that Objective Number 4 has also been achieved. On the CAF's maintenance staff, therefore, rests the major responsibility for keeping more than 100 combat airplanes airborne, thus ensuring that the CAF will not become just another aviation museum limited to static displays.

It is not only the passing of years that presents Vince Carruth with such an enormous challenge. It is also the CAF's geographic location in the Lower Rio Grande Valley of Texas, where salt air from the Gulf of Mexico twenty miles away and a climate dripping with humidity most of the year exert corrosive forces on wood and metal matched by only a few theaters of war from 1939–45. As this is written, for instance, a twin-engined British Mosquito fighter-bomber squats forlornly on the Harlingen airport apron, awaiting hard-to-find innards for an ailing engine so that it can be flown again. With each passing day, Carruth notes, the humidity is wreaking havoc on its plywood-covered fuselage and wings. The "Mossie" was scheduled to be flown to a dry California desert home, but meanwhile, for lack of perhaps an inexpensive but elusive engine part, it's flying nowhere.

Carruth notes, too, that the very nature of American wartime aircraft manufacture works against him. The thousands of planes cranked out assembly line fashion by midnight-oil-burning plants during the dark war years simply weren't *intended* to last as long as a few have. In some cases, as proof, adjoining fittings

Typical of the condition in which the Confederate Air Force found many of the World War II planes in its collection.

were made of materials that everyone at the time knew would cause electrolysis, the chemical decomposition and deterioration that occurs when certain incompatible metals are placed together. "During the war, it didn't really matter, because aircraft engineers knew that electrolysis wouldn't occur right away, and the planes were not intended for long use," Carruth explains. "Besides, they had no choice; metals were scarce as hen's teeth during the war and the planes were needed badly. Now, one of the first things we do with a new acquisition is to inspect every single fitting and part, replacing any that are corroding."

The degree of maintenance problems varies from airplane to airplane. "The P-51s I mentioned aren't nearly as big a headache as some of our rarer birds, simply because there were more of them around after the war. But if, for instance, we were to break a landing gear on the Navy SBD—and that's a *very* rare bird—we'd find ourselves between a rock and a hard place where a replacement is concerned."

Because of the unique nature of the CAF, there are no parts-swap catalogues or newsletters of the kind that the antique automobile restoration fraternity has wisely organized. "In other words," Carruth explains, "when we need a certain part, we can't look in a book and find that Joe Doakes over in Fishcreek, Tennessee, has just what we want for sale. It's mostly a word-of-mouth proposi-

Most of the aircraft built for World War II simply weren't meant to be flying years afterward. That's why the task of maintaining them is so difficult. Here, some routine work on a fighter engine.

tion, and a good memory. Our 'colonels' are now located all over the world; when we need a part, we pass the word around and sooner or later it seems to turn up."

The CAF's growing public exposure as a result of its many years of existence, and publicity generated by its air shows, has helped, too. Occasionally, because the organization is far better known than in its fledgling days, parts come in unsolicited. "As an example, one guy wrote us that he had a bunch of gear for a Navy Helldiver," Carruth remembers. "He'd picked the bird up at surplus and now was selling it off piece by piece. He didn't have an engine, but he had just about everything else: cowling, engine mounts, collector rings. Could we use any of the stuff? Hell, yes, we could use it; we bought everything he had. Our Helldiver was running fine at the time, but those parts are mighty fine insurance against a day in the future when it isn't."

Naturally, all of this takes money . . . bushels of it. As explained in Chapter 1, the important green stuff needed to keep the Ghost Squadron airborne comes from four major sources: membership dues, air show gate revenues, aircraft sponsorships, and donations. Tax deductible sponsorships have become increasingly important not only to finance aircraft acquisition and restoration, but to offset the mushrooming costs of operation—spiraling aviation fuel prices, as an example—as well.

The cost of a sponsorship ranges from $350 upward. A sponsor need not be a pilot, and the CAF, founder Lloyd Nolen emphasizes, adheres to a rigid set of rules to ensure utmost aircraft safety; putting up sponsor money doesn't entitle a nonqualified donor to fly that particular airplane.

"Flying military combat type aircraft requires specialized training in aircraft systems, cockpit management, flight procedures, and a thorough knowledge of the limitations of each type," Nolen says. "Since the primary mission of the CAF is to preserve these aircraft, only well-qualified pilots will be considered for pilot duties. We're not running a flight school at Harlingen." (However, the CAF does maintain a fine training program for pilots otherwise qualified who wish to upgrade their skills to "combat status.")

What are the rewards of sponsorship for those who can't fly the ships their dollars have given a new lease on life? "If you'll look our planes over closely," says Nolen, "you'll find the answer. There's a lot of competition within the CAF to keep our planes in top condition; we have no awards or trophies or that sort of thing, but you can feel the pride of participation when you see how well our birds are cared for."

Considering the age of the aircraft it flies and the fact that most of the flying is other than "straight and level," the CAF has a commendable safety record. But although crashes are rare, they can tote up repair bills at a staggering rate. During the 1976 Harlingen air show, for instance, a Messerschmitt Me-109 bellied in during a low-altitude maneuver and although the pilot walked away unhurt from the result, the sight of the plane's underside was calculated to drive Vince Carruth to tears. It was, in a word, a mess. Estimated cost of repairs was $60,000; of that, $12,000 was needed for a replacement propeller alone. But to no one's surprise, almost $7,000 of the needed cash was raised on the spot when an appeal for donations was broadcast over the public address system.

Lastly, where money is concerned, there's always S. H. Collier, founder and chairman of the board of the First National Bank of Mercedes, Texas, since 1957, and an unabashed sentimentalist where fine machinery, including World

The B-17 is a thirsty lady. A CAF maintenance crewman prepares to top off a "Fort"'s fuel tanks.

War II airplanes, is concerned. A motorcycle dispatch rider for General "Black Jack" Pershing during World War I, Collier time and again has authorized four- and five-figure loans to the CAF, doubtless vetoing the more conservative wisdom of his own board of directors, rather than see a historically important 1939–45 era war bird molder into dust.

Between the dues, the sponsorships, the gate fees, the loans, and the volunteer donations, the CAF manages to stay financially afloat year by year, even in the face of soaring inflation and despite the ravages of time. "The way the money comes in sometimes surprises even me," Lloyd Nolen notes. "None of us 'colonels' is wealthy, we're all working stiffs with businesses to run. But whenever we put out a plea for money, we hope there's somebody out there who'll hear us."

Ghost Squadron Colonel Ed Messick briefs his staff prior to a CAF air show. Flying formations and maneuvers are meticulously planned and executed.

An air show briefing. Texas Stetsons, helmets and goggles, and an occasional Stars-and-Bars cap of the Confederacy—all are standard headgear.

Oops! *The pilot walked away from this crash of a Messerschmitt Me-109 due to land-ing gear failure, but the plane itself will need considerable tender loving care before flying again.*

The Ghost Squadron's annual air show in Harlingen is an enormously popular event. In addition to performances by its own aircraft, the shows feature hijinks by modern jet aircraft, such as the Navy's Blue Angels shown here, and propeller plane aerobatics, too.

At Harlingen's Rebel Field, these expressions say it all.

INDEX

Joseph E. Brown has written eight books and published hundreds of articles in magazines as varied as *Smithsonian, National Wildlife, Popular Mechanics,* and *Esquire.* Mr. Brown also wrote the brief biography of Frank Tallman that prefaced *Flying the Old Planes.*

Dan Guravich is a professional photographer whose work has appeared in numerous leading magazines and books as well as in commercial advertising. He has been an aviation enthusiast since boyhood and holds a private pilot's license.

Brown and Guravich combined their talents in 1980 with the publication of *The Mormon Trek West.*